The Analytic Tradition

PHILOSOPHICAL QUARTERLY MONOGRAPHS

VOLUME 1   The Analytic Tradition: Meaning, Thought and Knowledge
Edited by David Bell and Neil Cooper

The Analytic Tradition

Meaning, Thought and Knowledge

PHILOSOPHICAL QUARTERLY MONOGRAPHS
VOLUME 1

Edited by David Bell and Neil Cooper

Basil Blackwell

Copyright © Basil Blackwell 1990

First published 1990
First published in USA 1991

Basil Blackwell Ltd
108 Cowley Road, Oxford, OX4 1JF, UK

Basil Blackwell, Inc.
3 Cambridge Center
Cambridge, Massachusetts 02142, USA

British Library Cataloguing in Publication Data
A CIP catalogue record for this book is available from the British Library.

Library of Congress Cataloging in Publication Data
The Analytic tradition: meaning, thought, and knowledge/edited by
David Bell and Neil Cooper.
p. cm. — (Philosophical quarterly monographs: v. 1)
ISBN 0-631-17686-1
1. Analysis (Philosophy) 2. Frege, Gottlob, 1848–1925. I. Bell,
David Andrew. II. Cooper, Neil. III. Series.
B808.5.A532   1990
146′. 4 − dc20   90–38301
                                                              CIP

Typeset in 10 on 12pt Ehrhardt
by Graphicraft Typesetters Ltd., Hong Kong
Printed in Great Britain by
T.J. Press Ltd, Padstow

Contents

Introduction

If we date the beginnings of analytic philosophy from, let us say, the publication of Frege's *Grundlagen*, or his '*Über Sinn und Bedeutung*', then the tradition has been with us now for more or less 100 years. Its classical, or better perhaps, its 'heroic' phase – represented for example by the works of Frege, Russell, Moore, Wittgenstein, Carnap and the philosophers of the Vienna Circle – established with remarkable speed a distinctive set of philosophical concerns, an equally distinctive vocabulary, and a network of methodological procedures that to this day dominate philosophical practice throughout the English-speaking world. And yet neither the nature, the origins, the development nor indeed the value of this 'analytic tradition' has been of significant concern to those who have worked within it: analytic philosophy has been, and remains, largely unself-conscious and almost entirely ahistorical. There are, however, signs that this situation is beginning to change – and the present collection of papers is indeed itself one symptom of a growing willingness on the part of contemporary analytic philosophers to examine the nature and the history of their own tradition.

Although the essays in this collection address themselves to a wide variety of topics and figures, a number of common themes recur in many of them. One is the profound importance of Frege, not only historically – as a direct influence on Russell, Wittgenstein and Carnap, and through them, indirectly, on the entire subsequent development of the tradition – but also philosophically, as a thinker whose contemporary relevance is incontestable. Tyler Burge and Michael Dummett explicitly address problems to do with our understanding and evaluation of Frege, but distinctively Fregean themes also occur in the papers by Peter Hylton, Chris Hookway and Bill Hart.

Burge is concerned to develop and substantiate nothing less than a new, historically accurate, interpretation of Frege's notion of sense. Although, as Burge points out, 'Frege's conception of sense has fathered all the major approaches to "meaning" that have preoccupied philosophers in our century', subsequent philosophers have typically had intuitions, principles and goals different from and even inimical to those of Frege himself. The philosophical traditions most heavily influenced by Frege have, by and large, been empiricist, naturalistic and concerned at least in part with the language of common discourse. As a result, Burge argues, the profoundly rationalistic orientation of Frege's doctrines has been either neglected or misinterpreted. He includes, as participants in this 'historical process of obfuscation', Russell, the Vienna Circle movement, Carnap, Quine, Dummett, Kripke and others. Burge's alternative reading takes Frege's rationalism seriously, and in particular it emphasizes the role Frege ascribes to idealized thoughts, which leads him to sever the link between, on the one hand, the genuinely *Fregean* sense possessed by a linguistic expression and, on the other hand, its conventional meaning – what competent users of the expression would normally understand by it.

According to Dummett, one of the basic tenets of analytic philosophy, originating with Frege and subscribed to, amongst others, by Schlick, early and late Wittgenstein, Carnap, Ryle, Ayer, Austin, Quine and Davidson, is that 'the philosophy of thought is to be equated with the philosophy of language' (*The Interpretation of Frege's Philosophy*, p. 39). But while the intimacy of the connection that Frege forged between thought and linguistic sense was in many ways a virtue, enabling him to achieve for the first time in the history of philosophy a plausible account of the nature and inner structure of thoughts, it was also a vice; for in connecting thought with sense, and sense with language so intimately, Frege in effect ruled out the possibility of there being a *generalized* notion of sense or meaning, capable of applying not only to discursive thoughts but also to those intentional acts and cognitive states that are either unverbalized or, like perceptions, fundamentally non-linguistic. Dummett argues that just such a generalized account of non-linguistic sense can be found in the works of Frege's great contemporary Edmund Husserl, whose notion of a *noema*, the bearer of intentionality, is capable of univocal application to such diverse acts and states as thought, perception, memory, imagination and emotion. But while Dummett finds Frege's account of sense ultimately unacceptable, he finds Husserl's account indeterminate and merely programmatic. In the end Dummett leaves us with an uncomfortable dilemma: either, like Frege, we employ a concept of sense or meaning that is essentially linguistic, in which case we seem to be unable to account plausibly for the internal relations between discursive and non-discursive intentional acts and states, or, like Husserl, we sever the connection between meaning and language, in which case it appears that we are left with no model at all of the structure and content of our thoughts.

Künne's paper also returns to the time before the emergence of the 'Analytic-Continental Split' when philosophers like Russell, Moore, Frege, Meinong, Brentano and Husserl could rightly be considered members of a single philosophical community across which successful communication and informed debate were still possible. Focusing on the reaction by G. E. Moore to the Husserlian analysis of mental acts and, in particular, to Husserl's treatment of intentionality, Künne clarifies the differences between modes and qualities of acts, between nominal and propositional acts and, most crucially, between the object, the content or sense, the quality and the sensation-material of a given mental act. Künne concludes that, although some of the objections levelled by Moore at Husserl's theory of intentionality are misdirected, others are indeed pertinent and require modification of that theory.

Like Burge, Hylton is concerned to increase our understanding of an historical figure – in this case Russell – by removing the temptation to read his works anachronistically, as if, that is, Russell were writing today, addressing problems of direct contemporary relevance, and in terms immediately accessible to the modern philosopher and logician. Hylton argues that, on the contrary, Russell's logicist programme, and indeed Russell's very conception of logic itself, differ radically both in motivation and in content from anything to which logicians in the second half of the twentieth century would typically subscribe. By revealing Russell's conception of logicism as an anti-Kantian weapon, and by examining his early accounts of knowledge, truth, and reality (as well as his more technical, and perhaps more familiar, notions of proposition, propositional function, variable, class and the like), Hylton paints a philosophical portrait of the early Russell free from the anachronistic distortions that too often mar our picture of him.

Problems concerning scepticism, its expressibility and its coherence, have been central in the analytic tradition, and are the focus of the contributions by Tom Baldwin and John Skorupski. Baldwin concentrates on the contributions made to the solution of such problems by G. E. Moore. It is generally acknowledged that Moore's various attempts to refute scepticism were ultimately unsuccessful. There exists less agreement, however, concerning the precise doctrinal and methodological assumptions under which he took himself to be working. Indeed, given both the clarity of his style and the doggedness of his determination to make every argumentative move explicit, there exists a surprisingly wide divergence of opinion as to just what Moore was up to, just what *sort* of philosopher he was. Baldwin's paper addresses this problem, and takes issue with those who, like Clarke and Stroud, have interpreted Moore's response to scepticism as the naive and ultimately dogmatic response of the philosopher's 'plain man',who believes that the threat of scepticism can be deflected by nothing more than a sufficiently robust common sense. On the contrary, Baldwin argues, the genuine sophistication of Moore's theory has been obscured by the imposition onto it of an interpretative framework that is not Moore's, and which is, moreover, incompatible with his theory. An essential element in that framework is the Carnapian distinction between 'internal' and 'external' scepticism; and if Moore is construed as working within it, then it is possible to show that his supposed anti-sceptical challenge is simply misdirected – for an 'internal' response to 'external' scepticism is bound to be inadequate. Baldwin suggests, however, that this is not at all what Moore was up to, and that if we read him as employing instead the Cartesian distinction between practical and theoretical doubt, and as construing the latter as *second-order* doubt, then Moorean anti-scepticism becomes more intelligible and, indeed, more defensible.

One theme common to a number of the papers in this collection, and an important element in the analytic philosophical tradition as a whole, is what in the *Tractatus* Wittgenstein called 'the requirement that sense be determinate'. The contributions by Burge, Hookway, Sacks and Hart deal with aspects of this topic; Hookway and Sacks examine, though in very different ways, the extent to which this requirement is mandatory, and the acceptability of the consequences of giving it up.

Hookway concentrates on vague predicates. He shows the centrality of the demand for determinateness of predicate-sense (with its consequent rejection of many actual predicates in natural language) to a certain sort of analytic philosophy – the sort primarily associated with, say, Frege, Carnap and the early Wittgenstein, along with their heirs and successors. But he also detects in the writings of Frank Ramsey, the later Wittgenstein and, above all, C. S. Peirce, a quite different tendency: to assert not merely that vagueness or indeterminacy of sense is benign and hence tolerable, but that it is, rather, *a virtue* – something in the absence of which we would simply be unable to say, or think, or do the things we want. What these thinkers have in common Hookway indentifies as a distinctively pragmatist approach to semantic, logical and epistemological problems; and by examining Peirce's treatment of these issues he makes plausible the claim that the demand for determinacy of sense can in fact be resisted, without thereby making the possibility of natural science, classical logic, mathematics or everyday knowledge unintelligible.

In its formative phase, analytic philosophy was much concerned with the question: What must language be like if it is to perform the role required of it by the sciences – whether mathematical, logical or physical? One initially plausible and widely accepted answer to this question involved the claim that to be scientifically respectable the sentences of a natural or formal language must possess a determinate truth-value, and this in turn was taken to imply that they must express a determinate sense. Sacks examines the metaphysical assumptions inherent in this proposal, and traces their development and eventual demise at the hands of philosophers like Goodman, Quine, Wittgenstein and Putnam. Sacks isolates two such metaphysical assumptions: first, that reality is itself determinate, and hence that only a language whose expressions are without ineliminable vagueness of sense can adequately describe it. And, second, that the nature of reality is independent of any language in whose terms that reality is conceived or described. The history of the development of metaphysics within the analytic tradition, according to Sacks, is the history of the increasingly radical attempts to subvert either or both of these theses, and to articulate cogent alternatives to them.

The demand that sense be determinate is one form that a pervasive but largely unarticulated *ideal of clarity* has taken in analytic philosophy; and Hart's essay traces the vicissitudes this influential ideal has undergone, and the various forms it has assumed in the development of that tradition. He identifies two theses which together yield a strong, rationalist conception of what philosophical clarity should consist in. According to the first, the 'semantic ideal of rationalism', philosophy should model its output on that of mathematics: it should ideally result in statements whose sense is exact, impersonal and independent of context, and whose truth is both timeless and without qualification. According to the second, the 'epistemic thesis of rationalism', semantic clarity of this sort is itself the strongest, perhaps even the sole guarantor of knowledge and understanding. Hart distinguishes between four broad phases in the history of analytic philosophy – the early years from 1884 to 1918 (say) and dominated by Frege, Russell, Moore and Wittgenstein; the logical positivism centred, between the wars, round Schlick and Carnap; the linguistic or 'ordinary language' philosophy of the 1950s and 1960s; and the most recent period of the American Hegemony – and in the first half of his essay he examines critically the conception of clarity, and in particular the fate of the epistemic thesis of rationalism is each of them. The philosophy of the later Wittgenstein does not, however, fit comfortably into this fourfold classification; and yet that philosophy makes clarity a more explicit and central theme than do any of the others. The second half of Hart's essay therefore addresses the problem of what we are to make of Wittgenstein's (ironically obscure) pronouncements on that topic.

The opening paper of this collection is by John Skorupski, and is part of an attempt to place the concerns and procedures of analytic philosophy within the broader context of contemporary culture and ideas – to see analytic philosophy, that is, as both reflecting and contributing to developments in twentieth-century thought as a whole. And in this respect he argues that the view of sceptical questions as intrinsically meaningless should be seen as one of the distinctive features of 'modernism'. He aims to bring out not only what is novel in this view, but also its continuity with aspects of an earlier philosophical tradition to which Descartes, Hume and Kant belong. What he calls 'the modernist strategy' takes the analysis of meaning to be the most fundamental philosophical activity. It then seeks to demonstrate that (in Wittgenstein's words) 'Scepticism is *not* irrefutable, but obviously nonsensical, when it tries to raise doubts where no questions can be asked.' In defending the cogency of this strategy, Skorupski is led both to examine a number of issues central to present-day analytic philosophy (to do, for example, with the distinction between 'internal' and 'external' questions, the tenability of naturalism, realism, verificationism and the like), and also to explore the intimate relations in which these issues stand to Kant's transcendental idealist response to Humean naturalism. He concludes that, even though it is at present rather discredited, the 'modernist strategy' *is* in fact capable of demonstrating the unintelligibility of radical scepticism – though in avoiding transcendental idealism it finds itself committed, surprisingly, to a perspective within which what is true in naturalism turns out to coincide with what is true in absolute idealism.

David Bell

Acknowledgements

The essays in this collection are published here for the first time. Most were originally presented at a conference entitled 'The Nature and Origins of the Analytic Tradition in Contemporary Philosophy', held in Munich in April 1986. The conference was funded by the Volkswagen Stiftung, and took place in the Kardinal Wendel Haus: thanks are due to both organizations for their generosity and efficiency. Thanks go also to Dr Mark Sacks, Prof. John Skorupski and, especially, Prof. Willhelm Vossenkuhl for their invaluable and numerous contributions to the success of the conference. In addition, David Bell is personally indebted both to the Radcliffe Trust and to the Alexander von Humboldt-Stiftung, for two Research Fellowships during tenure of which this work was edited.

List of Contributors

Tom Baldwin is Lecturer in Philosophy at Cambridge University

David Bell is Senior Lecturer in Philosophy at Sheffield University

Tyler Burge is Professor of Philosophy at the University of California, Los Angeles

Neil Cooper is Professor of Philosophy at Dundee University and Editorial Chairman of *The Philosophical Quarterly*.

Michael Dummett is Wykeham Professor of Logic at Oxford University

Bill Hart is Senior Lecturer in Philosophy at University College London

Chris Hookway is Reader in Philosophy at Birmingham University

Peter Hylton is Professor of Philosophy at the University of California, Santa Barbara

Wolfgang Künne is Professor of Philosophy at Hamburg University

Mark Sacks is Lecturer in Philosophy at Liverpool University

John Skorupski is Professor of Philosophy at Sheffield University and Professor-elect at St Andrews University.

1

The Intelligibility of Scepticism

John Skorupski

I

This century has shown extraordinary fertility in adding to the stock of philosophical methods and ideas. Fertility in such profusion can take the appearance of a revolution in the very essence of philosophy, restarting it from zero. Sometimes philosophical movements in this century have presented themselves exactly thus. On the other hand, it is also possible to place the new techniques and ideas in relation to the philosophical tradition; placing it in turn – throwing into relief new features and assumptions in it, and finding novel continuities with it. In a similar way, twentieth-century art, for example the 'second' Viennese school of Schoenberg, Berg and Webern, can be presented as utterly new or (as Schoenberg himself saw it) as an opening and widening which throws the classical tradition into new significance.

The problem of scepticism is one of the simplest, profoundest and most beautiful of questions in the classical philosophical tradition. It is also one of the points at which both the continuity and the transformation which I have referred to can be most clearly traced. For there is a response to scepticism which first appears only in the twentieth century. It is one of the things that give the 'analytic tradition' a distinct character – and one of the justifications for taking the most important thread of that tradition to be a centring of philosophy on the analysis of meaning. I think it is also one of the ingredients in the analytic movement which give one good reason to see that movement as part of modernism. But equally, as I shall try to show, it is a natural development of reflections on the relationship between naturalism and the possibility of knowledge which go back to Hume and Kant. The combination in modernism of continuity with radical new turning is here illustrated at the deepest level.

With these thoughts in mind, I shall call this twentieth-century response to scepticism the *modernist strategy*. Sceptical arguments usually proceed by fixing on some of our most basic common sense beliefs about the world, advancing a radically opposed possibility, and asking what reason we have for preferring the common sense view to its alternative. (How do I know I am not dreaming? How do I know the world did not come into existence five minutes ago?) The modernist strategy seeks to show that the sceptic fails to ask the question he intends to ask – where he thought there was a question there is none. For he either asks an intelligible, and answerable, question, or he fails to ask any intelligible question.

Or again: there are internal and external questions. The internal question has an internal response; the external question is in some way defective, it is a 'pseudo-question'. The distinction has been very influential. It is made by Carnap, and versions of it are present in the early and the late Wittgenstein (in particular, in *On Certainty*).[1] In 'ordinary-language philosophy' many treatments of scepticism deploy considerations such as the impossibility of doubting everything, the 'paradigm-case argument' and so on. In doing so they too seem to distinguish between legitimate questions and answers, which are asked and given within language games, and illegitimate or meaningless questions which seek to come from outside them; and they try to dispel or dissolve the latter by an analysis of the conditions of meaning.

All of these approaches fall within what I am calling the modernist strategy, and all of them are currently somewhat unfashionable. In English-speaking philosophy there has been a marked reassertion of the basic Anglo-Saxon equilibrium – that is, a philosophy which is both empiricist and scientifically realist, and in which sceptical arguments are allowed at most a purgative role, without ever posing an ultimate challenge to science and common sense. Many attempts to implement the modernist strategy have – rightly – come to seem weak or shallow. And new and subtle analyses of the concept of knowledge have been developed which have at least forced greater complexity on to the statement of classic sceptical arguments.

That, however, is not to say that they have answered them. If recent accounts of knowledge are correct, the sceptic should concede the possibility that he does *know* many things about the world – for example, that there is a table here. For to deny it would itself be an assertion about his relationship to his environment, requiring reasons in support. But he can still legitimately ask what reason there is to believe that there is a table here, or to believe that he knows there is. Sceptical arguments continue to pose a potent challenge, even after we have become more accurate in our understanding of the word 'know'.[2]

What I am calling the modernist strategy is, in one way, extremely familiar. Yet it does not seem to me that its essentials are well understood. Authentically new philosophical ideas take a long time to sink in – in fact they can seem old even before they have done so. The object of this paper is to set in relief the essentials which underpin the modernist strategy and to assess their significance. I shall not go into details about how they appear in the writings of important philosophers of this century – it would be a difficult and illuminating task to do so. However I do hope to exhibit them for what they are: a profoundly interesting line of thought which goes to the heart of our understanding of ourselves and our relation to the world. Philosophy cannot ignore the modernist strategy or simply go round it to what came before.

II

Even though the strategy is familiar it will still be useful to begin by setting it out in some detail. Suppose the sceptic asks how I know that I am not – right now – the subject of an experience-simulation experiment being carried out by medical researchers. He asks me to imagine that they have the technical capacity to produce, by direct stimulation of the central nervous system, any state of sensory experience they wish to, and any sequence of such states.

I certainly cannot simply rule out *a priori* the possibility that that is technically feasible. There is a perfectly intelligible question here: how do I know that I am sitting at a desk, typing into a word-processor – and not lying in a bed with a simulation device clamped to my cranium? Or better: what reason do I have to prefer the one view to the other?

The plain answer is that it is extremely unlikely – vanishingly unlikely – that I am being deceived by medical researchers;[3] and extremely likely – practically certain – that I am typing at a desk. Soberly speaking, I know perfectly well that medical technology has not progressed to the point where such sensory stimulation is possible. And who are the medical researchers? Why are they doing this? Why do I not remember any 'cut' in my previous experience?

No doubt I would appeal to such points if I had to justify my practical certainty. Still, I do not deny the *possibility* of its turning out, in future, that I was after all, being deceived by medical researchers. I recognize, in principle, that I may in five minutes time undergo a sequence of experiences which will convince me that a simulation device does exist and that I have been the subject of an experiment with it. It may then be explained to me that the cup of coffee I swallowed half an hour ago contained a tasteless drug which put me into an instantaneous coma, during which I was transported to the medical laboratory, where a sequence of experiences was produced by direct central stimulation in such a way as to cause me to believe that I was typing into a word-processor – which was exactly what I had been intending at that very moment to do.

I recognize this as a possibility in principle, but I am plainly justified in placing a great deal of money on a bet that it will not turn out to have been the case – let us say within the next twenty-four hours, or two weeks, or a year. This is the 'internal' response. It attaches a probability amounting to practical certainty to the proposition that I am typing at my desk.

There are possible circumstances in which it would not do so. Imagine me to be familiar with prototype simulation devices – I know that one is being worked on in the medical laboratories of my university; imagine I share a flat with the medical research students who are working on it. They go in for practical jokes and have already tricked me a number of times. . . . I might be in genuine doubt whether I was really sitting at a desk, typing. This would be an 'internal' doubt.

It is not the kind of doubt that the sceptic intends to raise. His grounds for dissatisfaction with my internal response are easy to see. He will point out that my reasons for thinking it vanishingly unlikely that I am being deceived relate to a set of premises, a set of beliefs about the world. Relative to these propositions, the probability that I am being deceived by medical students is indeed exceedingly low. But what are my grounds for believing them to hold? How do I know that they are not themselves grounded on experience caused by an experience-simulation device? By the same token: suppose I were to have the experiences which would justify me, as I think, in believing that I was being deceived by medical researchers. How would I know that those experiences themselves were not the deceptive products of a simulation device (or of an evil demon or a dream)? In both cases, of course, one could once again read the question internally, and respond accordingly. But it would be wilfully obtuse to do so: the sceptic evidently intends to make the point that every iterated internal response can be undercut by a further question. No evidence can be brought to bear on the question whether I am being deceived or not, for whenever I treat something as evidence I am doing so from *within* a substantive conception, a 'theory', of the relation between myself and the world.

The sceptic is raising a metaphysical or hyperbolical doubt. The supposition that I am being deceived by medical researchers, as he intends to advance it, cannot have any degree of probability attached to it – high or low. And that being so, he further concludes that nothing could give me grounds for attaching any degree of probability to the supposition that I am typing at my desk.

Here of course is the point at which the modernist strategy comes into play. Its familiar claim is that when no evidence could even in principle be brought to bear on the question, the question is meaningless. To answer it either in the affirmative or the negative would be to make no genuine assertoric move. The disciplines of assertion would have been thrown off.

If one has closely followed the sceptic's argument, this response is apt to seem thin and unconvincing. The question, as intended by the sceptic, does undeniably seem intelligible. When it is – as one wishes to say – properly understood, it produces a distinctive sense of disorientation, free fall. It mines under one's most basic sense of self and world. In reply, the modernist strategy argues that this disorientation is not the product of coming to see any genuine possibility. It results from thought going out of gear (or 'language going on holiday') – attempting to take a perfectly intelligible question in an impossible way. The form of words 'Are medical researchers deceiving me by means of sensory stimulation?' is perfectly intelligible taken in the normal way. There are normal ways of assessing answers to it. It is only because we have that normal understanding of it that we have the illusion of understanding it in the way that produces the sense of free fall, in which normal evidential supports lose all their rigidity.

The strategy does not suggest that the questions or suppositions by which the sceptic seeks to express his doubts are meaningless. They are all perfectly intelligible. The point is rather that the sceptic imagines that they can be given a reading which they do not and could not have. Their sense depends on taking them in a way that allows them to be assessed. That sober stance can be taken towards the most outrageous hypotheses. Even the extreme supposition that I am the result of a cosmic accident which produced a brain in a vat, with no intervention by any intelligent agent at all, could be assessed soberly. Patiently I consider whether it is probable or improbable.... I conclude that, as things are, there is every justification for rating it immensely improbable. But I could imagine, with sufficient ingenuity, states of evidence which would diminish that improbability a little, or at the very least leave me not knowing what to say.[4]

III

It is not enough, of course, merely to assert that if a question is unanswerable it must be meaningless. The sceptic after all insists that his question *is* unanswerable. No doubt most people's reason for dismissing sceptical questions as pointless is just that – that they are unanswerable. But that is a different matter. Those people are not saying that sceptical questions are literally inexpressible. The modernist strategy is not to be confused with the practical man's reaction; it is not a thinly disguised version of the dogmatism (healthy or otherwise) of the natural attitude. Nevertheless its reason for holding that no real questions are being posed is indeed the utter unanswerability of the supposed questions – the fact that nothing could conceivably count as an answer. So – unlike the practical man's reaction – it requires the backing of a general perspective on meaning: on the conditions which must hold for a sentence to have sense. Only with that backing can the idea of distinguishing an intended philosophical or 'external' reading of the sceptic's questions, and dissolving it as senseless, be carried through. How else could one justify the move from unanswerability to unintelligibility?

There is a perspective on meaning which has been influential in the analytic tradition, and which – if it is correct – would underpin the modernist strategy in the way that is required. Particular forms of it were developed in American pragmatism and in the writings of the Vienna Circle. It can be found, perhaps in most subtle and dialectically developed form, in the late Wittgenstein. I shall call it the *epistemic conception of meaning*.

Obviously if this epistemic conception is to underpin the modernist response to scepticism it must itself be capable of being worked out in detail and shown to be coherent. And that, moreover, has to be done in a way which still leaves the modernist strategy offering something distinctively new. In the rest of this section I shall consider how the modernist strategy differs from Kant's transcendental idealism and I shall point out some important constraints which this difference imposes on it. In the remaining sections I consider whether the epistemic conception can coherently meet those constraints, and whether, even if it can be distinguished from transcendental idealism, it is not after all subtly idealist in another way – a form of absolute idealism. I shall do little more than raise these latter questions – a full discussion of them would of course take much more than a single paper.

The essence of the epistemic conception is that meaning is cognitive role. Our interest here is in assertoric sentences and the conception, as we shall consider it, holds that understanding such a sentence is a matter of appropriate assertoric and inferential dispositions: namely, the ability to recognize a state of experience and belief as licensing assertoric utterance of the sentence, and the ability to recognize inferences in which the sentence appears (as a non-redundant premise) as valid or invalid. The meaning of a sentence is given in terms of its assertion-conditions and its inferential power.

Opposed to this conception is what I shall call the *classical pre-understanding of meaning*. 'Classical' because it begins to be questioned in philosophy only at the beginning of this century, and 'pre-understanding', because it is in no way an *explicit* assumption in the philosophy that came before. Its existence and significance could begin to be explored only when conceptions of language-mastery developed which threw it into relief by providing alternatives.

On the classical pre-understanding of meaning, to understand a sentence is to grasp its truth-condition. So far, so platitudinous; but grasp of a sentence's truth-condition is pictured as something determined independently of one's mastery of how rules of evidence bear on it. It has the potential of transcending that mastery, that is, of yielding an understanding of the sentence even when no rules of evidence can bear on it. If, in contrast, the meaning of a sentence is given by its assertion-conditions and inferential power, then grasp of the truth-condition – semantic content – is not primitive but must rather be seen as constituted by grasp of assertion-conditions and inferential power – cognitive role: grasp of semantic content will not be distinct from grasp of cognitive role and will not be able to stand against it or go beyond it.

What lies at issue between these contrasting approaches to meaning, evidence and inference will emerge more fully. But compare, to begin with, the modernist response to scepticism with Kant's response to the scepticism of Hume. Hume attempted to put the study of mind on a purely scientific footing. Human beings were to be seen as natural entities. He also set out a profound statement of inductive scepticism. On his principles there could be no reason to accept any assertions, unless they be assertions about one's immediate states of consciousness. Kant found this sceptical conclusion to be intolerable, and its source he identified as lying in Hume's naturalism – in the view that the mind is only a part of nature.

Whatever else is obscure about Kant's transcendental idealism, one thing is clear – it involves the rejection of naturalism. If, given naturalism, knowledge is impossible, we must contrapose and reject naturalism. The great cultural influence of Kant's critique stems from this: that it upstages the natural attitude – the perspective of common sense and its outgrowth, science. If Kant is right, the natural attitude cannot give the absolute truth about the world and our situation in it. Its truths are 'empirical'; and the significance of scepticism is that it forces us to recognize a transcendental level at which their limitations are seen. Indeed talk of 'naturalism' as a philosophical position gets its fully developed meaning only in relation to this Kantian critique – by contrast with transcendental idealism. After Kant, the challenge to a naturalistic philosophy is to find a defence of itself as epistemologically coherent.

This view of Kant as the pivotal figure who recognized the transcendental significance of scepticism goes back in British philosophy to T. H. Green.[5] More recently, Barry Stroud (see, in particular, 1984) has emphasized the parallels between Kant's distinction between empirical and transcendental, and the modernist distinction between internal and external. On both the Kantian and the modernist view, the ordinary beliefs of the natural attitude are properly assessed by natural standards of reasoning. Both the Kantian critique and the modernist strategy 'insulate' these natural standards from sceptical short-circuits.[6] The insight to be gained from scepticism is reflective. It has no first-order lesson to teach the natural attitude as such; but it shows that the domain in which natural canons of inference are licensed to operate has limits.

Certainly the metaphor of insulation is suggestive and, for Kant at least, it is fully appropriate. There *is*, in his view, a domain of reality which is off limits, or on the other side of the insulating material. But is it equally appropriate for the modernist? If his strategy is fully successful, it ought not to be: this, in fact, is just the question on which the claim that modernism provides an authentically novel, and genuinely deflationary, response to scepticism turns.

Hume's scepticism, like the scepticism of antiquity, is uninsulated. He has a use for it: he wants to show by means of it that common beliefs do not result from the application of reason. The 'sceptical solution' of 'sceptical doubts about the understanding' affirms, of general beliefs formed by induction, that we cannot help believing them. But it refuses to affirm that we have reason to believe them. The Humean philosopher is often willing to affirm *I cannot help believing that* p. But he cannot on his principles affirm *There is reason to believe that* p. He cannot endorse statements in which this latter operator has dominant scope. So he cannot affirm that he has reason to believe his own principles. He can only insist that he cannot, in the study, help believing them – though it is also part of his position that in the normal circumstances of life he cannot help disbelieving them. If this right, then human belief indeed finds itself in an extraordinary predicament.

There is a tradition of naturalistic philosophy which is less hectically paradoxical than Hume's. It does not endorse sceptical arguments and put them to use; rather, it completely ignores them in favour of constructing a 'naturalized' science of science. Perhaps the earliest work which falls clearly in this category is J. S. Mill's *System of Logic*:[7] naturalized epistemology sketches out our basic methods of reasoning and solves puzzles about them, but when it comes to justifying them it restricts itself to appealing to a reflective equilibrium of rules and judgements.

In this spirit Nelson Goodman proposes a 'dissolution' of the 'old' problem of induction:

> An inductive inference [just like a deductive one] is justified by conformity to general rules, and a general rule by conformity to accepted inductive inferences. Predictions are justified if they conform to valid canons of induction; and the canons are valid if they accurately codify accepted inductive practice.[8]

Now this indeed ought to be the path of wisdom. But in the face of Hume's analysis and Kant's critique, surely some backing has to be provided for it? Whence the word 'justified'? Why is avoidance of scepticism not evasion? If a backing can be provided, relying on those spontaneous inferential dispositions which survive reflection might be fully vindicated in the internalist way of Goodman and Mill. In its absence, it seems no more than a dogmatic reassertion of common sense. Hence Green's contempt for naturalistic philosophy after Kant.

At this point the filiation of modernity and tradition is clear. For unlike Millian naturalism, the modernist strategy *engages* with classical epistemology. It seems to answer the Kantian challenge head on. It does so not by discharging naturalism but by discharging the classical pre-understanding of meaning, and replacing it by the epistemic conception; and in doing so it radically undercuts the whole nineteenth-century debate between naturalistic empiricism and various forms of Kantian or post-Kantian idealism.

If we deny, as the epistemic conception denies, that a language-user can first grasp what it is for a sentence to be true and then consider – as a separate question – what rules of evidence might in principle bear on it, we simultaneously deny a sense to the question whether ultimate rules of evidence, taken as a whole, are conducive to truth. (Which is not to deny that that question can significantly be raised of any one of them.) We come to see how our mastery of rules of evidence can be, in a certain weak sense to be considered below, *a priori*. The prospect opens of our being able to endorse a vital point in the Kantian critique – the need for an *a priori* element if knowledge is to be possible – while retaining the premise of naturalism.

This prospect, however, requires that the epistemic conception should not itself be a metaphysical position, among other metaphysical positions. Properly understood it must be seen to shrink into insignificance as a mere truism about what understanding consists in. The modernist must argue that the classical pre-understanding contains a spontaneous metaphysical illusion, and that the epistemic conception is simply the dispelling of such illusion. This latter conception is, to be sure, a philosophical thesis, in the sense in which that includes *anti*-philosophical theses which are needed for true philosophical enlightenment – or release. When it is isolated in the form of a general statement, however, the danger arises that it will itself mutate into a philosophical thesis in the bad sense. (Of course there remains the question of why and how this happens, and in general of how spontaneous metaphysical illusions are generated.) So what from one point of view – that of spontaneous, innocent, philosophical first-thoughts – must appear a hard-to-swallow doctrine, must from another – the finally achieved – point of view recede into a set of empty platitudes, or 'reminders'. Having brought the epistemic conception to centre stage, the modernist strategy must eventually succeed in fading it back into the background.

Some further points follow from this. If the sceptic succeeds in asking no question which he intended to ask, there is every justification for ignoring his intentions. There is after all no proposition which he is putting forward which can be refuted. The best thing may be simply to answer in deadpan fashion the only questions he does succeed in asking. These answers will be internal and taken in themselves will not be a piece of philosophy, but in their context they will be a philosophical act – a piece of performance philosophy. That would be a reason for responding to the sceptic in the manner of Moore. I do not suggest that it was Moore's reason, but I think it is one reason why his performance remains fascinating – why, for example, it fascinated Wittgenstein.

There is however a limit to the number of times the performance is worth repeating. If the only point of allowing the sceptic's question to be raised lies in the educational value of responding to it in a way which purposely ignores his intention – why bother, once enlightenment has been achieved? There only remains for the epistemologist the respectable project of providing a naturalistic codification of principles of evidence – for which, as I have said, Mill's *System of Logic* is the earliest clear model. The modernist cannot therefore treat naturalized epistemology with the contempt reserved for it by T. H. Green.

Naturalism, on the modernist view, is not to be seen as a metaphysical doctrine opposable by another – 'transcendental realism' as against transcendental idealism. But neither can it be seen simply as a very large, but internal, statement. (Of the kind which a transcendental philosopher ought theoretically to be able to accept – though the relation between empirical and transcendental ego is of course a central difficulty for Kant.) If the modernist philosopher espouses naturalism he espouses it neither as a metaphysical doctrine nor as an empirical one but as an anti-metaphysical one. He asserts the final unintelligibility of any alternative. He is not arguing with Kant on transcendental ground; he is saying that the ground which Kant claimed to occupy is non-existent. He will be as reluctant to formulate 'naturalism' as a thesis as he is to formulate the epistemic conception as a thesis. In talking about these theses in the way we have done we describe the point of view of the modernist strategy from outside it. Only if the modernist strategy is unsuccessful can they be isolated from the natural attitude as disputable metaphysical doctrines.

It follows that the distinction between internal and external must be treated with care. From a fully worked-out modernist viewpoint, the terminology is dangerously misleading, because it suggests there *is* something on the outside, from which the inside needs insulating. Insulation would be something that had a metaphysical cost, as it does in Kant. But on the modernist view, there is no genuine insulation – no two sides between which insulating material needs to be inserted.

IV

So much for the 'modernism' I have in mind, and the role in it of an epistemic conception of meaning. But now for the questions. In rejecting the 'classical pre-understanding' *are* we simply dispelling a confusion? Are we not in fact rejecting something more? Are we not rejecting a certain natural realism, or notion of objectivity, as surely as the transcendental idealist does? A view of the world as 'objectively there, independently of us', which is part and parcel of the natural attitude itself?

In Barry Stroud's view, there is an 'idea of ourselves and of our relation to the world' which 'lies behind the sceptical reasoning' and is

deeply powerful and not easily abandoned. As long as it is even an intelligible way of thinking the sceptical conclusion will seem to be defensible against attack. In trying to give expression to the idea it is natural to resort to what seems like nothing more than the merest platitudes. If that is so, trying to avoid scepticism by throwing over the old conception will not be easy – it will involve denying what seem to be obvious truths.

The 'obvious truths' are special cases of a general platitude:

the world around us that we claim to know exists and is the way it is quite independently of its being known or believed by us to be that way. It is an objective world.

An example of the platitude is that if

> I believe that there is a mountain more than five thousand metres high on the continent of Africa . . . what I believe will be true, or false, depending solely on the heights of the mountains in Africa . . . No statement of precisely *what* I understand, therefore no account of what 'There is a mountain more than five thousand metres high in Africa' means, will include anything about human beings or human knowledge or human thought. In particular it will not include anything about whether that sentence itself is or can be known to be true or could be reasonably asserted in certain circumstances. That would introduce an extraneous reference to human beings or human knowledge into a statement solely about the non-human world (pp. 76–7).

These are certainly truisms. Do we, in rejecting the classical pre-understanding and affirming the epistemic conception, reject them? Understood in the plain sense, the statement that the way the world is is dependent on the way I believe it to be would be a plainly false causal assertion (trivial qualifications being understood). Making that point is just producing one of the reminders to which 'naturalism' boils down. So if we do accept the statement at some level we do seem to be committed to idealism in some form at that level. If endorsing the epistemic conception forces acceptance of the statement, the modernist strategy fails.

Stroud thinks that the verificationism of Carnap and the Vienna Circle requires us to reject the truism at a certain level and only provides a response to scepticism by doing so. He refers to 'what might be called the 'pre-Copernican' idea that our perception and knowledge simply conform or fail to conform to objects' which 'Kant thinks makes an explanation of knowledge impossible'. Against this Kant holds, he says, the 'Copernican' view that ' "outer things" cannot be regarded as things in themselves independent of us . . . idealism rather than realism must be accepted in the philosophical explanation of our knowledge.' Stroud thinks that Carnap's position is equally Copernican, that is, idealist.

> Perhaps it is not 'empirical' idealism, 'internal' to the framework of our knowledge of the things around us, but it is idealism or non-realism nevertheless. If not, there would be no explaining how knowledge is possible (pp. 195–6).

Stroud's point is that Carnap succeeds in building defences against the sceptic only by rejecting the naturalistic platitudes at the external level. Carnap holds that our statements about physical objects only have truth-values in the context of the framework statement that there are physical objects. Internally speaking, the truth of 'There are physical objects' is on a par with 'There are mountains in Africa' and indeed a simple deductive consequence of it. But externally speaking, it only holds because we have 'decided' that it should hold – and we could have decided to adopt some other framework. Externally speaking, we can say that it would not have been true that there are mountains in Africa if we had not adopted the physical object framework. But internally speaking, it is plain that our decisions or beliefs in no way feature among the truth-conditions of that statement. So Carnap does propound an external idealist doctrine which does need to be insulated from the inside. It does not help to insist on the difference between the formal and the material mode. If Carnap's thesis ('There are physical objects' is true *because* we have chosen a physical-object framework) does successfully block the question 'How do we know that "There are physical objects" is true?' it does so either because the sentence does not make a factual claim, or because a decision about a framework can make a worldly fact obtain. The first alternative is transcendental idealism: yielding a transcendental reading in which the sentence is non-factual, an empirical reading in which it is factual, and a mystery about how the two readings are related. The second is empirical idealism – or sheer magic.

Stroud is right to put Carnap's position in the idealist camp, but Carnap's position is only one way of implementing what I have called the epistemic conception. The question still remains whether *any* version of the epistemic conception must reject – if not internally, then externally – the 'idea of ourselves and of our relation to the world' which 'lies behind the sceptical reasoning' and is expressed by 'merest platitudes'. Will it always be possible, in any version, to formulate externally some such Stroudian conditional as the one above, about 'There are mountains in Africa'?

Before we can take up these questions we must notice some important points about the epistemic conception and clarify further its bearing on sceptical arguments.

V

Michael Dummett has often argued that philosophical realism, at its most general, ought to be understood as taking the form of a conception of meaning. The conception he has in mind is, in essentials, what I have called the classical pre-understanding. It is that conception brought to the surface and made explicit. However, what Dummett opposes to it – 'anti-realism' – goes beyond a simple

rejection of the classical pre-understanding. It merges that rejection with a positive view of truth which I shall in a moment argue is inessential to it. Nevertheless, in identifying the contrast between what I have called classical and epistemic
conceptions of meaning, and in making clear how much turns on it, Dummett
established an immensely illuminating perspective on the analytic tradition.[9] My
account in this paper is thoroughly indebted to it.

    Is it illuminating, though, to call the rejected idea 'realism'? Calling it 'realism'
gives it much the sound of Stroud's pre-Copernican notion of objectivity. But
Stroud seems to hold that the only way of rejecting pre-Copernicanism is by
espousing idealism. Pre-Copernicanism, it seems, is *essentially* expressed by certain platitudes which form an innocent part of the natural attitude. If that is what
realism is, the modernist strategy had better not be found to be anti-realist.

    However, it should not be assumed that rejecting what Dummett calls realism
is embracing idealism. The negative term 'anti-realism' usefully leaves that issue
open. The anti-realist's intention, at any rate, may be to oppose a metaphysical
doctrine, without espousing any alternative metaphysical doctrine. That would
accord with the line of thought which we are studying in this paper. The question still remains whether the rejected metaphysical doctrine is usefully termed
'realism' – it might be better to take the classical pre-understanding as the underlying thesis which both idealist and realist have in common, realism being the
unstable fusion of a naturalistic view of mind with the classical pre-understanding of meaning: the failure to distil the former from the latter. This would avoid
the clumsiness inherent in holding that idealism rests on an underlying realist
premise. But on the other hand, there is genuine point in calling the rejected
metaphysical view realism. (When it is formally defended it develops into a form
of realism about meanings which the idealist himself is likely to reject as naive,
and which may indeed be deployed in opposition to idealism, as by Frege, Moore
and Russell. But the pre-understanding and its influence is not to be identified
with the explicitly developed philosophical thesis.)

    It is not necessary to pursue the issue of terminology here; but it should be
noted that Dummett's own version of the epistemic conception is anti-realist in a
very much less downbeat way. Dummett intertwines with the epistemic conception of meaning (EM) what I shall call an epistemic conception of truth (ET). On
this latter view truth equates with assertibility. (It might be assertibility in an
ideal limit, or by an ideal inquirer, but I shall ignore refinements of this kind –
which in any case detract from the force of the basic idea, or at least cloud its
original rationale.) ET holds that we can make no sense of a sentence being true
(or false) other than in terms of the availability of a procedure for determining it
to be true (or false). This is the generalization of intuitionism in mathematics – of
the conception of truth as proof. It is the doctrine that leads the Dummettian
anti-realist to his suspicion of bivalence.

    It is important to know whether ET is a necessary part of the package adopted when one rejects the classical pre-understanding and adopts EM, for the issue has a direct bearing on the question whether EM is a philosophical doctrine, in the sense in which the modernist opposes philosophical doctrines. An epistemic view of truth forces us to depart in some way from the 'pre-Copernican' platitudes. And Stroud is right to say that rejecting these commits us to idealism. On the naturalistic view, a mind can be nothing more than (or supervenes on nothing more than) a complex casual process which is itself part of a larger causal order. Evidence is a contingent causal relation between a state of affairs and a knower. There are many states of affairs from which no readable causal signal reaches any actual knower, and which no actual knower could in fact get into a position to receive a readable signal from. So there are many states of affairs which hold without any mind being able to acquire evidence that they hold. Naturalism itself entails, as one of its internal consequences, that truth is not epistemically constrained. On the naturalistic view, there must be propositions which are true but which we can in fact acquire no evidence for holding true. This platitude follows from our general conception of ourselves in the world – it is *internal* to our fabric of beliefs.[10]

The truth of a proposition cannot entail its assertibility. Equally, the assertibility of a proposition cannot entail its truth. Given naturalism, all propositions are radically defeasible: fallibilism prevails. A proposition which is assertible in a given state of information may always cease to be assertible in an enlarged state.

However in section III we observed only that the modernist strategy forces rejection of the classical pre-understanding of meaning. It was not apparent that it presupposed anything about the nature of truth. Is it in fact possible to take an epistemic view of meaning while leaving truth alone – proposing no constitutive account of it at all?

The question is a difficult and deep one. The issues at stake can only be sketched here. Notice first of all that there is indeed a clear argument from ET to EM. It proceeds by means of the uncontroversial principle that to understand a (fact-stating, assertoric) sentence is to grasp what must be the case for it to be true. If we are given an independent argument for the epistemic conception of truth, then we can use this principle to argue to the epistemic conception of meaning: understanding meaning is grasping truth-conditions, truth equates with assertibility, so understanding meaning is grasping assertion-conditions.

But does the converse hold? We might argue thus: if the meaning of a sentence is determined by assertion-conditions, the content of an assertion of that sentence will be that its assertion-conditions obtain. For what other feature of the sentence do we discern in grasping its meaning? But since, by the uncontroversial principle, what is asserted is that the truth-conditions obtain, these must equate with assertion-conditions.

So long as EM is thought of as identifying meaning solely in terms of assertion-conditions, this has force. For then indeed, what difference *are* we grasping in claiming to distinguish the meaning of *P* and *It is assertible that P?* What we grasp, of course, is their different use as premises in inferences. But the real import of EM should be that meaning is constituted by correct use – and inferential as well as assertoric practice is an essential ingredient of correct use. So the proper conclusion is that the cognitive role of a sentence is constituted by its inferential power as well as its assertion-conditions; once this is recognized there is no obvious route from EM to ET.

It will remain the case that a significant sentence must have assertion-conditions; so there will be no intelligible sentence whose truth is radically evidence-transcendent (in the sense that no state of belief and experience, achievable in any possible world, would justify one in holding it true). Or more accurately, even this claim is, as it stands, somewhat too strict – the reasons why will be considered in section VII. But for the moment the point to notice is that it does not itself force endorsement of ET. What it says is that an intelligible sentence must be assertible in a possible information state. It does not follow that an information state in which the sentence – or its negation – is assertible can *in fact* be achieved; nor does anything follow about whether or not the sentence has a truth-value if no such information state can in fact be achieved. The connection with truth is no more than that a meaningless sentence cannot have a truth-condition.

On this line of approach cognitive role is fixed by inferential power as well as assertion-conditions, and truth-conditions are recovered from cognitive role. Use – cognitive role – must constitute truth-conditions – semantic content. Yet there is at the same time a sense in which use is regulated by truth-conditions. If there is an epistemic conception of meaning which can underpin the modernist strategy, it must be able to give a perspicuous picture of this dialectic between cognitive role and semantic content. Such a position, I believe, is found in the later thought of Wittgenstein. It is expressed in the variety of 'reminders' which are harnessed – with Wittgenstein's usual reservations about slogans and theses – to the slogan that meaning is use; and it is grounded in the rule-following considerations. Rule-following is constituted by nothing other than practice (perhaps – for those who go along with Wittgenstein on this – an essentially communal practice); yet there is a perfectly proper sense in which a particular act within the practice is explained by saying that it follows the rule.

But what is the status of these lines of thought – where are they coming from: from within or from without?

Stroud points out in his closing discussion that verificationism itself requires defence – and if it is to provide a fully naturalistic response to the sceptic, that must be an internal, non-transcendental defence:

I have tried to show how verificationism would directly oppose the traditional conception [of objectivity] by implying that everything meaningful could be known to be true, or to be false; that the 'empirical' way of understanding things is the only way there is. But I argued that that could be used to establish the incoherence of the traditional conception only if there were some independent support for the verifiability principle. And it remains to be seen whether any such support could itself be understood only 'empirically', while having the philosophical consequences it is meant to have (p. 274).

Notice first that Stroud here takes it that verificationism implies 'that everything meaningful could be known to be true, or to be false'. If 'could' is relative to evidence actually available, even if not actually possessed, then such verificationism is stronger than the position of the Dummettian anti-realist. For he allows that a statement can have meaning, even though all available evidence may warrant neither its assertion nor its denial. *A fortiori*, Stroud's verificationism is stronger than the position being considered here. The Dummettian anti-realist denies that a statement which is in fact undecidable can be said to have a truth-value – or at least he refuses to affirm that it has one; the present position does not.

Granting these important differences, however, Stroud's closing challenge applies as much to the epistemic conception of meaning as to 'verificationism'. Any argument for the epistemic conception must be understandable 'empirically'.

The claim that 'meaning is use' should be understood in just this way. It is ready to shrink into a set of constitutive banalities. Understanding just consists in appropriate assertoric and inferential dispositions. What else could it consist in? ('This table is made of matter.' What else could it be made of?) Wittgenstein's explorations can be presented as a naturalistic investigation of the notions of understanding and inference. Were the investigation to issue in acceptance of both epistemic theses, hence, in a form of idealism, it would undermine itself. But if ET can be detached from EM, that is not so obvious.

I shall not inquire further into the possibility of detaching EM from ET in this paper.[11] In the remaining sections I shall assume that it *is* possible; and on that assumption explore further the relation between idealism and the modernist strategy – understood as underpinned in this way.

First we must establish how such a position blocks sceptical arguments while yet not forcing us to reject pre-Copernican platitudes at any level.

VI

I can never rule out the possibility that a proposition I am warranted in asserting in my current state of belief and experience (information state – IS for short) will cease to be warranted in an enlarged IS. But that in itself does not remove my current warrant to assert it: to recognize that my information warrants me to assert it *is* to be warranted to assert it. The belief that I am typing into a word-processor is justified in my current IS. I cannot rule out the possibility that an enlarged IS will defeat it, and will justify me in concluding that I am the subject of an experiment in simulation. But the mere possibility does not itself constitute positive evidence – evidence which should weaken my grounds for belief.

Consider this more closely. If I am warranted in believing that P, am I warranted in believing that no enlarged IS will defeat the proposition that P? No: if I am warranted in believing that P, I am of course warranted in thinking my belief true. However, from the premise that my belief is true it does not follow that no enlarged IS will defeat it. It is possible for an enlargement of my current evidence to defeat a true belief which I am now warranted in holding on that current evidence.

So long as the possibility of an enlarged IS defeating a currently warranted assertion is a merely abstract one, grounded in the general defeasibility of evidence, then I am justified in thinking that if such an IS were to ensue, it would be misleading. But suppose I have *specific* ground, in my current IS, for thinking that a defeating IS will ensue. That is a different situation. A specific ground may weaken my warrant for asserting that P, proportionately to its strength. For example a regular history of defeated theories on a subject would rightly weaken our trust in any theory on that subject. But this provides no global collapse of fallibilism into scepticism.[12]

All of this takes for granted the legitimacy of our basic standards of reasoning. But if the sceptical questions could be taken in their intended way, they would, of course, put those very standards in doubt. It is here that EM does its work. Return again to Kant: on Kant's view naturalism issues in the negative thesis that no proposition which has genuine content is *a priori*. And this in turn leads to the sceptical *impasse*, for there can be reason to believe any proposition at all only if some substantive ('synthetic') propositions have *a priori* standing.

Now we have already observed that on the naturalistic view all propositions are in principle revisable in the light of experience – and to that extent we have agreed with Kant. Given naturalism, no proposition is classically, *strongly a priori*. But it does not follow that no proposition can have a rational claim on our thinking prior to experience: that none is *weakly a priori*. We accept certain principles in our reasoning as prior postulates: canons of induction, ground rules of good explanation, various propositions of logic and mathematics, guidelines of scientific inquiry such as principles of continuity, conservation and sufficient reason. Such principles are weakly *a priori* in that they have an authentic initial claim as rules of reason but can be defeated under sufficient pressure from experience. Rationality requires that they be given first refusal. That is intelligible on the epistemic conception of meaning. For if understanding a sentence is being able to recognize what warrants its assertion, then spontaneous acceptance of certain rules of evidence and reasoning must be part of the very process of acquiring mastery of our rules of language. Yet these principles are still not 'analytic', and their authority can still in the long run be undermined by empirical inquiry.[13] An example which might be used to illustrate this point is the principle that two straight lines cannot enclose a space. The disposition to infer, where two apparently straight lines are found to enclose an area, that they cannot really be straight, can plausibly be regarded as partially constitutive of understanding 'straight' – in which case the principle is weakly *a priori*. But that disposition can be checked or subtly modified by experience-based theory: current physical theory gives us ground for holding it to be false.

Rejecting the classical pre-understanding would defuse sceptical questions and block the self-undermining sceptical consequence which the Kantian critique draws from naturalism. But we must ask whether the resulting position still generates the idealistic conditionals which Stroud finds in Carnap's argument.

Carnap wanted to say that certain specifiable propositions (there are physical objects, there are numbers) have an external status inasmuch as we can be said to choose to endorse them. There is indeed an internal sense in which someone may affirm that there are physical objects, à la Moore. Or that there are numbers. (There are many numbers greater than the number of planets, so there are numbers.) But there is also an external sense, in which the claim that there are numbers amounts to a stipulation, made for convenience. That Carnapian line of thought allows Stroud to group Carnap with Kant in the idealist camp. For it seems that specifiable elements of our system of beliefs can now be seen as *a priori* because resulting from our own input. There is an external or transcendental level at which it can intelligibly be said that external objects exist because we have decided that they do.

But the position we are considering would not endorse Carnap's external claims about such propositions as 'There are numbers.' It is thoroughly fallibilist and it is holistic. Guiding principles can be retroactively confirmed by their success in organizing data – or disconfirmed by their failure in comparison with alternatives. Contrary to what might be thought, application of this holism is not incompatible with holding that the sceptic seeks to ask an unintelligible external question. On the contrary, it brings out its full subtlety. Stroud's criticism of Carnap does not turn, in fact, on Carnap's endorsement of the epistemic conception of meaning, but on his particular way of implementing it. It turns on Carnap's allegiance to a distinction between the form and the content of our knowledge which is characteristic of the Austrian and German analytic tradition and presumably traces back ultimately to Kant. The difficulty arises when an external perspective is allowed – a perspective in which certain identifiable elements in the system of what we take, internally, to be *factual* beliefs are perceived as 'really' non-factual. This is an essentially Kantian idea, and it is not surprising that it should require a Kantian form of idealism to underwrite it.[14]

As we have seen, the doubt the sceptic seeks to raise *can*, strictly speaking, be answered by a straightforward appeal to natural standards of reasoning. That, indeed, is the only possible *answer*. But naturalism in the Mill/Goodman style is wise not to bother with it. The answer would not address the sceptic's intention, for his questions, as they are intended, would put the reliability of those natural standards of reasoning – taken as a whole – in doubt. So what is needed is an analysis which shows why the intentions are empty, and the supposed questions non-existent. What must be shown is that, if it seems legitimate to ask whether our reasoning propensities, taken as a whole, lead to truth, that is only because our philosophical thinking is shaped by the classical pre-understanding of meaning. When we reject the pre-understanding, we reject the idea that it makes sense to ask the question. In all of this Carnap and Wittgenstein – the two Viennese modernists as one might say – are perfectly right. But none of it requires that we should make any distinction between the form or framework of our knowledge and its content. There does not have to be any conventional yardstick whose length it is meaningless to question. Any of our standards of reasoning could come to be rejected in the process of inquiry. The only point required is that it makes no sense simultaneously to question them all.[15]

VII

I have now set out the philosophical ideas which seem to me to provide the strongest foundation for the modernist strategy. Does it finally achieve the elusive objective – that of turning sceptical questions into pseudo-problems while avoiding idealism? The objective is indeed elusive and there remain difficulties to be met. In the final two sections I shall consider two major doubts.

We have seen that naturalism makes it a platitude that there are true propositions for which we have no evidence. That is, we have perfectly good grounds for asserting

1   There are propositions which are true even though no-one has any evidence for asserting that they are.

So this general proposition is in good standing. It has perfectly good assertion-conditions. Yet there can be no grounds for asserting any substitution-instance:

2   There are birds in my garden right now, even though no-one has any evidence for asserting that there are.

For if we have grounds for asserting the first conjunct in (2), we have grounds for denying the second. And if we have grounds for asserting the second, we can have no grounds for asserting the first. The difficulty raised here is not just for the epistemic view of truth. It is a difficulty for the epistemic view of meaning. For if (2) has no assertion conditions, how can it have sense?

(2) has no direct assertoric role in the language game on its own. There are no circumstances in which it can be used to make a simple assertion. Its only role is as a constituent in a complex assertion; embedded, for example, in the context 'It is possible that . . .', 'It could be true that . . .', or in tensed contexts ('It was the case that . . .')

We want to insist on the principle of compositionality: the meaning of a complex expression is a function of the meaning of its constituents. Given compositionality, if the complex sentences in which (2) occurs have a meaning – and they undoubtedly do, because they can be used to play an assertoric role – (2) itself must have meaning. However none of this determines the direction, so to speak, in which meaning flows.

Considering meaning as semantic content – i.e. as characterized by a systematic compositional semantics – we shall see these complex sentences as building on (2). They follow (2) in the semantic order – first (2) is built up from its syntactic constituents and a truth-condition for it derived; then the complex sentences are built out of it by further applications of sentential operators, or by dropping a constituent sentence and replacing it by quantifiers and bound variables, and truth-conditions for them are derived. It is the drive towards smoothness of semantic structure that delivers a semantic content for (2).

But the complex sentences do not follow (2) in the cognitive order. In the dimension of cognitive role, the complex sentences have priority. Thus our grasp on (2) derives in part from our grasp on (1) and our understanding of the systematic semantic structure which tells us that (2) is a substitution instance of (1).

In the semantic order, truth-conditions for substitution instances of (1) are derived before the truth-condition for (1) is derived. But in the cognitive order we get a grip on the assertion-conditions of the general statement and we recognize its substitution instances as having meaning because we hold to the structural uniformity in which an existential sentence has truth-conditions only if its instances have truth-conditions. The existential sentence has the primary cognitive role, but we invest its substitution instances with semantic content: this structural imperative modifies the principle that every semantically significant sentence has assertion-conditions, and thereby the strict correspondence of cognitive role and semantic content.

Note the sharp contrast between our account of the epistemic conception of meaning and an anti-realism based on the intuitionistic perspective. That perspective underwrites a Berkeleyian argument to idealism. Consider

3   There are objects which are not being thought about.

Berkeley in effect argues: Let a be such an object; then a is not being thought about: Contradiction. But *a* is an arbitrary name, and cannot present an object to my thought relationally. I do not get to (3) by existential generalization; I cannot give myself in thought an object which is not being thought about. Yet on the intuitionist view (3) is assertible only if an instance is assertible. Since no instance is assertible (3) must be meaningless. The same will apply to (1); since no instance is assertible (1) ought not to be assertible and should therefore be meaningless too.

It is not the epistemic conception of meaning which is at fault here, but the idea that it must be associated with rejection of classical in favour of intuitionistic logic. However, there need be no such association if we can block the inference from EM to ET. I suggested earlier that nothing in the epistemic conception of meaning as such forces acceptance of the epistemic conception of truth. What we are now considering are cases which force its rejection. For there are general propositions which must be recognized as true – (1), or (3), or others of similar structure – though their substitution-instances have no conditions of assertion. The drive towards smooth semantic structure leads us to endorse these instances as meaningful, and we must also accept that they have truth-values – otherwise a general proposition would be true, when no instance of it was.[16]

But have we now opened up a line of response for the sceptic? Is he not precisely relying on the intelligibility of something of the form 'P and it is not assertible that P'? Consider, for example, the hypothesis that 'The world came into being five minutes ago, even though there is no evidence that it did.'

There *is* a way in which that hypothesis can be brought within the scope of our normal attitudes of assessment. 'Evidence' will then be understood in the normal sense – the sense in which, while I, strictly speaking, have no *evidence* that McQuingle is the fraudster, I nevertheless have pretty good indirect or general reasons for thinking that he is. (I do not have *evidence* for thinking that my house was not destroyed by a bomb five minutes ago. But I am still perfectly justified in taking it for granted that it has not been: such bomb-explosions are unheard of in that part of Sheffield.) Understood in this way, we have good reason to reject the hypothesis. The normal canons of common sense and scientific inquiry rule it out as flagrantly *ad hoc*. Anyone who straightforwardly considers it more probable or even equi-probable to our normal view, suffers from some defect of rationality. On the other hand – still plainly speaking – these points give no basis for excluding the possibility that arcane, theoretical and indirect reasons might emerge for taking it seriously, or that there could have been such arcane reasons, which we would have recognized as such. But we do not have them. So we are justified in denying the hypothesis, but we do not rule out the very possibility of finding grounds for asserting it.

The sceptic will say that what he intends is the possibility that the world came into existence five minutes ago even though no grounds *whatsoever* are available or could be available for holding that it did. So he means to exclude all grounds, including the most indirect theoretical ones. The possibility as he intends it is one for which nothing in principle could count as evidence.

But then this has become a case of what EM excludes as an intelligible possibility. Consider the following three existential sentences, which give successively stronger readings of 'P and it is not assertible that P':

1   (∃P) (P and we are not in possession of evidence that P)
2   (∃P) (P and we cannot in fact achieve evidence that P)
3   (∃P) (P and there is no perspective in principle available (i.e. in which a knower could have been sited) which would justify assertion that P)

(1) and (2) are 'internally' assertible: their assertibility arises within the empirical fabric of common sense/science as such and they do not depend on a metaphysical position. (All that is required is that, since we are part of the world, our detailed knowledge of particular states of affairs can only be local and perspectival.)

But allowing (1) and (2), and their instances, is not enough to license the possibility that the world tracelessly came into existence five minutes ago, as the sceptic intends it. The statement which expresses that possibility would be an instance of (3). So the crucial point is whether there are internal grounds warranting assertion of (3).

Of course the 'modernist's' argument has to be that there are not. It is just here (he claims) that the sceptic has to slip in a dose of metaphysical realism. Our fabric of belief does not in itself force (3) on us – fortunately, in view of the self-undermining consequences that would have. But in allowing (1) and (2) we have marked out a line which the sceptic projects. Here we see very clearly how the metaphysical illusion is generated by our natural beliefs, and the way in which they shape our language.[17]

VIII

The position we have reached seems genuinely different from transcendental idealism. There are no philosophical truths 'on the outside', not even unsayable Stroudian conditionals. But we have not yet settled accounts in full with the 'pre-Copernican' notion of objectivity. In one sense, we endorse the pre-Copernican view: we endorse the platitudes which, Stroud implies, express it – and there is no external level at which we deny them. On the other hand, in rejecting the classical pre-understanding of meaning we reject a certain pre-understanding of objectivity; we make it impossible to raise the question whether our methods of inquiry taken as a whole lead to truth, even though any one of them could come under question.

That is quite consistent with the natural attitude, which accepts that particular explanatory inferences may turn out wrong, but does not question the method of inference to the best explanation as such. Yet there is reason to wonder whether complete fidelity to the natural attitude has been restored. In the evolution of our explanatory conceptions, and of our philosophical ideas about what is good explanation, any strut may need to be restructured and improved. Such gradual replacement could eventually produce a wholly new fabric. Can it be guaranteed, though, that there is only one best path of evolution? May there not be different paths, developing an irreducible multiplicity of overarching best explanations? And is there not a tension between allowing this possibility and continuing to insist, against the sceptic, that our methods of reasoning can achieve truth?

We should distinguish between global and local underdetermination. Local underdetermination occurs when available data, in a specific domain *within* our overarching framework of physical theory, are insufficient to adjudicate between rival explanations of those data. Examples occur in the historical rather than the micro-explanatory sciences: geology, the fossil record and evolution, archaeology, cosmogony – the origins rather than the nature of things. Another area is the constitution of particular objects which we cannot explore, for example, because they are too distant, or because they offer environments which are too hostile for probing. In these cases, we say, *within* the context of general physical theory, that the evidence is insufficient to determine the history or the make-up of some particular thing.

Global underdetermination obtains if all available data, all the data we could advance to, are compatible with more than one view of the ultimate nature of things – more than one set of irreducibly primitive theoretical concepts in physics. That is so if there is more than one optimal global theory. Is the possibility of such global underdetermination intelligible? Or is it another pseudo-possibility, like the sceptic's possibilities? If it is not a pseudo-possibility, there must be circumstances in which we would at least begin to be justified in asserting that global undertermination obtains.

Optimal theories would differ among themselves non-trivially but would be of equal overall explanatory power, as judged by all the criteria of good explanation which we could be brought to recognize. But that is not all. It would have to be the case that, as proponents of the respective theories tried to improve them, the theories neither converged, nor fell into a stable rank order, nor came to be superceded by a new theory which non-trivially differed from all of them. Unless we had grounds for thinking that that would continue to be the case indefinitely, we would not be in a position to assert that we had two optimal theories.

Obviously it is difficult to imagine circumstances in which we would have grounds for saying this, and our grounds could never be definitive. However, a long history of theoretical debate can be imagined in which every attempt by one theoretical tradition to trump or assimilate another, quite distinct, one was always matched by an effective reply, without any sign of convergence setting in. At some stage of this process, the conclusion that no such attempt would ever be successful, that convergence would never set in, would start to be plausible. We can recognize that as the kind of situation which, as it continues, makes the underdetermination thesis ever more plausible, and that is enough to show that the thesis has sense.

The question then arises of how we would react if it occurred. There must be an element of guesswork in any answer to that. But I suggest that there would in fact be a strong tendency to resort to an instrumentalist view of the theories advanced by both traditions. At this point there are well-explored options.

One kind of instrumentalism would hold that there is no way things absolutely are beyond the way they are observed to be. This positivist response has the difficulties of positivism – how can the observable measure the real, if observers are just part of the world, and if there can be very different observers with different perceptual powers? We make ourselves into different observers every time we equip ourselves with new senses by developing new instruments. We surely do not thereby bring into existence new domains of reality.

A second kind of instrumentalism would also withhold truth-values from theoretical sentences, but it would not equate the real with the observable. In which case, unless there is some radically non-empirical form of access to the real – a possibility naturalism renders unintelligible – it will follow that we cannot know how things in themselves really are. This position does endorse metaphysical realism: it would endorse proposition (3) in the last section, just as the Kantian has to. (There is a way things in themselves are, even though no possible knower could be so placed as to know it.)

But instrumentalism, of either kind, is not the appropriate response if we accept the account of meaning which underpins the modernist strategy. Each cognitive tradition could represent its own particular theoretical judgements, within its own framework, as reliably, though not infallibly, tracking the facts. So consensus among subscribers to that cognitive tradition could – internally speaking – be explained by correspondence. Within each tradition, 'the answer represents how things are' would be seen as constituting the best explanation of convergence. So each cognitive tradition can, by hypothesis, apply the correspondence notion with full cogency – internally. And the internal notion of correspondence is the only notion we have made sense of. Rejection of any other notion is the essence of the epistemic conception of language mastery.

If I am right in thinking that the natural response would nevertheless be to retreat to instrumentalism, does that not show that in our philosophical first-thoughts we are 'metaphysical realists' after all, and that those first-thoughts are rooted in the natural attitude? Not in itself. Metaphysical realism, understood as the view that there are ways things are for which no naturalistically possible knower could in any possible circumstances have evidence, is ruled out by the positivistic instrumentalist. So it would depend on which kind of instrumentalism we resorted to. But in any case the position of the positivistic instrumentalist still differs from that which should be accepted by the modernist. Why then does the 'natural' response veer towards instrumentalism?

Because, one feels inclined to say, modernism gives up the view, or rather intuitive commitment, that *there is a single way the world is*. This gestures at something expressible only as an 'external' perspective. From it, we see each tradition as constructing a world-picture, driven by imperatives of predictive power and simplicity. Of course we have just seen that *within* each cognitive tradition particular judgements can be seen as tracking the world in this way. But the external stance involves the further step of seeing both traditions as reactions to a single world, providing in each case different, but equally optimal, tools for thinking about it. So both traditions become options, and the underlying world determines neither.

The modernist will insist that no such metaphysical vision is inherent in the natural attitude. What is rooted there is, rather, a link between objectivity and convergence: if we become persuaded that however much evidence becomes available, nothing will force rational convergence on one response to a given theoretical question, we shall concede that there *is* no objectively correct response to the question. So there is no objective issue as to which cognitive tradition is right, and *a fortiori*, no factual issue.

On the modernist strategy, therefore, global underdetermination would only serve to pinpoint the fallacy in asking of an optimal system of belief, as a whole, whether it is true. There would, to be sure, be a sense in which we could say that it was true – the sense in which the proposition would follow from our acceptance of each belief in the system as true. The fallacy would lie in taking a whole optimal system, comparing it with another, and asking which corresponds to fact. But the only sense we have made of correspondence is the 'internal' sense (this is not to reintroduce an unsayable external sense), and that notion of correspondence is consistent with holding that, if there could be a plurality of optimal cognitive traditions, there would be no fact as to which was right.

As C. D. Broad said, Kant's analogy with Copernicus is odd. For Copernicus (and others) made us a part of a natural world which stretched infinitely beyond us, whereas Kant put the constructive mind outside the natural world. There is a temptation to say that in rejecting the intelligibility (as the assertion is intended) of 'There is a single world', while still insisting that all the parts of our fabric of belief have truth-values, we follow the path of absolute idealism – a relativized absolute idealism; so that at the limit, absolute idealism coincides with fully thought-through naturalism.

However, the true modernist should hold that there is absolutely no idealism involved. A better analogy for him might be the rejection of Euclidean geometry, which allows us to appreciate that space-time may be finite but unbounded: so that despite its finitude, no question can be raised about what is *beyond* it. Similarly, the thought-system of any naturally possible community of knowers will be determined by their finite cognitive powers, but there will be no boundary of knowability, with something on the other side. But it is not really a question of the degree of analogy between these various modern developments – in epistemology, or in physical geometry (or in set theory or quantum physics). The point is that all of them have a similar effect. They are all aspects of the dissolution of a classical synthesis – of the world-view which might with some justice be called Copernican, and which seemed so completely intuitive while it prevailed.

Notes

1 Carnap, 1956. One source of the distinction between internal and external questions is Wittgenstein's *Tractatus* – though it is not applied there to epistemological issues – and through the *Tractatus*, Frege's paradox of the concept *horse* which is not a concept.

That pedigree encourages the idea that answers to external questions cannot be said but can be shown – by our 'syntax', 'grammar', or choice of scheme of representation; so it concedes a kind of sense to external questions. Here there are evident Kantian analogies, which will be discussed below; though they diminish if the line between form and content is made variable, as in *On Certainty*.

However, the view of 'external' questions as nonsensical can be taken quite strictly; as it was, for example, by Frank Ramsey – in which case the metaphor of 'internal' and 'external' becomes misleading, and the affinity with Kant reduces towards zero. We shall see that a full working-through of the modernist strategy porduces this latter view.

2 On these analyses of the concept of knowledge I may know something even though I have no reason to believe it (See Ramsey, 1978 – a great deal of elaboration is provided in Nozick, pp. 172–97.) Thus, if I am sitting at a desk, the answer to the question: How do I know that I am? would be that that fact produces my belief that I am in appropriate and reliable ways. If the sceptic accepts such an analysis he will of course concede the possibility that I do know that I am sitting at a desk. (So long as I believe that I am.) But he will question whether I have any reason to believe that I am sitting at a desk, or to believe that I know I am sitting at a desk.

3 The term 'plain' is from Clarke.

4 I can imagine coming to be convinced by new data that I am indeed physically realized as nothing more than a brain in a vat, and further coming to appreciate that the chance of that being the result of any designed intervention is on the face of it extremely low. Perhaps I am discovered and instated by a transplant in an available or a synthetic body. Perhaps further inexplicable cases are discovered in the remote corner of the universe where I was found. And so on. We must accept that sufficiently bizarre cases would throw the plain response into complete bafflement.

5 Though Green's main ground for claiming that naturalism makes knowledge impossible is not its sceptical consequences but its undermining of the very intelligibility of notions of knowledge, meaning and reference; its 'insufficiency to account for an intelligent, as opposed to a merely instinctive or habitual, experience' (p. 3). (The

remark is about associationism, but is intended to apply to naturalistic psychology as such.)

6 'insulate' is from Burnyeat who also sees Kant as the turning point in this.

7 This statement is argued for in Skorupski, 1989.

8 Goodman, p. 64. Goodman presents this as the view Hume intended. But that cannot be right, since, as we noted, Hume did not think inductive rules were *justified*: it was a positive part of his view of the mind that they were not. And this gave him an important role in the nineteenth-century development of 'irrationalism'. The passage does however, express just what Mill intended. The difference between the two kinds of naturalistic tradition should not be diminished. (The most recent Humean philosopher is Sir Peter Strawson – Strawson, 1985.)

9 This is not to say that I agree with Dummett's general picture of the development of the analytic tradition – in particular, with his view of Frege as crucial in the formulation of the issue between 'realism' and 'anti-realism'. See Skorupski, 1984.

10 This is a crucial claim, of course, which calls for more development than I can give it here. It raises questions about what can be regarded as internal to common sense and scientific methods of reasoning. (One might for example compare the question of whether Newtonian physical theory could justify 'internally' the postulation of absolute space.)

11 I examine the arguments for, and coherence of, a position which endorses EM without ET in Skorupski, 1986 and in forthcoming work.

12 Winkler argues that anti-realism is consistent with scepticism. His account of anti-realism comes close to the position I have suggested here, which endorses EM but not ET, and his account of the Wittgensteinian grounds for EM is also close to mine. But he holds that I do not know X unless I have ruled out the possibility that not-X. This is not true on a reliabilist view of 'know'; however the argument should not be a narrow one about 'know'. Reading 'Ap' as 'My information state justifies me in asserting that p', 'Ap, $A(p, A(p \rightarrow q)$, Aq' does seem to me to be a valid principle. However 'Aq' may be true even if I have not 'ruled out' the possibility that not-q (i.e. by bringing independent evidence to bear on the question of whether q).

13 More on why they are not analytic in Skorupski, 1987.

14 Note however that Carnap, 1949, specifically distinguishes truth and confirmation – a first step in developing an epistemic account of meaning which posits no distinction between 'form' and 'content'. (Carnap appeals to Tarski's semantic theory of truth and points out that if truth is equated with confirmation it would be necessary to abandon the law of excluded middle.)

The distinction between form and content also pervades Wittgenstein's thought – and in particular, in *On Certainty*, even though Wittgenstein there allows that propositions may have a shifting status. But the idea that 'hinge' propositions, as he sometimes calls them, are non-factual remains open to the same sort of objection that Stroud raises against Carnap.

Davidson has suggested that the 'dualism of scheme and content' is 'a dogma of empiricism, the third dogma' (p. 189). However, there is surely nothing particularly *empiricist* about it: it should rather be seen as belonging to the Kantian inheritance of Viennese philosophy.

15 We cannot intelligibly challenge the abstract pattern of inference to the best expla-

nation, with its criteria of predictive power and simplicity, though of course the best explanation relative to given data may always turn out wrong. But the logic which underlies deduction of empirical results, and the understanding of what is 'simple' can change.

16 Similar treatment should be given to such sentences as 'I am unconscious', (the example is Moser's, in Moser, 1988), 'This does not exist' etc. In all these cases the drive towards smooth semantic structure is the central fact.

Moser's paper is a critique of 'semantic justificationism', particularly of the views of John Pollock. The treatment of meaning and justification outlined here has, it seems to me, strong similarities to Pollock's, though the specifics of my account of the relationship between the levels of cognitive role and semantic content (see Skorupski, 1986, and forthcoming work) may well differ from what he would adopt. The most recent statement of Pollock's views is Pollock, 1987.

17 Further analysis is needed (as observed in note 10) of how and when the 'internal' shifts to the 'external' and of the way in which (3) posits something unintelligibly external. Compare Wright on the 'Superior perspective' in his section 4; similar issues are raised by Thompson Clarke.

References

Burnyeat, M. F. 1984, 'The sceptic in his place and time', in R. Rorty, J. B. Schneewind and Q. Skinner *Philosophy in History*, Cambridge: Cambridge University Press

Carnap, R. 1949, 'Truth and confirmation', in *Readings in Philosophical Analysis*, eds H. Feigl and W. Sellars, New York: Appleton-Century-Crofts (translation, with adaptations, of 'Wahrheit and Bewahrung', *Actes du Congres International de Philosophie Scientifique'*, 1936)

Carnap, R. 1956, 'Empiricism, semantics and ontology', in *Meaning and Necessity*, Chicago: University of Chicago Press

Clarke, Thompson 1972, 'The Legacy of Scepticism', *Journal of Philosophy*, 69

Davidson, Donald 1984, 'On the very idea of a conceptual scheme', in *Inquires into Truth and Interpretation*, Oxford: Clarendon Press

Goodman, Nelson 1979, *Fact, Fiction and Forecast*, (3rd edn), Hassocks: The Harvester Press

Green, T. H. 1882, 'Introduction to Hume's Treatise on Human Nature', *A Treatise of Human Nature*, by David Hume, eds T. H. Green and T. H. Grose, London

Moser, Paul K. 1988, 'Meaning, justification and scepticism', *Philosophical Papers*, XVII, 77–101

Nozick, Robert 1981, *Philosophical Explanations*, Oxford: Clarendon Press

Pollock, J. 1987, *Contemporary Theories of Knowledge*, London: Hutchinson

Ramsey, F. P. 1931, 'Philosophy', in ed. R. Braithwaite *The Foundations of Mathematics*, London: Routledge and Kegan Paul

Ramsey, F. P. 1978, 'Knowledge', in *Foundations*, ed. D. H. Mellor London: Routledge and Kegan Paul

Skorupski, John 1984, 'Dummett's Frege's (Critical Study), *The Philosophical Quarterly*,

34, pp. 402–14, reprinted in *Frege, Tradition and Influence*, ed. Crispin Wright, Oxford: Basil Blackwell

Skorupski, John 1986, 'Anti-realism: cognitive role and semantic content', in *Language, Mind and Logic*, ed. J. Butterfield, Cambridge: Cambridge University Press

Skorupski, John 1987, 'Empiricism, verification and the *a priori*', in *Fact, Science and Morality*, eds G. Macdonald and C. Wright, Oxford: Basil Blackwell

Skorupski, John 1988, Critical review of C. Wright, *Realism, Meaning and Truth, The Philosophical Quarterly*

Skorupski, John 1989, *John Stuart Mill*, London: Routledge

Skorupski, John forthcoming, 'Realism, inference and the logical constants', in *Realism and Reason*, eds J. Haldane and C. Wright, Oxford: Clarendon Press

Strawson, P. F. 1985, *Scepticism and Naturalism*, London: Methuen

Stroud, Barry 1984, *The Significance of Philosophical Scepticism* Oxford: Clarendon Press

Winkler, Kenneth P. 1985, 'Scepticism and anti-realism', *Mind* XCIV, 36–52

Wright, C. 1985, 'Facts and certainty', Henriette Hertz Philosophical Lecture, *Proceedings of the British Academy*, London, LXXI, 429–72

2

Frege on Sense and Linguistic Meaning

Tyler Burge

Frege's conception of sense has fathered all the major approaches to 'meaning' that have preoccupied philosophers in our century. Some of the progeny have developed the Fregean conception. Others have rebelled against it. All have borne its mark. Certain key elements in Frege's conception have, however, disappeared in interpretations of his view. These elements derive from his rationalist predilections and from his primary concern with idealized thought. The philosophical traditions most heavily influenced by Frege have been empiricist, preoccupied with language and suspicious of the notion of thought – idealized or not. So the neglect is natural. I think that some of the neglected elements in Frege's conception are of profound philosophical importance. They are critical to a philosophical understanding of language, cognitive processes, and conceptual change. I shall not, however, be building on Frege's conception in this paper. Rather I shall approach it historically.

I

Frege introduces the notion of sense by giving it three functions.[1] The first is that of accounting for 'cognitive value'. Senses are 'modes of presentation': ways things are presented to a thinker – or ways a thinker conceives of or otherwise represents entities in those cases where there are no entities. Not all modes of presentations are senses. But where modes of presentation are senses, they are associated with linguistic expressions. Being a sense is not essential to the entities that are senses. Being a (possible) mode of presentation to a thinker is what is fundamental. A sense is a mode of presentation that is 'grasped' by those 'sufficiently familiar' with the language to which an expression belongs. The second function of the notion of sense in Frege's theory is that of fixing the *Bedeutung*, the denotation or fundamental semantical value, of semantically relevant expressions. The third is that of serving as the denotation of expressions in oblique contexts.

Our primary concern is with the first function. Although the third is essential to Frege's overall theory, I think it less fundamental for understanding his conception of sense, at least initially, than the first two. The second function has been widely discussed, and I shall say only a few words about it now.

Frege explicates the notion of fixing a *Bedeutung* in a purely logical way: for each sense there is at most one *Bedeutung*. It is also clear, partly from the first function, that a sense is a way of thinking of *Bedeutung*. Beyond the foregoing, Frege says little.

The urge to say more has led some to interpret this second function in verificationist terms: sense is construed as a procedure for determining *Bedeutung*.[2] Thus the sense of a name would be a means of finding or recognizing an object; that of a predicate would be a way of determining whether an object satisfies it; that of a sentence would be a method of verification or falsification. To deal with a variety of problems of interpretation, these procedures have been regarded as highly idealized – for example, as what a collection of experts or a superior being would do. I think that there is little justification in the texts for this procedural interpretation of Frege's notion of sense. I shall return to it later.

The main import of the second function lies in its connecting thought and judgement with truth, the *Bedeutung* of sentences. The first function indicates that the notion of sense is designed for an account of thought and judgement. The primary logically relevant function of thought and judgement is to 'strive after truth'.[3] Thus sense provides a logically relevant connection between judgement and truth. This connection grounds Frege's celebrated insistence that in construing the sense of an expression one consider only the expression's contribution to the deductive inferential potential and 'truth-conditions' of the sentences in which it is contained.

Let us now concentrate on the first function of the notion of sense in Frege's theory. The first function is to represent the way entities are presented to a thinker, or the way a thinker conceives of or otherwise represents entities in those cases where there are none. Frege's development of his theoretical notion of sense, through consideration of linguistic phenomena such as the paradox of identity and through his remark that sense is what is grasped by those 'sufficiently familiar' with a language, has led many to assimilate his conception of sense to modern notions of conventional linguistic meaning.[4] This interpretation cannot be sustained. My primary purpose is to explain in some detail why.

II

As background for what ensues, one must bear in mind Frege's repeated claim that his primary concern in producing his logical theory is to theorize about thought and truth, not language. He says that language often obscures the actual structure and nature of thought. Of course, he also held that one could not think most of the thoughts one thinks except by means of language. So, as he says, he is forced to concern himself with language even though it is not his main interest. Thus natural language is cast in the role of a villain on which one must perforce rely, both in order to think and as a source of clues about the nature of thought. But natural language is an imperfect instrument for thought. And Frege believed that only a language yet to be fully fashioned – a 'perfect language' (one ideally suited to the expression of thought, especially *a priori* thought) – would express thought, and senses, in a perspicuous manner.

One might be inclined to assimilate this point of view to more modern conceptions according to which the form and semantical characteristics of a language can be understood only by reference to its 'deeper structure'. There is something to be said for this interpretation. But taken in the way it would normally be understood, it underestimates how far removed, for Frege, thought and sense may be from a language's surface.

I shall be arguing that no amount of investigation of the actual usage and understanding of one's language is, according to Frege, sure to reveal the 'deeper structure' and nature of sense and thought. One may have to achieve genuine advances in non-linguistic knowledge before one can fully master the senses and thoughts that one's language expresses. This point renders Frege's view and modern methodologies for studying language quite different.[5]

We can begin to appreciate the full extent of the difference between sense and conventional linguistic meaning by developing Frege's statements about understanding and about *vagueness*.

We enter this subject by posing an interpretative puzzle. The puzzle consists of an argument that leads from Frege's statements and a plausible further premise to an inconsistency. Resolving the inconsistency as Frege would will, I think, deepen our understanding.

The puzzle arises out of the conjunction of three claims that Frege makes. The first is that vague expressions lack a *Bedeutung* (e.g. PPW 112; 155; 179/ NS 133; 168; 193–4; PMC 114/ WB 183; 'About the Law of Inertia', 360–1/ KS 122–3). Frege states this principle repeatedly. We need not discuss his reasons.

The second is that all of the expressions in conventional mathematics and natural science, and some of the same terms in ordinary discourse, are not sharply understood – are not backed by a sharp grasp of a definite sense – even by their most competent users (PPW 221–2; 216–7; 211/ NS 239–40; 234; 228;

FA vii in conjunction with FA sections 1, 2; FA 81; cf. also 'About the law of inertia', 360/ KS 122).

If the best mathematicians lack such a grasp, one might reason, conventional mathematical usage is surely, by Frege's lights, vague. And if mathematical expressions are thus vague, surely most other expressions are too. This is the premise I foreshadowed.

The third element in the puzzle is Frege's repeated citations of this or that expression from mathematics or ordinary discourse as having such and such a *Bedeutung*. Indeed, Frege consistently writes as if lacking a *Bedeutung* is an aberration, except in fiction.

The three claims, together with the reasoning following the second, are jointly inconsistent. For if one holds that even the best mathematicians do not have a firm grasp of a sense that fixes a sharply bounded *Bedeutung* for concept words and concludes from this that most mathematical and other (concept) expressions are vague; and if one holds that vague concept expressions lack *Bedeutung*; one cannot go about assigning *Bedeutungen* to most of the concept expressions of mathematics and ordinary discourse. Here we have a puzzle. Did Frege find his way through it?

III

Although the puzzle centres on *Bedeutung*, much of its interest bears on sense. So in discussing it, we shall keep track of both notions. In arriving at an interpretation, one must bear in mind the fact (not seriously questionable, I believe) that Frege was committed to the view that senses of concept expressions fix definite, sharp *Bedeutungen* where they have any *Bedeutung* at all. Frege conceived of senses as eternal abstract entities that have their logical and semantical properties independently of the activity of actual minds or language-users. Neither senses themselves nor their applications to *Bedeutungen* could be vague. This in itself constitutes a difference between Frege's conception and the ordinary conception of conventional linguistic meaning. But this difference will stand out in sharper relief once we have unravelled the puzzle.

Let us begin by considering whether one could avoid attribution of the third of the three claims. One possible line would be this: 'Despite what Frege says in illustrating his doctrines, he does not really mean that our expressions have definite senses or *Bedeutungen*. For if they are vague, they do not, by his own account, have *Bedeutungen*; and if the most competent users of the expressions do not fix definite *Bedeutungen* through their linguistic practices, the expressions would seem also to lack definite senses. The fact that Frege does not speak this way could be attributed to his desire not to complicate his expositional task unduly. He conveyed his idealized picture of sense and *Bedeutung* through his examples. But he did not see imperfect natural language as embodying his idealization.'

There are two options within this general line. We might say that Frege thought that ordinary expressions in mathematics and elsewhere had a sense but lacked a *Bedeutung*. Or we might say that he thought such expressions lacked a sense as well. Let us take up the second option first.

There is an early passage in *Begriffsschrift* (1879) (B 27) where Frege says of a particular vague expression that it lacks a 'judgeable content'. But he does not indicate how far he intends his remark to be generalized. And since 'content' is a technical expression that Frege later thought blurred the sense – *Bedeutung* distinction, one cannot rest much weight on the remark. More significantly, there is a letter to Peano (1896) that reads as follows:

> The fallacy known by the name of 'Acervus' rests on this, that words like 'heap' are treated as if they designated a sharply bounded concept whereas this is not the case. Just as it would be impossible for geometry to set up precise laws if it tried to recognize threads as lines and knots in threads as points, so logic must demand sharp limits of what it will recognize as a concept unless it wants to renounce all precision and certainty. Thus a sign for a concept whose content does not satisfy this requirement is to be regarded as without *Bedeutung* from the logical point of view. It can be objected that such words are used thousands of times in the language of life. Yes; but our vernacular languages are also not made for conducting proofs. And it is precisely the defects that spring from this that have been my main reason for setting up a conceptual notation. The task of our vernacular languages is essentially fulfilled if people engaged in communication with one another connect the same thought, or approximately the same thought, with the same proposition. For this it is not at all necessary that the individual words should have a sense and *Bedeutung* of their own, provided only that the whole proposition has a sense. Where inferences are to be drawn the case is different; for this it is essential that the same expression should occur in two propositions and should have exactly the same *Bedeutung* in both cases. It must therefore have a *Bedeutung* of its own, independent of the other parts of the sentence. In the case of incompletely defined concept words there is not such independence: what matters in such a case is whether the case at hand is the one to which the definition refers, and that depends on the other parts of the proposition. Such words cannot therefore be acknowledged to have an independent *Bedeutung* at all. This is why I reject conditional definitions of signs for concepts (PMC 114–15/ WB 183).

This passage raises a number of interpretative problems that I will not go into. It could perhaps be read as supporting the view that Frege thought that virtually all words in ordinary discourse lack a definite sense. Perhaps each would be attached to a cluster of senses, no one of which it definitely expresses. But the passage certainly does not demand this interpretation. There is nothing in the passage to indicate that Frege is assimilating virtually *all* words in natural discourse to 'heap'.

The main point of the passage is that one must insist on explicit rather than contextual definitions. Frege is laying down a requirement about how we should analyse language for the purposes of logic (as contrasted with the purposes of the vernacular). Similar requirements apply to the project of defining 'number' (cf. FA, middle sections). But Frege repeatedly assumes that 'number' has a definite sense and denotation. For example, he writes of a certain large finite numerical expression that it has a 'perfectly definite sense' (FA 114).[6] Words like 'heap' seem to be treated as special cases, not as paradigms of all linguistic usage.

It should be noted that this passage suggests a distinction between the notion of sense and the notion of conventional or idiolectic linguistic meaning. The implication of the passage is that the relevant vague notions, like 'heap', do not have a definite sense or denotation. Different people in different contexts, or the same person in different contexts, may associate different thoughts with sentences containing the word, in such a way that there is no saying what thought component is the sense associated with the word. Sometimes such thought components will apply to 'the case at hand' (say, counting it a heap); other times, they will not. One cannot associate any particular sense with the relevant vague word on all its occasions of use, though it may have different senses on different occasions.

There is no suggestion that such words are strictly without what we would call meaning. They contribute to the fulfillment of the 'task of our vernacular languages' by facilitating communication. It might well be that despite variations in putative extension among language-users (or by a given user at different times), one could attribute a constant meaning – a constant norm for understanding – to the word. I see no reason to think that Frege would have denied that an attribution of vague linguistic meaning was possible, based on an account of vague linguistic usage. Frege's own analogy suggests that he would not have denied this. There is no suggestion that one couldn't give a theory of knots and threads. It just would not be directly relevant to geometry. Similarly, an account of vague usage would not be an account of sense.

Let us return to the option of solving the puzzle by denying that most ordinary and mathematical expressions have a definite sense. The primary trouble with the option is that there is no evidence that Frege thought that nearly all the expressions we actually use lack a definite sense. In fact, he often seems to suggest that it is relatively easy to get an expression to express a sense. He writes:

If one is concerned with truth . . . one has to throw aside concept words that do not have a *Bedeutung*. These are . . . such as have vague boundaries . . . [But] the context cited need not lack a sense, any more than other contexts in which the name 'Nausicaa', which probably does not denote or name anything, occurs. But it behaves as if it names a girl, and it is thus assured of a sense (PPW 122/ NS 133).

Here it is clear both that senses are easily attached to words and that vague concept words do not, or need not, lack sense. It is also at least suggested that the vague words comprise a relatively small, delimited class.[7]

Frege argues in numerous places that the objectivity of science and the possibility of communication depend on sentences' expressing (objective) sense (e.g. G&B 46/ KS 170; PMC 80/ WB 128; LI 32ff., 24ff./ KS 362ff., 358ff.). And he repeatedly states or implies that the sense of a sentence (at an occurrence) is a function of the senses of its parts (G&B 54/ KS 178; PWW 192/ NS 208–9; LI 55ff./ KS 378ff.).

These general doctrines about the commonness of sense-expression are buttressed by numerous statements that this or that expression has a sense: 'the morning star', 'the celestial body most distant from the Earth', 'the least rapidly convergent series', 'the Moon', 'Odysseus' and so on are cited in 'On Sense and Denotation' alone. In fact, the general tenor of Frege's remarks is that only rationally defective expressions (like 'the concept horse', as he later decided (PPW 177–8/ NS 192–3; PPW 193/ NS 210), really lack a sense. Although the examples I have cited concern singular terms, many of the cited singular terms contain concept words. So by the composition doctrine, the singular terms could not have senses unless their component concept words had senses. Moreover, there are passages in which Frege explicitly speaks of concept words in conventional usage as having a definite sense (e.g. PPW 122, 209/ NS 133; 225–6). The view that nearly all expressions lack a definite sense has no clear textual basis and runs against an overwhelming number of remarks Frege makes.

We turn now to the option of taking Frege to hold that nearly all expressions in ordinary, conventional mathematics and ordinary discourse lack a denotation without lacking a sense. This option might seem to receive support from the following unpublished passage written in 1914:

In the first stages of any discipline we cannot avoid using the words of our language. But these words are, for the most part, not really appropriate for scientific purposes, because they are not precise enough and fluctuate in their use. Science needs technical terms that have precise and fixed *Bedeutungen*, and in order to come to an understanding about these *Bedeutungen* and exclude possible misunderstandings, we give explications. Of course, in so doing we have again to use ordinary words, and these may display defects similar to those which the explications are intended to remove. So it seems that we shall then have to do the same things over again, providing new explications. Theoretically one will never really achieve one's goal in this way. In practice, however, we do manage to come to an understanding about the *Bedeutungen* of words. Of course we have to be able to count on a meeting of minds, on others guessing what we have in mind (PPW 207/ NS 224).

The practice of substituting technical expressions for ordinary expressions, even those like 'number', is prominent in *Grundgesetze*, written much earlier. Here Frege does perhaps suggest that nearly all non-technical words are 'not precise enough and fluctuate in their use'.

Nevertheless, Frege does not say in this passage that non-technical words, much less ordinary mathematical expressions, are in general bereft of *Bedeutung*. In fact, the passage clearly presupposes that the relevant words *have* a *Bedeutung*. The problem that concerns him is that there is some difficulty in determining or understanding exactly what *Bedeutung* a person denotes with an ordinary word. The problem is lack of standardization. The remarks of this passage appear to apply primarily to expressions of ordinary language. And Frege is issuing a general indictment, not one specifically concerned with vagueness. Imprecision and fluctuation of use cover not only vagueness but ambiguity; lack of interpersonal standardization; lack of a generally agreed-upon specification, in other terms, of the *Bedeutung*; and the dependence of expressions (demonstratives or indexicals) on context.

The problem with this option for solving the puzzle is similar to the problem with the previous option. Frege repeatedly writes as if fiction and serious mistakes are the primary sources of failures of denotation. When he discusses vague, denotationless concept words, the examples he offers are always presented as if they were special cases – 'heap', 'bald' and so on. By contrast, Frege gives numerous examples of concept words – both in conventional mathematics and in ordinary discourse – that are explicitly ascribed denotations. (PPW 120–1; 177; 182; 229/ NS 130–1; 192; 198; 247, G&B 113/ KS 278; and so on).

If he were to hold that nearly all concept words in mathematics, natural science, and ordinary discourse are vague, and thus lack a *Bedeutung*, he would have to hold that nearly all sentences in actual use strictly speaking express neither truths nor falsehoods. There is no suggestion of a 'secret doctrine' to this effect. (The closest approach to it that I can find is PPW 242–3/ NS 261–2.) Indeed, again, his basic argument for the existence of sense depends on the assumption that we share knowledge, hence express true thoughts, in the sciences. Neither of the options that we have considered for denying the third step in the argument is a credible expression of the spirit or letter of Frege's writings.

There is no questioning the attribution of the first step of our argument – the claim that vague expressions lack a *Bedeutung*. Frege's remarks are frequent, straightforward and explicit. What of the second step – the claim that expressions of mathematics, science and ordinary discourse are not sharply understood, even by their most competent users? Understanding it is a complex undertaking – the central element in solving our puzzle. I shall be developing an interpretation of the second step throughout the rest of the paper.

IV

On several occasions, Frege states or implies that the sense of an expression, often a mathematical expression, is not clearly or sharply grasped even by the most competent users of the expression. This theme emerges most clearly in his late writing. But the idea informs Frege's work almost from the beginning. Let us start by considering some passages from *Foundations*:

> What is known as the history of concepts is a history either of our knowledge of concepts or of the meanings of words. Often it is only through great intellectual labour, which can continue over centuries, that a concept is known in its purity, and stripped of foreign covering that hid it from the eye of the intellect (FA vii).

A cognate passage occurs seven years later, in 1891:

> For the logical concept, there is no development, no history ... If instead of [this sort of talk] one said 'history of the attempt to grasp a concept' or 'history of the grasp of a concept', it would seem to me far more appropriate; for the concept is something objective that we do not form and is not formed in us, but that we try to grasp and finally, it is hoped, really grasp – if we have not mistakenly sought something where there is nothing (KS 122).[8]

The significance of these two passages can be appreciated only when the context of the first one is noted. That passage occurs in the introduction to *The Foundations of Arithmetic*. It is almost immediately followed in sections 1 and 2 by a long complaint that most of the fundamental notions of arithmetic have not been 'sharply determined' or 'sharply grasped' (section 1) by mathematicians, past or present. He cites the notions of function, continuity, limit, infinity, negative and irrational numbers.

The whole book is thus cast as an attempt to produce, for the first time, a sharp grasp of concepts (later, senses and concepts through senses) that are associated with conventional mathematical usage, but that had never before been 'sharply grasped'. In the course of the book, Frege gives several further examples of applications of mathematical expressions that past usage and understanding had left indeterminate, but which his own understanding purports to fix determinately (FA pp. 68; 80–1; 87, 96–8, 100–1; 102–3).

The mist metaphor recurs thrice in 1914. Here is one occurrence:

> How is it possible, one may ask, that it should be doubtful whether a simple sign [in common use] has the same sense as a complex expression if we know not only the sense of the simple sign, but can recognize the sense of the complex one [that purportedly analyses it] from the way it is put together? The fact is that if we really do have a clear grasp of the sense of the simple sign, then it cannot be doubtful whether it agrees with the sense of the complex expression. If this is open to question although we can clearly recognize the sense of the complex expression from the way it is put together, then the reason must lie in the fact that we do not have a clear grasp of the sense of the simple sign, but that its outlines are confused as if we saw it through a mist. The effect of the logical analysis of which we spoke will then be precisely this – to articulate the sense clearly (PPW 211/ NS 228).

A second occurrence appears in a critical discussion of ordinary mathematical practice. Frege makes the point that ordinary mathematicians often grasp the same senses. In particular, they 'attach the same sense to the word "number"'. But because they are so cavalier about their definitions, they do not 'get hold of the sense properly'. They do not manage to attain a definite mastery of the sense they think with. He says that the sense appears to them

> in such a foggily blurred manner that when they make to get hold of it, they reach for it in the wrong place. One reaches perhaps erroneously to the right, the other to the left; and so they do not get hold of the same thing, although they wanted to. How thick the fog must be for this to be possible! (PPW 216–7/ NS 234; the third occurrence of the mist metaphor occurs later in the same essay PPW 241–2/ NS 260–1, and will be mentioned below.)

The comedy of this passage is double-edged. Frege produces a deliciously absurd picture of his opponents. But the terms of the metaphor indicate a notion of understanding on Frege's part (as grabbing some elusive phantom) that inevitably seems incongruous to modern minds.

Frege goes on to blame the failure of mathematicians to 'grasp' or 'get a proper hold' of the senses that they attach to the word 'number' on a failure to lay down and abide by good definitions. There follows a lengthy discussion of Weierstrass's failures to provide clear definitions for his primary mathematical expressions. Frege is obviously taking Weierstrass as an example of one of the mathematicians who 'attach the same sense to the word number', but do not get hold of it pro-perly. Frege thinks Weierstrass does not grasp sharply the sense that he associates with his own word. Frege ends this discussion with the remark that Weierstrass's grasp of the notion of number is very unclear. And he diagnoses the trouble as follows: 'He lacks the ideal of the system of mathematics.' (PPW 221/ NS 239)

The obvious implication of these passages is that the most competent users of the relevant expressions may not have achieved a sharply bounded understanding of a sense – a 'sharp grasp' of a definite sense – that they attach to the word they use. Conventional usage and understanding may not give those users a clear understanding of a definite sense that the expression already expresses.

From this remark it is natural for us to infer that the relevant expressions are vague. For if conventional use and understanding *by even the most competent users* does not constitute mastery of a sense that fixes sharp boundaries, it is natural to conclude that the expression's 'sense' and proper application simply lack sharp boundaries. Attributing this inference to Frege is, however, the mistake that leads to our puzzle.

For Frege did not draw this inference. The clear implication of the above cited passages is that the relevant expressions *have* a definite sense, or denote a definite concept. The problem is that no-one has yet grasped it fully or clearly. The defect is in our understanding and use, not in the abstract senses themselves, nor even in our expressions' relations to their senses. There is, moreover, no sugges-tion that such senses lack a sharply delimited denotation.

Thus, although Frege believed something that for most modern philosophers would appear to entail that the senses of most mathematical expressions were vague, he did not accept the entailment. He might well concede that what we would call an expression's 'conventional linguistic meaning', as fixed by conven-tional or actual usage, is vague. (Recall the knots and threads passage.) But he thought that the expression might nevertheless have a definite *sense* with a sharply bounded denotation.

Now this fact, not the mere resolution of the puzzle, is the primary point of interest. Frege's views about vagueness are in themselves not particularly im-portant. They are significant almost entirely because they are symptomatic of interesting aspects of his conception of thought and sense: Frege's failure to draw the inference is, I think, a sign that his conception of sense differs substantially from any ordinary conception of conventional linguistic meaning.

For all the controversy that has surrounded the term 'linguistic meaning' as a theoretical tool, I think it clear that we have a rough and ready, reasonably coher-ent conception that is expressed in standard dictionary entries and in intuitively acceptable explications of the meanings of terms. Conventional linguistic mean-ing, according to this ordinary conception, is a complex idealization of conven-tional use and understanding. The meaning of a term is revealed in its use and is articulated in dictionary entries and in reflective explanations of its use by competent users. If conventional use and best understanding are not sharp, then conventional meaning is certainly not sharp. An analogous point can be made for the notion of idiolectic meaning. On this common conception, it would be absurd to say that an expression had a definite, non-vague conventional linguistic meaning – or, alternatively, a definite range of application – even though all extant understanding and all actual usage failed to fix sharp boundaries for the expression's application. Similar points hold for modern conceptions of idiolectic linguistic meaning. It would be absurd to to say that an expression had a definite, non-vague idiolectic linguistic meaning, even though all the individual's abilities to articulate the expression's meaning, and all the individual's actual usage failed to fix sharp boundaries for the expression's application. (Cf. n. 4)

So it appears that for Frege the capacity of a word to express a sense is partly independent of the user's understanding and use of the word, and even of conventions about the word's usage, in a way that distinguishes his notion of sense from almost any ordinary notion of linguistic meaning – conventional or idiolectic.[9]

V

Before proceeding, I want to note that Frege does not explicitly emphasize the contrast with conventional (or idiolectic) linguistic meaning that I am highlighting. I believe that he never thought the issue through in any depth. The view that I have attributed represents a prominent strand in his thinking. And I think that he never gave it up. But there are passages that suggest that Frege was not focusing on the matter, passages in which some further specification of the view would be natural had Frege clearly formulated it to himself. There are also passages which suggest that Frege wanted to avoid questions that this conception very naturally raises.

According to the conception that we have been developing, the sense and *Bedeutung* of an expression in conventional mathematics might be quite definite even though all past and present applications and all extant abilities to explicate a word fail to fix sharp boundaries. Frege indicates, however, that the *Bedeutung* of a mathematical expression sometimes changes in the course of its history. Frege indicates in 'Function and Concept' that the *Bedeutung* of the word 'function' has changed in the course of the history of mathematics. More is now included in the *Bedeutung* than had been earlier, Frege counts inclusion of transition to the limit as an essential broadening of the original *Bedeutung* of 'function'. And he counts the admission of new arguments and values (such as negative numbers) for standard mathematical operations as evidence that the *Bedeutung* of the expression has been extended.

A similar point applies to the expression 'number'. In 1914 he writes:

Originally the numbers recognized were the positive integers, then fractions were added, then negative numbers, irrational numbers, and complex numbers. So in the course of time wider and wider concepts came to be associated with the word 'number' . . . And the same happened with other arithmetical signs. This is a process which logic must condemn and which is all the more dangerous, the less one is aware of the shift taking place. The history of science runs counter to the demands of logic . . . No science can master its subject matter and work it up to such transparency as mathematics can; but perhaps also, no science can lose itself in such thick mist as mathematics if it dispenses with the construction of a system. As a science develops, a certain system may prove no longer to be adequate, not because parts of it are recognized to be false but because we wish, quite rightly, to assemble a large mass of detail under a more comprehensive point of view in order to obtain greater command of the material and a simpler way of formulating things. In such a case we shall be led to introduce more comprehensive, i.e. superordinate, concepts and relations. What now suggests itself is that we should, as people say, extend our concepts. Of course . . . we do not alter a concept; what we do rather is to associate a different concept with a concept word . . . The sense does not alter, nor does the sign, but the correlation between sign and sense is different . . . If we have a system with definitions that are of some use and aren't merely there as ornaments, but are taken seriously, this puts a stop to such shifts taking place . . . In fact, we have at present no system in arithmetic. All we have are movements in that direction. Definitions are set up, but it doesn't so much as enter the author's head to take them seriously and to hold himself bound by them. So there is nothing to place any check on our associating, quite unwittingly, a different *Bedeutung* with a sign or word. (PPW 241–2/ NS 260–1).

This passage is not incompatible with the passages I previously centred upon. Indeed they are complementary. This last one occurs in the same essay as the most explicit remarks about the best mathematicians' lacking a clear grasp of the senses they all attach to terms they commonly deal with. The mist metaphor even recurs in this passage.

But seen very schematically, the two groups of passages suggest different models of progress in science. On the first model, progress is a matter of obtaining a better, clearer grasp of thoughts that one is already dimly thinking and unperspicuously expressing. Better theory results in deeper understanding and clearer explication of some of one's own thoughts and senses. One might have been thinking various thoughts at different times, even though one is using a single expression. But deeper theory cuts through the mist and explicates a given sense long associated (however inconstantly and uncomprehendingly) with an expression. On the second model, theoretical improvements issue in new connections between words, on one hand, and senses and *Bedeutungen*, on the other. One replaces old concepts (and senses determining them) with new ones in one's thinking.

If the first model is to have any place at all, it must be complemented with the second. Sometimes actual usage is just too far removed from some conceptions to attribute those conceptions to the users. When the users eventually arrive at such a conception, and express it in old words, we have to see them as having altered the senses of the words. On the other hand, this point is compatible with the idea that *sometimes* a user expresses a conception that is more definite and richer than the users could articulate given his or her state of knowledge.

There remain vexed questions of practice and principle about where to draw the line. I believe that Frege never concentrated on the differences between the two models, or worried about the issues regarding change-of-belief *versus* change-of-'meaning' that have become prominent since his time. As noted, some of Frege's discussion seems fashioned so as to lay these issues aside.[10] I shall, however, continue to concentrate on the first model on the ground that it represents something philosophically important and distinctive, even if undeveloped, in Frege's thinking.

VI

How *could* an expression express a definite sense if its being related to that sense were not entirely explicable in terms of how its users actually use and understand the expression?[11] Frege does not directly confront the question. But his work seems to indicate a certain type of answer. Saying that the expression 'Number' denotes a definite concept and expresses a definite sense, despite the insufficiencies of current understanding and usage, is (for Frege) made possible by the belief that the ultimate justification of current mathematical practice supplements current usage and understanding in such a way as to explicate a definite concept and a definite sense that no one may currently be able to thoroughly understand or articulate. Weierstrass's inadequate understanding of the senses he thought with would be rectified if the 'ideal of the system of mathematics' had properly informed his thinking.

Frege's conception of sense expression has two fundamental presuppositions. The *first* is that mathematics and other cognitive practices are founded on deeper rationally understandable aspects of reality, than anyone may have presently understood. The implications of a practice can reach beyond the procedures and dispositions of the practitioners.[12]

The *second* presupposition is that mastery of these deeper rationales is to be treated as involving insight into the true senses of expressions. It is to be understood in terms of conceptual clarification. Deeper insight into the nature of things is simultaneously deeper insight into rational modes of thinking about the nature of things.

Both presuppositions derive from the rationalist tradition. They combine to form a rather special conception not only of the nature of sense expression, but also of the enterprise of philosophical analysis. I mean this latter phrase not in a narrow sense that would apply specially to 'analytic' philosophy – the tradition that grew out of Frege and came in our century to dominate the English-speaking philosophical world. I mean by 'philosophical analysis' something that would apply to much of the philosophical activity of Socrates, Plato, Aristotle, Descartes, Leibniz and Kant, as well as to twentieth-century 'analytic' philosophers more specially concerned with language. Any activity at least partly aimed at understanding our 'conceptual scheme', our cognitive practices, is analytic in this broad sense. Frege shared with the rationalist tradition the confidence that a deep rationale underlay many of our practices. He also shared the view that this rationale made its imprint on those practices in such a way that understanding the rationale was achieving insight into what was part of the practices even before the understanding was achieved. Since Frege develops the second of the two cited presuppositions in some depth, at least implicitly, I shall begin by discussing it. I shall return to the first afterward.

There are in Frege's writings two contrasting themes about the grasping of senses. Frege does not explicitly juxtapose and reconcile them until relatively late in his career (1914). But both themes and the makings for reconciliation are present from early on. One theme emphasizes how relatively easy it is to express and grasp a sense. We have already noted a variety of passages in which Frege suggests that normal linguistic activity is often sufficient to *express* a sense. Frege also states (GB 58/ KS 144) that a sense expressed is grasped by everyone 'sufficiently familiar with the language'. He does not say what constitutes sufficient familiarity. But the surrounding context certainly suggests that the requisite familiarity is not an exceptional accomplishment. In the same passage, Frege cites names and (presumably) other context-dependent devices as exceptions to the remark that knowing the language is sufficient to grasp the sense. But he indicates that people nevertheless commonly 'attach' a sense to the relevant term in a context, presumably grasping it in so doing.

There are also numerous passages in which Frege says that thinking paradigmatically involves grasping a thought, grasping the sense of a declarative sentence. There is no suggestion that thinking is especially difficult to engage in. (Frege's own virtuosity in this regard may have blinded him to difficulties that the rest of us face!) In fact, Frege bases one of his arguments for the existence of senses on the assumption that mankind commonly grasps them in common. All of these passages indicate that senses are routinely grasped in the hurly-burly of cognitive life.

On the other hand, there are passages where Frege indicates that grasping a sense or thought is a matter of degree, and that thoroughly grasping thoughts is an achievement worthy of some renown. There are, for example, the two passages from 1884 and 1891 in which Frege says that what is usually called the history of a concept is better termed the history of attempts to grasp a concept (FA vii, KS 122). Frege elaborates the point in a passage from 1897 (PPW 138/ NS 150). He is arguing that thoughts are changeless, in precise analogy to the earlier arguments that 'concepts' do not change: 'We might cite, as an instance of thoughts being subject to change, the fact that they are not always immediately clear. But what is called the clarity of a thought in our sense of this word is really a matter of how thoroughly it has been assimilated or grasped, and is not a property of a thought.' Taken together, these remarks suggest that 'thorough grasp' is a difficult matter.

The suggestion is amplified in Frege's late writing (1914). Where there is a failure to provide a satisfactory explication of mathematical terms, there is, he writes, a failure to understand the terms. Writing of Weierstrass, Frege says in an unusually smug passage:

He had a notion of what number is, but a very unclear one; and working from this he kept on revising and adding to what should really have been inferred from his definition . . . And so he quite fails to see that what he asserted does not flow from his definition, but from his inkling of what number is (PPW 221/ NS 239).

He continues:

But how, it may be asked, can a man do successful work in a science when he is completely unclear about one of its basic concepts? The concept of a positive integer is indeed fundamental for the whole arithmetical part of mathematics. And any unclarity about this must spread throughout the whole of arithmetic. This is obviously a serious defect and one would imagine that it could prevent a man from doing any successful work whatsoever in this science. Can any arithmetical sentence have a completely clear sense to someone who is in the dark about what a number is? This question is not an arithmetical one, nor a logical one, but a psychological one. We simply do not have the mental capacity to hold before our minds a very complex logical structure so that it is equally clear to us in every detail. For instance, what man, when he uses the word 'integral' in a proof, ever has clearly before him everything which appertains to the sense of this word! And yet we can still draw correct inferences, even though in doing so there is always a part of the sense in penumbra. Weierstrass has a sound notion of what number is and working from this he constantly revises and adds to what should really follow from his official definitions. In so doing he involves himself in contradictions and yet arrives at true thoughts, which, one must admit, come into his mind in a purely haphazard way. His sentences express true thoughts, if they are rightly understood. But if one tried to understand them in accordance with his own definitions, one would go astray (PPW 222/ NS 239–40).

Here Frege issues a sharp statement of the point that the best mathematicians may fail to have a clear grasp of senses or thoughts they think with. Nevertheless, he emphasizes that the expressions such mathematicians use express definite senses, definite thoughts (*Gedanken*). The presupposition of the whole passage is that the science of arithmetic and the words that Weierstrass uses already express the relevant senses and denote the relevant concepts. The lack of clarity or definiteness resides purely in the person: it is 'psychological' not 'logical' or 'arithmetical'. The mathematician is thinking with the sense, and expressing it in his writing, but not grasping it clearly.[13]

Frege articulates the same view, in a passage we quoted earlier (PPW 21/ NS 228), at the conclusion of a long and interesting discussion of philosophical or foundational analyses – analyses of the sort that he had pursued in trying to establish logicism. The suggestion is that insofar as an analysis like the one he attempted in *Foundations of Arithmetic* is true but still subject to doubt, the difficulty resides in the person's inability to grasp the sense clearly.

These last two passages from 1914 contain the resolution of the apparent tension between the passages that suggest that grasping the sense of an expression is relatively easy and those that indicate that it is quite difficult. It is possible to express a sense and think by 'grasping' senses even though one lacks a 'clear' or 'thorough' 'grasp' of the sense. The sort of grasping that is necessary for successful communication and ordinary thinking is different from the sort (or level) of grasping necessary to articulate the senses of one's expressions through other terms.

In one respect, Frage's distinction between levels of understanding is quite ordinary. We commonly attribute thoughts and statements to people on the basis of their linguistic expressions even though those people cannot produce acceptable definitions or explications of the terms they use. That is, we interpret our attributions in standard ways even though the people to whom we are making the attributions are unable to articulate the standard meanings of the expressions they use. This practice extends even to cases where the people in question misunderstand the relevant expressions.

The striking element in Frege's view is his application of this distinction to cases where *the most competent speakers, and indeed the community taken collectively*, could not, even on extended ordinary reflection, articulate the 'standard senses' of the terms. The view is that the most competent speakers may be in the same situation as the less competent ones in expressing and thinking definite senses which they cannot correctly explicate or articulate. Definite senses are expressed and 'grasped' (with merely the weak implication that they are thought with), even though no one may be capable of articulating or explicating those senses (grasping them clearly and analytically).

Frege does not introduce a distinction between sorts or levels of sense expression that parallels his distinction between sorts or levels of understanding or 'grasping'. Here it is clear that sense expression is not seen as supervenient on use and individual or communal capacities in the way that conventional (or idiolectic) linguistic meaning is commonly taken to be.

As I indicated earlier, I think that Frege's conception attempts to bridge the gap between actual understanding and actual sense expression by means of a normative concept – that of the deeper foundation or justification for actual understanding and usage. It would be incorrect to see Frege's notion of sense expression as separated from that of actual understanding and use. But it does depend on the possibility of a projection beyond actual understanding and use.

Even the ordinary notion of conventional linguistic meaning depends on a projection. Actual usage is interpreted in terms of a standard that is drawn from such usage. But the standard depends on a certain sort of rationalized ordering of that usage. Think of how dictionary definitions are arrived at. Frege's idealization is, however, much more radical. His conception of an 'ideally competent speaker' is much further removed from that of actual competence than is the conception of an ideally competent speaker that is current in discussions of conventional (or idiolectic) linguistic meaning.

Frege's ideal speaker is not simply an ordered composite of what is – or would be, under certain fairly ordinary conditions – recognized to be the best extant usage and understanding. Frege's ideal speaker may have an understanding that is fundamentally better than, even substantially different from, anything anyone has yet achieved. Understanding in the relevant sense is seen as an achievement that brings with it insight into substantive truths. In this, Frege is at one with the leading representatives of the rationalist tradition. (Cf. FA vii, PPW 12–13; 222/ NS 16–17, 240) As with Plato and Descartes, deep understanding of one's thoughts – and of the senses (forms, ideas) one thinks with – is not separable from the deepest sort of knowledge (KS 122–4; 369, PPW 33/ NS 37).

Analyses that articulate the senses of expressions do not constitute degenerate knowledge for Frege, any more than logic and arithmetic themselves do. Nor are they true 'purely in virtue of sense'. Analytical insight into the nature of one's senses or thoughts may involve a legitimate feeling of having been 'committed' to the relevant knowledge all along – may produce some sense of reason's recalling its origins. But from the point of view of what informs one's explications, one's actions, and one's operative understanding, such knowledge may count as new and substantive. It is not *merely* reflection on one's thoughts or meanings in the sense that the empiricist-positivist tradition in this century would represent it. This aspect of Frege's view has been seriously neglected because it is so out of keeping with the meaning-is-use approaches that stretch from the Vienna Circle to the present.

What is original about Frege's interpretation of the relation between conceptual insight and the deepest sort of propositional knowledge is his reversal of the traditional order of priority, and his emphasis on the role of theory in attaining such knowledge. Traditionally, among rationalists as well as empiricists, conceptual mastery was considered a precondition for judgement. And such mastery was interpreted in terms of what were presumed to be non-conceptual abilities, such as vision. This model is almost completely absent in Frege's work. There are, as I noted earlier, significant traces in Frege of the pre-Cartesian, Platonic picture of *a priori* knowledge as outer vision: vision of an eternal reality that informs and constitutes one's reason. But the traditional picture does not inform Frege's work in the traditional way. His model is not vision but theory.

Kant preceded Frege in insisting on the priority of judgement over non-propositional cognitive capacities. But Frege went beyond this Kantian view in two ways. In the first place, he developed a logical theory that demonstrated the fruitfulness of an account of judgement in analysing non-propositional parts and non-propositional cognitive capacities.[14] That is, Frege gave deep and detailed grounds for accepting the order of priority that Kant announced.

In the second place, Frege held that the analysis of judgement – and more generally, logic – was inseparable from *theoretical activity*. Unlike Kant, Frege was an original logician. Perhaps because of this he was more sensitive to the difficulties of arriving at a satisfactory logical theory and to the possibility that reflection on logical matters, as well as in other domains, had to be tested in a comprehensive theoretical context. For Frege, logic had to be discovered. It was not transparent to reflection. It had to be discovered through checking proposals as applied to discriminating reflection on ordinary theoretical usage in logic, mathematics and other domains. Frege thought that one could be sure of attaining thorough grasp of the senses of one's terms only through understanding their logical roles and their proper roles in a good theory. Such roles were guaranteed to be perspicuously revealed only in a logically perfect language that was ideally adequate to its subject matter.

Frege is a traditional rationalist in his belief in *a priori* knowledge, in his association of the deepest substantive knowledge with conceptual mastery, and in his modelling philosophy itself on logic and mathematics. But he goes beyond the tradition: Even *a priori* knowledge and non-propositional understanding (or conceptual mastery) were construed as grounded in logical analyses of theory, and checked against good theoretical usage. What makes Frege modern and entirely original is his combination of his traditional views about aprioricity, understanding and philosophy with a pragmatic understanding of the epistemology of logic.

Thus Frege held a fallibilist and theory-based account of *a priori* knowledge, understanding and philosophical inquiry.[15]

Frege expresses his pragmatic perspective on understanding and *a priori* knowledge only occasionally. But it appears at all periods of his career. For example, in an unpublished manuscript from 1880–1, he writes:

> All these concepts have been developed in science and have proved their fruitfulness. For this reason what we may discover in them has a far higher claim on our attention than anything that our everyday trains of thought might offer. For fruitfulness is the acid test of concepts, and scientific workshops the true field of study for logic (PPW 33/ NS 37).

The same point is developed at somewhat greater length in a passage of 'About the Law of Inertia' (1891). There Frege holds that thorough grasping of concepts has resulted to a large extent from recognition that the accepted delineation (*Begrenzung*) is 'blurred, uncertain, or not the one that was sought' (362/ KS 123). He develops the idea (KS 122–4) that only through the development of scientific theory, whether in physics, chemistry or logic, does one achieve a thorough grasp of one's concepts. Similar remarks occur in the later period. (Cf. KS 369, BL 7; 25/ GGA I; x; xxvi)

Partly because of Frege's work, and the work of those such as Wittgenstein, Carnap and Quine who were influenced by it, the connection between understanding and theory has become a commonplace. What is still unassimilated, in my opinion, is the way Frege attaches ideal understanding and actual sense expression to ideal theory. It is his explication of sense expression in terms of theorizing beyond any that may have actually been carried out that sets his conception of sense apart from more ordinary conceptions of conventional (or idiolectic) linguistic meaning.

VII

I wish now to turn briefly to the first of the two presuppositions behind Frege's view that the ultimate foundation and justification of current linguistic practice may supplement ordinary understanding in such a way as to attach it to a definite sense that no one may currently be able to articulate adequately, or thoroughly grasp. The presupposition is that some of our practices are founded on a deeper rationale or on deeper aspects of 'reality' than anyone may have presently understood.

This presupposition is, of course, bound up with deep and contentious philosophical issues. Systematic development of the idea is anything but trivial. Although I think that the idea need not be developed in foundational terms,

Frege clearly regarded his senses, at least in some contexts, in the light of some final state of cognitive achievement.

One naturally thinks here of some Peircean conception. Although like Peirce Frege had a notion of ideal science, he did not construe it in terms of agreement, or in terms of any epistemological notion (such as the application of best canons of reason to all possible evidence). Such accounts would not express the notion of an ideal science for Frege because he thought that there is no conceptual guarantee that any human agreement, or any humanly applied epistemic methods, would not be mistaken. He thought it conceivable that everyone might agree on what was not correct. Where a theory is incorrect, there would always remain room for a better theory that might provide better understanding of the senses of terms in the original theory.

There are, of course, epistemically orientated accounts of ideal science that recognize these limitations and try to idealize beyond them: we should not limit the account to *human* agreement or observational capacities, or to what is available to *us* as possible evidence, or to *our* inductive methods. All these might be improved upon. But when one projects beyond human practices, the idealizations become much less clear. Moreover, they become subject to the suspicion that they are covertly relying on the assumption that they are practices that are ideal in the sense that they yield a *true theory*. Such reliance would make epistemic notions presuppose semantical notions, giving up the spirit of Peirce's idea. But short of reliance on semantical notions, it is unclear how such epistemic explications can give a satisfactory account of the notion of ideal science – and hence of Frege's notion of sense. In any case, for Frege, the notion of truth is not to be reduced to epistemic terms.

For Frege, thoughts, the senses of declarative sentences, are conditions on truth. Conditions on truth are best understood, and senses are best articulated, from the standpoint of a comprehensive true theory. This is not to say, of course, that only expressions in a true theory have sense. The forerunners of such a theory also express senses, even if the senses are not thoroughly grasped. Moreover, non-denoting terms express senses. So even theories that are on the wrong track and have no justifying rationales express senses, possible ways of thinking. The point is rather that adequate explication of the senses of expressions is *guaranteed* only in a theory that cannot suffer further improvement or correction.

Frege did not attempt the reduction in reverse. He did not try to explicate epistemic notions by means of his notion of truth. He was as aware as anyone that the notion of truth does not provide an epistemic touchstone for judging the credibility of theories (cf. the opening pages of 'The Thought'.) Thus he seems committed to the view that one has no epistemic guarantee, beyond all conceivable doubt, that one has arrived at a true theory.[16] But one is guaranteed an understanding of one's senses only from the point of view of an 'ideal science' – a true theory. So how to explicate the senses of one's terms is in principle just as subject to theoretical debate as whether one's theory is true. The terms and methods of debate are surely different. But there is no difference as regards an epistemic guarantee that one is right.

The notion of truth provides a normative ideal that (in inevitable conjunction with concrete epistemic practices) enables us to conceive of terms having senses that are not fully explicable in terms of usage and understanding. An ideally competent speaker is one who can give ideally thorough explications and has an ideally thorough grasp of the senses of the expressions of his language. Having tied adequate explication and thorough grasp to having fundamental knowledge, and having tied fundamental knowledge to common theoretical activities (rather than indubitable insight), Frege must see full understanding as guaranteed only by completely fundamental and completely satisfactory (true) theory. It is this combination of a rationalist notion of understanding with a pragmatic epistemology that makes Frege's view unique and intriguing.

Since Frege did not develop this conception, it is important to reflect on it – and be prepared to develop it – in a flexible way. The view is most immediately attractive as applied to terms in mathematics and the empirical sciences. It is less plausible, at least initially, with respect to ordinary expressions that have no role in the sciences. The idea that one might obtain some significant improvement in our understanding of them may seem rather far-fetched. And surely, one is inclined to think, there are some expressions in ordinary discourse for whose understanding we would simply refuse to recognize any further authority than communal practice.

It is noteworthy that Frege always applies his remarks about the most competent users' incomplete understanding of their own expressions to terms that have a role in a scientific enterprise. Perhaps he would have given a different theory for non-scientific terms that are not grasped sharply. He may have held that such terms were associated with a cluster of senses. Where none of the senses is grasped sharply, no determinate thought is entertained. Or (what is more suggested by his actual remarks about vague terms) a definite sense might be assigned in the context according to how the thinker would draw a line if pressed. Perhaps he would have seen no need, in the case of ordinary non-scientific terms, for the possibility that a particular, unforeseen sharpening might be the correct one. Surely this possibility is sometimes closed.

On the other hand, the possibilities for rational improvement that extends elements already present in a practice are difficult to circumscribe. What underlies the attractiveness of Frege's conception, to my mind, is not some prior view of what a science is. It is a combination of two more general views. One is the view that full understanding of our thoughts and senses is not independent of knowledge of the subject matters about which we think. The other is that neither individually nor communally do we have infallible access to the truth about those subject matters. These two views jointly press one toward Frege's conception.

And they retain some force even as applied to thoughts outside the systematic sciences.[17]

Let us return briefly to our initial puzzle about vagueness. The puzzle helped signal the distinctive character of Frege's conception of sense. The account of sense that we have given helps, in turn, to illumine Frege's otherwise odd views about vagueness. Through theory one arrives at the sharpening of the application of expressions. This sharpening enables one to go beyond conventional or idiolectic linguistic meaning to arrive at a full understanding of one's expressions, a thorough grasp of their senses. Until a powerful theory is developed and logical analysis of its language is achieved, a full grasp of the senses of one's own expressions may be lacking.

Frege's conception of sense as deeply connected to that of a true theory also sheds light on, though it may not justify, his view that no senses have vague boundaries. Where senses are ways of thinking ideally or purportedly appropriate to a true theory, they are ways of thinking that ideally or purportedly reflect reality. Frege believed that vagueness could not infect reality itself – the objective entities which our thoughts denote. I suspect that only if one explicates reality in terms of mind or meaning does the notion of vagueness in reality make any sense. And Frege resisted such explications, partly out of allegiance to common sense, partly because of the sort of considerations that we have been rehearsing. So he concluded that senses, ways of thinking about reality, could not be vague. Only our grasp of senses could be.

This line of thought is, of course, more attractive for ways of thinking that are ideally fitted to reality than for ways of thinking that are merely purportedly fitted to reality. Some senses, as we noted, do not fit into an ideal science. They would not be expressed by a true theory. It is unclear how such an argument that senses cannot be vague could be applied to such senses. Perhaps the old charge that Frege's idealizations are too imperial still sticks. But it seems to me that his motivations are far more subtle and interesting than the traditional criticisms of his views on vagueness recognize.

I do not want to suggest that these issues are anything like as simple as I have been representing them. My primary point has been to try to indicate how Frege's odd-sounding views about vagueness are motivated by his realist conception of the world and his rationalist conception of sense.

VIII

I will close by noting in an extremely sketchy way some points about the subsequent historical fate of Frege's notion of sense.

Russell's views of understanding and knowledge began the historical process of obfuscation. From the beginning, Russell allowed little or no room for the idea that one could think with notions that one only partially understood. Russell assimilated understanding to a non-propositional, vision-like conception of knowledge, called acquaintance, which propositional abilities were supposed to presuppose. Much of the motivation for his semantical work lay in his notorious 'principle of acquaintance', which antedates 'On Denoting' (1905). According to this principle one had to be 'acquainted with' every constituent of a 'proposition' that one thought. The key point for us is that acquaintance was understood in terms of an infallible, direct and absolutely complete mastery of the propositional constituents. Eventually, Russell held that the only things with which we could be acquainted were universals, present sense data, and our selves. This approach led, of course, to much discussed difficulties with the theory of reference to individuals. But it did not allow serious consideration of the understanding of universals.

Encouraged by his interest in establishing logicism, Russell did emphasize that through analysis one could enlarge one's powers of understanding and gain insight into the foundations of notions that one is already thinking with. But because he treated understanding in terms of acquaintance rather than in terms of the use of a theory, Russell never allowed this emphasis to threaten the principle of acquaintance and the view of understanding and propositional thought that rests upon it. Thus the implicit tension between the principle of acquaintance and the natural view that with 'analysis' we obtain a better understanding of the analysanda never comes to a head in Russell's work.

Russell's communication of Frege's views to the rest of the philosophical world did nothing to call attention to the difference between his own views and Frege's on these points.

It is not clear to me to what extent the Vienna Circle reacted against Russell's vulnerable conception of understanding and to what extent it simply bypassed it. What is clear is that the Vienna Circle struck off in a very different direction. The early, more phenomenalist stage of the movement bears comparison to Russell's work in its interest in explicating understanding in terms of a construction from basic, rather specially certain types of cognition (the having of phenomenal experiences). But the prominence of this view diminished as the movement developed. Moreover, from the beginning the movement was much more ambitious about giving a detailed account of understanding than Russell was.

There seem to me to be two key ideas in the positivist programme that are relevant to our theme. One is the view that what there is to be understood, 'meaning', is to be reduced to actual procedures that express or constitute actual understanding. That is, meaning is identified with cognitive or theoretical usage. The other key idea is that both meaning and understanding are to be accounted for in terms of verification procedures.

The standard histories of the period concentrate on the second idea. But it seems to me that the first is equally momentous. Roughly speaking, it contains two moves: the reduction of what is understood to actual understanding, and the explication of actual understanding in terms of presently articulateable abilities or experiences. These moves seem to me to be fundamental, but largely unexamined in the work growing out of Vienna Circle movement.

The influence of these moves is evident in the explications of Frege that have been taken to be authoritative until recently. Carnap's explication of Fregean sense in *Meaning and Necessity* is a prime example. He writes, 'The concepts of sense and of intension refer to meaning in a strict sense, as that which is grasped when we understand an expression without knowing the facts.'[18] Quine takes up the same line, with fewer positivist commitments, when he explains Frege's conception, without comment, in terms of linguistic meaning. Most (though not all) of Kripke's criticisms of Frege depend essentially on identifying sense with an ordinary conception of linguistic meaning. Dummett's account of Frege's notion of sense, though much more nuanced and in many respects more insightful, takes up the same theme – again influenced by preconceptions about the relation between 'meaning' and 'use'.[19]

What made it historically difficult to appreciate the difference between Frege's conception of sense and modern notions of linguistic meaning was the domineering role of the idea that originated with the Vienna Circle: the reduction of what is understood to actual understanding and the explication of understanding in terms of actual articulateable abilities or experiences. The conception of meaning as use in the later Wittgenstein, the attempt to reduce philosophical problems to questions about ordinary language, and Quine's holistic liberalizations of verificationist conceptions of meaning, are all marked by these moves.

Parallel doctrines in the philosophy of mind are equally founded on the reduction of what is thought to what the thinker can presently do. Behaviourist and functionalist theories of mental content, Wittgenstein's puzzles about the possibility of following a rule, and Quine's claims that mind and meaning are fundamentally indeterminate – all depend on the idea that what is understood is to be reduced to or accounted for purely in terms of present abilities (where these are described in such a way as not to make explicit use of intentional notions like understanding or thought).

There is, of course, considerable force – not to say epistemic comfort – in this idea. But its dominance has engendered a certain blindness to the character and, I think, power of the very different point of view that motivated Frege. Appreciating and developing that point of view may help illumine some of the dark dead-ends of twentieth-century philosophy.

Notes

1   These functions are developed throughout Frege's work after 1891. But they appear in succession in 'On Sense and Reference' pp. 57–8; 58; 58–9 in *Translations of the Philosophical Writings of Gottlob Frege*. They are also discussed in my 'Belief *De Re*' (1977), section 4. References to Frege's writings will occur in the text, with abbrev-

iations set out in the bibliography. Where English and German paginations differ, both will be cited, separated by a slash. I am responsible for all translations of quotations from Frege, although often there will be little or no difference from already published translations. I will not say much on the vexed question of the translation of '*Bedeutung*'. I think that the current vogue of translating the term as 'meaning' is unfortunate, despite the support from ordinary translation practice outside of philosophy. The original choice, 'reference', was also unfortunate – though less so, in my opinion. The translation I prefer and have used here is 'denotation'. The translation goes back to Church, I believe. The advantage of this choice is that the term has an ordinary meaning ('meaning') which is roughly the same as the ordinary meaning of the term '*Bedeutung*' but also has various technical meanings that are not to be presumed the same as the ordinary meaning. In English-speaking philosophy, these technical meanings bear comparison to Frege's technical meaning for '*Bedeutung*', although the analogies (especially to Russell's and Mill's technical usage of 'denotation') must be handled with extreme caution. An alternative choice would be to leave the term '*Bedeutung*' untranslated. In the light of the moral of the present paper, as applied to '*Sinn*', this choice has much to be said for it: much gets lost and distorted under translation – especially translation between philosophical cultures.

2   Michael Dummett, *Frege: Philosophy of Language* (Duckworth, London, 1973), pp. 488ff.

3   I have discussed at some length the role of judgement and truth in Frege's system in 'Frege on Truth' (1986).

4   This view was almost universally held until a few years ago. It has received its most comprehensive articulation in writings by Michael Dummett. Dummett's characterization is very complex and not to be caricatured. But despite its many strengths, it seems to me fundamentally a misrepresentation.

The notion of conventional linguistic meaning has itself received numerous characterizations. I shall not attempt another. I shall assume, however, that conventional linguistic meaning is what is understood by an ordinary speaker of a language, or by the 'most competent' speakers of a language. I shall assume that in order to understand something in this sense, a speaker must be able on reflection to articulate, or recognize, without further instruction correct explications of the meaning, at least in those cases of meaning where explications are relevant to understanding. So, for example, those who understand the conventional linguistic meaning of 'chair' could on reflection articulate or at least recognize as correct a correct dictionary explication.

I should add that Frege's conception of sense is distinct not only from conventional linguistic meaning, but also from modern conceptions of idiolectic linguistic meaning. I shall concentrate on conventional linguistic meaning, because (except in the case of proper names and indexicals) Frege's notion of sense is much more likely to be confused with a conception of meaning that has social elements. But my discussion of linguistic meaning is meant to be neutral, except where the context indicates otherwise, on issues of the relative roles of individual and community in fixing meaning. Frege's notion of sense contrasts with all modern conceptions of linguistic meaning, including those concerned with meaning in idiolects. Of course, since he conceived of sense as a sort of linguistic 'meaning', sense is something with aboutness properties which is expressed through language. To this degree, Frege's conception of sense is a conception of linguistic meaning. So when I write of 'linguistic meaning' with the intent of contrasting such a notion with Frege's notion of sense, I am using this notion in a way that associates it with modern conceptions.

5   Another background point that serves as a clue to Frege's distinction between sense and conventional linguistic meaning lies in his remarks about proper names, demonstratives and other indexicals. He ascribes sense to names, but denies that there need be any conventionally agreed-upon sense. He frequently says that the senses of expressions like 'I', 'now' and 'yesterday' shift with the context and referent. Clearly their linguistic meaning, the accepted norm for conventional and idiolectic use and understanding of the language, remains the same through these shifts. Conversely, Frege sometimes counts the sense associated with two applications of two different indexical expressions ('yesterday' and 'today') the same, whereas the linguistic meaning is clearly different. These remarks are obviously incompatible with taking the sense of these expressions to be their conventional linguistic meanings.

It would be easy, though slovenly, to think of proper names and demonstrative expressions as special cases and to dismiss Frege's remarks about language getting in the way of thought as typical expressions of a logician interested in regimentation. But there is much more behind these remarks. They are symptoms of a radically epistemic conception of sense.

These background points are discussed at some length in 'Sinning against Frege', in my Review of Dummett's *The Interpretation of Frege's Philosophy* and in 'Frege on Extensions of Concepts'. The latter paper contains other grounds for distinguishing conventional linguistic meaning and sense. The present paper is a development of points first made in 'Frege on Extensions of Concepts'.

These points must be properly appreciated in order to assess the relevance of attacks on Frege over the last two decades. It has been common to hold that Frege had mistaken views about the 'semantics' of proper names, demonstratives and the like. Sometimes, with a dutiful nod toward 'the historians', a critic will say that 'Fregeans though perhaps not Frege' held certain mistaken views. I think that the historical issue is of more than historical importance. Frege held an entirely different conception of 'semantics' than do most of his modern critics. His conception of sense was introduced to serve this conception. Language was, in his view, an imperfect vehicle for thought; and thought itself was understood in a highly idealized manner that I shall try to articulate. By contrast, modern conceptions of language concentrate on explaining linguistic competence – what is standardly or normally understood by linguistic expressions.

If the philosophical interest and importance of modern conceptions of the 'semantics' of referring expressions is to be reasonably evaluated, one must be clear about what one is doing when one gives a 'semantical account' of the language. By paying too little attention to the range of possible conceptions of language (or semantics), modern critics of Frege often not only underestimate their target but fail to appreciate the nature of the philosophical problems that motivated his theory of sense. Since these problems remain philosophically important, discussions of them that fail to appreciate how they are understood in Frege's own work almost inevitably suffer substantively, as well as historically.

6   This occurrence of 'sense' (*Sinn*) is not corrected in the letter to Husserl of 5 May, 1891, that explicitly corrects a number of passages in *Foundations of Arithmetic* that blur the sense – *Bedeutung* distinction, cf. PMC 63.

7   Two pages later Frege writes that not being 'an empty sequence of sounds' is sufficient for a proper name's having a sense.

8   The first of these passages was written before the development of the sense – *Bedeutung* distinction (1891). It is likely but not certain that the second one was also. The talk of 'grasping' suggests, however, that the passages concern what is thought. Frege writes in 1897: 'We might cite, as an instance of thoughts being subject to change, the fact that they are not always immediately clear. But what is called the clarity of a thought in our sense of this word is really a matter of how thoroughly it has been assimilated or grasped, and is not a property of a thought.' (PPW 138/ NS 150)

9   It is important to recognize the difference betweeen this distinctive feature, which bears on the relation between senses and words, and two other striking features of Frege's doctrine of sense. Frege conceived of senses as eternal abstract entities that have their logical and semantical properties independently of the activity of actual minds. And he held that the content of all thinking could be characterized purely in terms of such entities. These latter two views, though perhaps congenial with the conception that we are discussing, are strictly independent of it. Of the three views, I find the first (the one I am concentrating on in this paper) promising, the second deeper and more interesting than commonly thought but extremely dubious, and the third mistaken. For criticism of the third view, see 'Belief *De Re*', and 'Sinning Against Frege'.

10 For example, Frege holds that for systematic purposes it is better to introduce new mathematical signs for old ones when one gives a new definition. He largely follows this practice in *Basic Laws*. At least once he writes of a given concept expression that 'as long as it remains incompletely defined [definiert]' in a way that fails to determine for every object whether that object falls under the denoted concept, it 'must remain undecided' whether the object falls under the concept. So the concept expression is vague (PPW 242–3/ NS 261–2). Perhaps Frege means only that as far as the incomplete definition goes, the word is left vague. Literally read, however, this passage is incompatible with the various passages, cited earlier, in which Frege speaks of the denotations of various mathematical concept expressions in conventional mathematics, even though no-one had given those expressions 'complete' definition. Frege is clearly more interested in giving an ideal system of mathematics than in providing a systematic account of the state of conventional mathematics before the ideal system has been discovered.

11 This sort of question is something that Wittgenstein pressed in his thinking about rule-following. It is also implicit in Dummett's insistence that a theory of 'meaning' be a theory of understanding and use. I think that the question is legitimate and profoundly difficult, though I think that Dummett is not very sensitive to the elements in Frege that ignore this insistence. Indeed, he often appears to attribute acquiescence in the insistence to Frege.

12 Interpreting this point requires delicacy. Frege was primarily interested in math-

ematics. And he was pursuing a foundationalist programme. I think that his conception of sense should not be tied too closely to these contingencies. Frege clearly intended to apply his conception of sense to domains other than the mathematical. And neither foundationalism nor reductionism are crucial to the conception. Sense expression is to be explicated in terms of better rationales than anyone may have grasped – regardless of whether these rationales provide a foundation in anything like the way logicism was supposed to provide a foundation for mathematics.

13   The remark comparing Weierstrass's plight with that of the ordinary mathematician when he thinks with the notion of the integral is useful in suggesting that thinking can go on without a clear, thorough grasp of the sense (the thought). On the other hand, it is important to recognize that although the notion of the integral has a fuller analysis that was coming to be grasped by the mathematical community, the notion of number that Weierstrass has not fully grapsed (and hence, presumably even the notion of the integral!) was not, in Frege's view, fully understood by any mathematician prior to Frege's own work. So the remarks that he applies to Weierstrass are applicable to the whole mathematical community.

14   This point is developed at considerable length in my 'Frege on Truth', especially the first and last sections.

15   This point makes it appropriate to say that for Frege philosophy is modelled on and continuous with science. But the relevant sciences are logic or mathematics, not natural science as it is for the positivists, Carnap, and Quine. In this view, Frege is again a traditionalist (emulating Plato, Descartes, Leibniz, and Kant.)

16   Frege does regard the basic truths of logic as self-evident. But he allowed that one might be mistaken about what was self-evident, if one had a less than thorough grasp of the thoughts involved. And the question of whether one has a thorough grasp is answerable by reference to the success of the theory in which the thoughts are embedded, cf. my 'Frege on Extensions of Concepts', pp. 30–4.

It is worth pointing out here that the 'final' explications of an expression are not, at least are not in general, expressions of the same sense. Frequently they are part of fixing the sense of the expression being explicated. Frege thought that only in the context of a proposition (and more generally, a theory) could the sense of scientific expressions be fully understood. The senses of expressions could be fully grasped only by grasping equivalences given by ideal scientific explications, or by otherwise understanding the contribution of those expressions to a theory. Of course, since most of the envisioned ideal explications would come as discoveries, it is possible to doubt them (even if the doubt depends on less than full analytic mastery of the senses), while not doubting the corresponding self-identities. So by Frege's test for the identity of senses, the senses of the *explicans* and *explicandum* would be different. Of course, many expressions will express senses but will not appear in ideal science at all (e.g. denotationless expressions). The point is not that senses are expressed only in an ideal science, and certainly not that every term is incompletely understood. The point is rather that terms in science may not be fully understood, and that full understanding is guaranteed only when one has an ideal science.

17   For a beginning at developing these ideas, see my 'Intellectual Norms and Foundations of Mind'.

18 Rudolf Carnap, *Meaning and Necessity*, p. 125. Carnap goes on to identify sense with intension, so that logically equivalent terms have the same sense. He explains logical equivalence in modal terms, thus further obscuring Frege's view. The explication of 'sense' in modal rather than cognitive terms continued in discussions of Frege into the 1970s and recur occasionally even now. Such explication of course has virtually nothing to do with Frege's original conception and his motivating problems.

19 W. V. Quine, 'Two Dogmas of Empiricism' in *From a Logical Point of View*, p. 21; Saul Kripke, *Naming and Necessity*, e.g. pp. 53–4; Michael Dummett, *Frege: Philosophy of Language* and *The Interpretation of Frege's Philosophy*. Some of these same points are discussed in my 'Sinning against Frege'.

References

Burge, Tyler, 'Belief *De Re*', *The Journal of Philosophy* 74 (1977), pp. 338–62

Burge, Tyler, 'Sinning Against Frege', *The Philosophical Review* 88 (1979), pp. 398–432

Burge, Tyler, Review of Michael Dummett, *The Interpretation of Frege's Philosophy*, *The Philosophical Review* 93 (1984), pp. 454–8

Burge, Tyler, 'Frege on Extensions of Concepts, From 1884 to 1903', *The Philosophical Review* 93 (1984), pp. 3–34

Burge, Tyler, 'Frege on Truth', in *Frege Synthesized*, eds Haaparanta and Hintikka (Reidel, Holland, 1986)

Burge, Tyler, 'Intellectual Norms and Foundations of Mind', *The Journal of Philosophy* 83 (1986), pp. 697–720

Carnap, Rudolf, *Meaning and Necessity*, 2nd edn, (University of Chicago Press, Chicago, 1956)

Dummett, Michael, *Frege: Philosophy of Language*, (Duckworth, London, 1973)

Dummett, Michael, *The Interpretation of Frege's Philosophy*, (Harvard University Press, Cambridge, Mass. 1981)

Frege, Gottlob, *Begriffsschrift und Andere Aufsätze* (B), ed. Angelelli, (Georg Olms, Hildesheim, 1967)

Frege, Gottlob, *Foundations of Arithmetic* (FA), trans. Austin, (Northwestern University Press, Evanston, 1968). (The volume contains both the German and the English. Pagination is the same as in the original.)

Frege, Gottlob, 'About the Law of Inertia', trans. Rand, *Synthese* 13 (1961), pp. 350–63

Frege, Gottlob, *Kleine Schriften* (KL), ed. Angelelli, (Georg Olms, Hildesheim, 1967)

Frege, Gottlob, *Logical Investigations* (LI), ed. Geach, (Yale University Press, New Haven, 1977)

Frege, Gottlob, *Nachgelassene Schriften* (NS), eds Hermes, Kambartel, Kaulbach, (Felix Meiner, Hamburg, 1969)

Frege, Gottlob, *Philosophical and Mathematical Correspondence* (PMC), eds McGuinness and Kaal, (University of Chicago Press, Chicago, 1980)

Frege, Gottlob, *Posthumous Writings* (PPW), trans. Long and White, (University of Chicago Press, Chicago, 1979)

Frege, Gottlob, *Translations from the Philosophical Writings of Gottlob Frege* (G&B), eds Geach and Black, 2nd edn, (Basil Blackwell, Oxford, 1966)

Frege, Gottlob, *Wissenschaftliche Briefwechsel* (WB), eds Gabriel, Hermes, Kambartel, Thiel, Veraart, (Felix Meiner, Hamburg, 1976)

Kripke, Saul, *Naming and Necessity* (Harvard University Press, Cambridge, Mass., 1980)

Quine, W. V., *From a Logical Point of View, 2nd edn*, (Harper Torchbooks, New York, 1961)

3
Vagueness, Logic and Interpretation

Christopher Hookway

1 Introduction: Vagueness, Natural Language and Logic

For many analytic philosophers, the presence of vague predicates constitutes, in Michael Dummett's phrase, 'an unmitigated defect of natural language' (1981, p. 316). According to Frege, when we are concerned with reasoning, or 'if it is a question of the truth of something', 'we have to throw aside concepts that do not have a meaning (*Bedeutung*)'; and he continues:

> These are . . . such as have vague boundaries. It must be determinate for every object whether it falls under a concept or not; a concept-word which does not meet this requirement on its meaning is meaningless (PW p. 122).

Similar passages could be found in the works of many other writers, all affirming that vagueness is an imperfection. Some attempt to conclude that there is only an appearance of vagueness in natural languages; most call for linguistic reform, or for the use of artificially constructed languages which are free from imperfection, whenever 'it is a question of the truth of something'.

Analytic philosophers who deny that vagueness is an imperfection mostly call for a revision in logic. They look for a system of deductive logic which systematizes inferences involving vague predicates. Such a logic would show which arguments involving vague predicates are valid; and, presumably, would help us to see how their logical behaviour differs from that of precise terms. They seek a formal logic of vagueness; and many would hold that only the construction of such a logic could convince us that vagueness is not an imperfection. In the following section, I shall set out some of the themes involved in these arguments by examining Frege's claims about vagueness more closely.

Wittgenstein, in his later writings, looks upon vagueness much more kindly. For example, in *Philosophical Investigations*, he describes some bizarre possibilities which our familiar notion of a chair leaves us uncertain how to describe: an apparent chair disappears when we approach it, only to reappear with all its familiar properties, and then to disappear again. We have no rules which determine whether it is a real chair or an illusion:

> But do we miss them when we use the word 'chair'; and are we to say that we do not really attach any meaning to this word, because we are not equipped with rules for every possible application of it? § 80

It is not a defect in a concept that it does not equip us to describe situations that will never arise. This theme recurs in Wittgenstein's writings, and he connects our tendency to view 'inexact' as a term of reproach, and 'exact' as a term of praise with a mistaken view of logic; this is the view that logic is 'something sublime', that it penetrates beneath phenomena to uncover a precise structure which provides 'the basis, or essence, of everything empirical' (1953, §§ 88–9).

It is a commonplace that Wittgenstein's later work has a 'pragmatist' flavour, due to the influence of Frank Ramsey upon his work around 1930. These views of vagueness – which contrast with the more Fregean position of his *Tractatus Logico-Philosophicus* – are one manifestation of this pragmatism. His discussion of 'chair' is followed by an examination of Ramsey's view of logic, which contrasts with his own earlier position. Moreover, Ramsey characterized his own position as differing from that of the *Tractatus* largely in the 'pragmatism' he had learned from Russell and his reading of an early anthology of Peirce's papers, *Chance, Love and Logic*. He accused the *Tractatus* of '*scholasticism*, the essence of which is treating what is vague as if it were precise and trying to fit it into an exact logical category' (1931, p. 269). Elsewhere, he describes the 'essence of pragmatism': 'the meaning of a sentence is to be defined by reference to the actions to which asserting it would lead, or, more vaguely still, by its possible causal effects' (1978, p. 57; 1931, p. 155). With its suggestion that the meaning of an expression is to be explained by its importance for (or effects upon) our practices, and the verificationism which it probably suggests, we can see further links with the themes from the *Investigations* which are described as 'pragmatist'. What is less clear, however, are the relations between these themes. Does a determination to take vagueness seriously form a unified whole with a kind of functionalist theory of meaning, and the rejection of an essentialist account of logic? Is the resulting set of views usefully described as 'pragmatist'?

I mentioned above that Ramsey was influenced by one of the classic American pragmatists, Charles Peirce. As well as defending a theory of meaning fitting Ramsey's description of pragmatism, Peirce complained that 'logicians have been at fault in giving Vagueness the go-by, so far as not even to analyze it' (5.446). He denied that vagueness was a 'defect in thinking or knowledge' and, in a suggestive comparison, insisted that it 'is no more to be done away with in the world of logic than friction in mechanics' (4.344, 4.512). Not only is 'a determinate sign an impossibility', but excessive precision, like excessive vagueness, is an *impediment* to the pursuit of truth. Although he claims to have 'worked out the logic of vagueness with something like completeness' (5.506), the systems of *formal* logic that he constructed do not seem to reflect this. He appears to deny that taking vagueness seriously requires us to construct special formal systems.[1] He used the word 'logic' more widely than is now common, to cover the ground he also described as 'semiotic' – the general theory of signs and interpretation. His investigations in the logic of vagueness are primarily semantic accounts of the use of vague predicates and classifications of the different kinds of vagueness.

In Wittgenstein, Ramsey and Peirce, there seem to be connections between a readiness to take vagueness seriously, a 'pragmatist' perspective upon issues of meaning, and some distinctive views of the nature or role of formal logic. I am sympathetic to the view that vagueness is not an imperfection, and I am attracted by broadly 'pragmatist' accounts of meaning. However, in view of the prevalance of the contrary view – and of the view that we can only take vagueness seriously by developing a special logic – my focus is upon whether it is possible to hold to this position. I shall mostly discuss Peirce, but my concern is with understanding some of the pragmatist tendencies present in analytic philosophy and with the underlying assumptions about meaning and logic which underly the opposing positions.

2 Frege, Wittgenstein and 'Pragmatism'

What reason has Frege for claiming that vague predicates lack meaning, and are no concern of logic? In section 56, volume 2 of the *Grundgesetze*, we read:

> [A] concept that is not sharply defind is wrongly termed a concept. Such quasi-conceptual constructions cannot be recognized as concepts by logic: it is impossible to lay down precise laws for them. The law of excluded middle is really just another form of the requirement that the concept should have a precise boundary (TPWF, p. 159).

and in a letter to Peano

> But logic can only recognize sharply delimited concepts. Only under this presupposition can it set up precise laws . . . Just as it would be impossible for geometry to set up precise laws if it tried to recognize threads as lines and knots in threads as points, so logic must demand sharp limits of what it will recognize as a concept unless it wants to renounce all precision and certainty (PMC, pp. 114–15).

The comparison with geometry occurs elsewhere too:

> If something fails to display a sharp boundary, it cannot be recognized in logic as a concept, just as something that is not extensionless cannot be recognized in geometry as a point, because otherwise it would be impossible to set up geometrical axioms. The technical language of any science must conform to a single standard: does it enable the lawfulness of nature to be expressed as simply as possible and at the same time with perfect precision ('The law of inertia', CP, p. 133).

The central point is that simple, precise logical laws could not be obtained if logic 'recognized' vague concepts; and the law of excluded middle is apparently an example of a fundamental logical truth which holds only for 'genuine' concepts. Frege offers no extended demonstration that no such logical laws are available – it seems to be accepted without much argument.

When Wittgenstein objects to Frege's denial that vague concepts have meaning, he does not respond directly to the challenge to find precise logical laws. Instead, he employs two different strategies. Firstly, he examines the ways we actually use concepts, the needs to which they answer, and reminds us that vague concepts can often answer to these needs far better than precise ones. For example, when uncertainty is expressed about whether a 'blurred concept' is a concept at all, he responds: 'Is an indistinct photograph a picture of a person at all? Is it always an advantage to replace an indistinct picture by a sharp one? Isn't the indistinct one often exactly what we need?'. And when Frege compares a concept to an area, denying that an area with vague boundaries is an area at all, Wittgenstein asks: 'But is it senseless to say: "Stand roughly there"?' (1953, § 71). The 'pragmatist' flavour of the remarks is evident: the meanings of our words, the character of our concepts, reflect the relations of their uses to our practical concerns and projects. Linguistic behaviour is a form of behaviour, and its tools can only be judged by their contribution to our achieving our communicative ends.

Secondly, he attempts a diagnosis of what has gone wrong. Logicians construct formal systems which provide idealizations of our ordinary practice. These systems can prove useful tools in evaluating reasoning and studying arguments. Of course, since they are idealizations, there will sometimes be a lack of fit between the model and our ordinary practice of argument – for example, in connection with some arguments involving vague predicates. Examination of our practice of evaluating arguments shows that we are aware of this, and that it rarely leads to error. But the logician misunderstands the nature of his formal system, and claims that his ideal pattern either is implicit in ordinary untidy usage, or like Frege, that it should be. The conclusion is that logic can only take seriously forms of discourse which do not risk exposing the idealizations involved in our logic. Once again there is a pragmatist flavour: we are to view logical systems as normative frameworks, whose meaning is to be understood by considering their role in our practices – they are not to be seen as capturing fundamental truths about some underlying or ideal reality.

In at least one respect, these arguments may fail to engage with Frege's concerns. Frege employs 'concept' and 'meaning' in a technical fashion, and the claim that vagueness is no concern of logic is compatible with the view that vague expressions are very useful for many practical purposes. He admits that 'the softness and instability of ordinary language' is 'necessary for its versatility and potential for development'. Its inadequacies only intrude, we might suppose, 'if it is a question of the truth of something' (CN, p. 86–cf. Dummett, 1981, p. 33). It is only then that logic comes into its own and vagueness should be spurned. We could imagine a Quinean holding that vague predicates have no role in a canonical notation for serious science, while being invaluable in the home and market place – this may be close to Frege's position. It is at this point that I wish to turn to Peirce; for his pragmatism, and his stress upon the importance of vagueness, emerge in the course of an extended attempt to justify the claim that serious inquiry, properly conducted, will take us to the truth about reality. The core of this argument is an approach to the philosophy of language and mind which provided philosophical foundations for his pragmatism, and also (through Ogden and Richards) influenced Ramsey and Wittgenstein. I hope that an examination of this will help us to see how the Fregean perspective upon vagueness can be avoided.

3 Pragmatism and Science

The term 'pragmatism' can be taken in a narrow and a wide sense. According to the former, it applies to a rule for clarifying the meanings of words and concepts. Peirce almost invariably uses the term to refer to such a rule which he first defended in 'How to make our ideas clear' published in 1878, and returned to on many occasions. If we wish to clarify a concept, he tells us, we should:

Consider what effects, which might conceivably have practical bearing, we conceive the object of our conception to have. Then, our conception of these effects is the whole of our conception of the object (5.402; W3, p. 266).

As his examples and later formulations make clear, we clarify the claim that some object o is F by deciding which claims of the following form we take to be true:

If *o* is F, then if action A were to be performed, experience *e* would result.

Thus:

If this powder is salt, then if we were to place it in water and stir vigorously, we would observe it dissolve.

If this object is hard, then if we were to make many attempts to scratch it, employing different objects to do so, few of our attempts would be successful.

and so on. (For further discussion, and more examples, see Hookway, 1985, pp. 49–51, 234–40).[2]

In its wider sense, we can think of pragmatism as an approach to philosophy which places stress upon the facts that human beings are agents, and inquiry and investigation are forms of activity. Scientific activity, for example, is understood as an attempt to put human agents into some sort of harmonious relation with their environment; and it is to be understood in terms of the goals of the activity and the means we have available for pursuing them. Questions of meaning and language are to be resolved by exploring the role of thought and speech in these activities: what kinds of concepts do we need for such purposes? What practices of linguistic behaviour are called for by serious science? It accords with this broader conception of pragmatism that Wittgenstein replaces questions about truth in mathematics with questions about the use of mathematical propositions (1967, p. 3). It encourages a broadly 'functionalist' approach to questions of thought and language: we approach them through an understanding of the contributions of concepts and utterances to the achievement of our aims. This is vague, and can only serve as a general characterization of the pragmatist flavour of much recent philosophy by remaining so. Hence, I shall descend to a particular example, examining two features of Peirce's philosophy which fit this pattern.

The first involves the underlying insight of his work on thought and language. One philosophical approach to meaning talks simply of expressions and their referents, or of sentences and the propositions they express. Little is said about how names can denote their bearers, or of how sentences can express propositions. Since the underlying concern is with describing (say) the truth–conditions of sentences, and with explaining the validity of inferences, it is supposed that we can abstract from the psychological details of how these dyadic relations are set up, and from the social framework which sustains them. While it is acknowledged that the relations of denotation and expression are mysterious in the absence of such explanations, philosophy of language can get on without them.

According to Peirce, by contrast, the fundamental semantic relation is triadic.

A name denotes an object only by being *interpreted* as denoting the object; a sentence expresses a proposition only by being understood or interpreted as expressing it. In general, something is meaningful by virtue of having the power to enforce a particular interpretation; and the relation between a sign (linguistic expression or thought) and its 'object' is mediated through an interpreting thought or utterance. In consequence, we can understand the contents of thoughts only by taking into account their interpretation in subsequent thoughts or their expression in utterances; and we can understand the meanings of utterances only by examining their interpretation through the thoughts and utterances of those who attend to them.

Interpretations are various, and Peirce has written extensively on the nature of interpretation and the different kinds of 'interpretants'; I shall very briefly mention a very few relevant considerations. The simplest kind of interpretation, I suppose, consists, in the thought that (for example):

That utterance of 'snow is white' expresses the proposition that snow is white.

or

That utterance of 'Brutus' refers to Brutus.

But an interpretation can 'develop' a thought through inference. I manifest my understanding of an utterance of 'snow is white' by inferring from it that snow is not red, or that snow is the same colour as flour, etc. Similarly, thoughts are typically interpreted through inference, in this fashion. Finally, a thought or utterance can be interpreted in a habit of expectation: my understanding of my thought that salt is soluble is manifested in my expecting any sample which is placed in water to dissolve – I am surprised if this does not happen. These different elements can be combined. For example, my understanding of the proposition that heavy clouds are forming over the mountains may be mainfested in my expecting a thunderstorm tonight – this expectation reflecting the impact of other beliefs about such cloud formations through inference. It follows from this that how I interpret a thought or utterance will depend upon the interests and concerns which occupy me at the time.

The second element of Peirce's thought that I wish to consider is his picture of *science* as a distinctive kind of activity, which involves the interpretation of thoughts and utterances through deliberation and discussion. Scientific activity is not directed at solving practical problems in the short run. The true scientist devotes his life to contributing to the eventual discovery of the truth. Peirce believes that methods are available which will ensure that, unless we are distracted by the search for personal glory or by the short–run demands of practice, the community of scientists will eventually reach the truth on all questions which are raised. There is supposed to be a proof that the scientific method will take us to the truth in the long run, although there is no reply to sceptical doubts about its short–run effectiveness. Our use of induction, for example, for the practical affairs of life is grounded in an unquestioned common sense, but can receive no logical vindication. The method of science involves proposing hypotheses, testing them experimentally by deriving predictions from them, modifying or abandoning them when our expectations about the results of experiments are surprised. The assurance that we shall eventually reach the truth is attributed to the logical character of certain patterns of statistical inference, and to the justified hope that our gradually developing standards of plausibility will equip us to propose, and take seriously, the theories which experience will eventually reveal to be true.

My concern here is not with Peirce's attempted *vindication* of the method of science: the argument is complex, and is entwined with Peirce's defence of a complex metaphysical framework which appears to involve a form of objective idealism. His account of how science proceeds – how we behave when 'it is a question of the truth of something' – is largely independent of this wider framework, and reflects his many years of experience as a practising scientist. I am interested in what can be said about the interpretative practices of serious scientific researchers. The pragmatist principle arises in this context. In order to function as a scientist efficiently, it is important that we do so in a reflective or self-conscious fashion. One thing that this involves is that we be reflective about how our 'scientific assertions' and beliefs can be interpreted: it is good methodology to seek a reflective clarity about those interpretations of our beliefs and utterances which could have a bearing upon scientific practice. Peirce claims that, if we apply the pragmatic principle, we become completely aware of the relevant features of the meanings of our terms: the principle is a rule for determining the 'ultimate logical interpretant' or content of our beliefs and concepts.

Once again, my primary concern is not with the thorny issue of how successful Peirce was at 'proving' his pragmatist principle. Rather, I want to point out some of the strategies he employs in arguing for it. One of these is familiar from writings on meaning by empiricists like Moritz Schlick. Peirce appears to think that a habit of expectation is the only kind of interpretation that takes us beyond the web of thoughts and words, enabling a thought or expression to be interpreted by something which gives it a definite content without itself needing to be interpreted. More interesting are arguments which appeal to what goes on in scientific practice and consider what kinds of interpretants we should favour to participate in these practices. I shall mention two of these.

First, the scientific method involves deriving testable predictions from hypotheses, and seeing whether they are surprised by the results of experiment or observation. The pragmatist principle guides us to a reflective understanding of which experimental results we should anticipate if an hypothesis were true. If all that there is to science is experimental testing, the claim runs, then the pragmatist principle reveals all the interpretations of an hypothesis which we would judge to be relevant to our scientific activity. If it is 'a question of the truth of something', that is all that we could need.

Second, a community of scientists is held together by a practice of *assertion*. If I assert something to you, then I am attempting to get you to believe it. I do so by producing an utterance which is conventionally recognized as a sign that I think it reasonable to believe that proposition. I expect your inference that I think it reasonable to hold this belief to be grounded in the fact that there is a practice of penalizing assertions of propositions which are false – unless the asserter has a reasonable excuse for being mistaken. Assertion provides the means for transmitting information from one member of the scientific community to another. It also provides the vehicle for scientific debate: once an assertion is made, another can criticize it, providing considerations which suggest that the assertion was improperly made or should be withdrawn. A cautious assertor should ensure that he is not likely to incur penalties before making an assertion. And the auditor of an assertion should be wary of the risks to which he is exposed when he accepts some testimony as something he will assert himself. In each case, what we need to know is what experimental results or observations would show the assertion to be unjustified. Once again, the pragmatist principle provides the information we need in order to participate in the practice of assertion in a reflective and cautiously scientific manner.

Peirce took these arguments to show that the pragmatist principle provided a valuable methodological rule for clarifying concepts, for those involved in the activity of science. The arguments rest upon examining scientific practice, and considering the semantic needs of someone who participates in it. His own worries about pragmatism – which occasioned most of his philosophical efforts during the first decade of this century – turned on whether he could prove that no further clarification was important for science. He was worried that we may have concepts available that would enable us to prefer one hypothesis to another empirically equivalent one on the grounds that it provided a 'better explanation' of the facts, entering into a more coherent or intelligible framework of theory. Whether he ever satisfied himself on this score is uncertain; and it would take us beyond the concerns of this paper to examine it more fully.

4 Vagueness and Assertibility

In one of his contributions to Baldwin's *Dictionary of Philosophy*, Peirce wrote that 'a proposition is vague when there are possible states of things concerning which it is intrinsically uncertain whether, had they been contemplated by the speaker, he would regard them as excluded or allowed by the proposition.' His disposition to accept the proposition is indeterminate simply because the question whether to apply it in these cases did not present itself. It is left 'doubtful just what [the sign's] intended interpretation was, not between two or more separate interpretations, which would be ambiguity . . . but as to a greater multitude or even a continuum of possible interpretations no two of which differ without the doubt being extended to the intermediate interpretations.' (R283, 1906).

There is an example in a draft for a logic text *Reason's Rules*:

[To] the question whether a certain newly found skeleton was the skeleton of a man rather than of an anthropoid ape, the reply 'Yes and No' might, in a certain sense, be justifiable. Namely, owing to our conception of what a man is having been formed without thinking of the possibility of such a creature as that to which this skeleton belongs, the question really has no definite meaning (R596).

Many other examples are given, such as colour predicates (5.448 n. 1). Peirce admits that the *question* he refers to has no definite meaning, but he has no doubts about the propriety of more familiar questions involving the concept *man*. By contrast, Frege appears to draw the more extreme conclusion that no sentence involving 'man' expresses a thought or should be used in inference.

Peirce often compares vague propositions to quantified ones, and it is natural to do so. Semantic accounts of vague expressions which exploit supervaluations, for example, do so explicitly.[3] A predicate M is a sharpening of 'man' if it agress with 'man' concerning all those objects whcih are definitely either men or not men, and is, in addition precise, yielding definite verdicts where 'man' yields none. A proposition containing vague predicates is then said to be true (false) if it is true (false) according to every sharpening of the vague predicates contained. So, the skeleton is of a man if it satisfies *every* sharpening of 'man'. We understand the truth-conditions of vague predicates when we see that they function analogously to universally quantified expressions. We should expect this picture to be attractive to Peirce. Since he thinks that a proposition is true only if all inquiry is destined to reach an unforced consensus upon its truth, he is surely committed to the view that it is true only if we should agree on its truth however it is sharpened. Up to a point, this is correct: he would agree that only in these circumstances does the question have a 'definite meaning'. However, it is important to understand that, whenever he makes a comparision between vagueness and quantification, the analogy he stresses is with *existential* quantification.

The point of the analogy emerges when we consider the assertibility-conditions of vague and existentially quantified propositions. Under which circumstances is the assertion that some book on my desk is green successfully challenged? How can it be defended? According to Peirce, the speaker, (the 'defender') reserves the right to stipulate the member of the universe of discourse by which it is to be judged. Perhaps better, he is sanctioned when it is shown that he cannot find a defensible instance of the quantified expression. Similarly, an assertion of a universally quantified assertion is defeated when the person addressed (the 'opponent') can find an instance of the quantified expression which is not defensible. In another words, the evaluation of the assertion depends upon a subsequent interpretation which renders it more determinate: an existential quantifier leaves it up to the speaker to fix the more precise assertion by reference to which it is to be evaluated; a universal quantifier assigns this role to the person addressed, who is concerned with whether to accept the testimony that he is offered. (The speaker is described as *defending* his utterance against the challenge that would expose him to sanction; the hearer, or opponent, will be anxious to refute the utterance if he can, since he desires to accept it only if he will not himself incur sanctions when he repeats the assertion.)[4]

Turning to vague expressions, the analogy with existential quantification emerges: if the speaker can produce a sharpening of the original predicate which accords with past usage and delivers an unequivocal verdict on the present case, then he has successfully met any challenge to his assertion. In that case, in the case described, both:

This is a human skeleton

and

This is not a human skeleton

may be defensible. The speaker reserves the right to determine which sharpening should be employed in evaluating his utterance. His assertion is criticized only if he selects a sharpening which renders it indefensible, or if the opponent can show that no sharpening of the assertion is defensible at all. Thus:

[Vagueness] is the antithetical analogue of generality [sc. universal quantification]. A sign is objectively *general*, in so far as, leaving to the interpreter the right of completing the determination for himself ... A sign is objectively *vague*, in so far as, leaving its interpretation more or less indeterminate, it reserves for some other possible sign or experience the function of completing the determination.

While it is false that 'A *proposition whose identity I have determined* is both true and false,' yet until it is determinate, it may be true that a proposition is true and that a proposition is false (5.448).

We have already encountered this in his willingness to countenance the answer 'Yes and no' to the question 'Is this a human skeleton?'

The distinctive pragmatist approach to semantic issues is evident in the style of argument used here. When Frege expresses doubts about the coherence of vague predicates, this is because he thinks that there are no precise laws of logic which explain their logical behaviour. When Peirce defends their coherence, this is through showing that they do not prevent our interpreting the utterances in which they occur: the focus is on the practice of interpretation, and upon how we can make them more precise through such a process.[5] Our two remaining tasks are to consider the views about the nature of logic which enable Peirce to remain unimpressed by the sorts of considerations which disturb Frege, and to understand the importance of these interpretative practices when we are concerned with discovering the truth.

5 Vagueness and Science

I shall take the second of these questions first: why does Peirce believe that vagueness is a virtue? He sometimes argues that vagueness is unavoidable by reference to the semantics of singular terms, but I shall not discuss these arguments here (see, for example, 3.93, 5.448 fn.). More immediately relevant here are three respects in which science calls for vague predicates.

As is well known, Peirce holds, by and large, to a hypothetico-deductivist account of the growth of science; one element in his realism is his assurance that any false theory would eventually be refuted by the test of experience, while only a true theory can survive the test of time. When we formulate a hypothesis for testing, we put it forward as approximately true: although *ad hoc* adjustments of theories to avoid empirical falsification are frowned upon, our initial hypothesis is only that some more precise theory grounded in the vague one proposed will turn out to be true. We hope that an unforced consensus will be secured on some precisification of our vague hypothesis. The refutation of some formulation of the hypothesis is not taken to refute the initial vague hypothesis: it refutes the formulation and sends us back to find a new better formulation of the hypothesis. Thus, when the tentative hypothesis is first put forward, it is understood that its precise interpretation is undetermined: it is suggested only that there is a way of interpreting it according to which it is defensible; and it is left to subsequent research to fix on how the hypothesis should be interpreted.

The familiar history of the kinetical theory of gases well illustrates this. It began with a number of spheres almost infinitesimally small occasionally colliding. It was afterward so modified that the forces between the spheres, instead of merely separating them, were mainly attractive, that the molecules were not spheres, but systems, and that the part of space within which their motions are free is appreciably less than the entire volume of the gas. There was no new hypothetical element in these modifications. They were partly quantitative, and partly such as to make the formal hypothesis represent better what was really supposed to be the case (7.216).

Secondly, Peirce allows a role for common sense certainties in grounding our claims to knowledge. Justification comes to a halt upon propositions which function as the 'bedrock of truth' which are accepted without grounds or justification. We regard them as 'the very truth' (5.505): 'if you absolutely cannot doubt a proposition . . . it is plain that there is no room to desire anything more' (6.498). Although these claims are, in fact, fallible, they are 'acritical'. This is an important concept for Peirce's philosophy (as well as being another point where his views strongly resemble those of Wittgenstein (see Wittgenstein , 1969 *passim*)): an acritical belief is one of which we are certain, which does not issue from the kind of process of deliberation or reasoning which can be subjected to critical monitoring. We do not know why we believe these things; we cannot imagine being able to doubt them; and they have a foundational role for our practices of inquiry and justification.

When he discusses how a fallibilist can accept that there are such certainties, Peirce writes: 'It is . . . easy to be certain. One has only to be sufficiently vague' (4.237). He claims that he can offer an a *priori* proof that 'veritably indubitable beliefs are especially vague' (5.507). If a belief is formulated precisely, 'a suitable line of reflection, accompanied by imaginary experimentation, always excites doubt of [it].' Once we can specify experiential results which would successfully challenge a claim, we can admit the possibility of its being false. So long as we do not specify what is burned by fire, and in what circumstances, little can falsify the vague common sense claim that fire burns (5.498). And, although no laboratory experiment could leave the proposition that there is an element of order in the universe 'more certain than instinct or common sense leaves it', still 'when anyone undertakes to say *precisely* what that order consists in, he will quickly find he outruns all logical warrant' (6.496).

Finally, it seems plain that Peirce thinks that perceptual judgements are unavoidably vague. These too are acritical: they are theory-laden judgements, which are fallible in the light of subsequent experience; but at the time of making them, we find them absolutely compelling while having no sense of any grounds upon which they are made. At 5.448 n. 1, he suggests that precision is not required of observational predicates. Considering two people discussing the colour of Charles II's hair, he points out that in spite of the facts that neither is a trained observer of colours, and that 'colors are seen quite differently by different retinas', 'if one of them says that Charles II had dark auburn hair, the other will understand him precisely enough for all their possible purposes; and it will be a determinate predication.' Colour predications work well enough for practical purposes although we lack any precise sense of what a particular colour attribution excludes. All that is required, to defend our claim, is that we can make a case for our attribution being a defensible interpretation of the pattern of use which has determined the meaning of the term. If the vagueness and variation is such that we do, in practice, find different observers making different judgements, then the term must be made more precise. There is no point seeking greater precision if this does not occur. When the term is more precise, we have to be more careful, more painstaking, in deciding whether it applies in any particular occasion; and it becomes less suited for casual reports of observation.

So, the practice of science is better served by vague predicates than by precise ones. It is compatible with this that we should aspire to greater precision, that one of the tasks of science should be the gradual elimination of vagueness from its theories. I suspect that Peirce believes that scientists properly, and naturally, attempt to remove the vagueness from their hypotheses. I suspect, too, that Peirce believed that science was approaching, as a limit, a point at which such vagueness was wholly eliminated. However, there is nothing internal to his account of the scientific method which guarantees this; and his assurance reflects other philosophical doctrines which are involved in his defence of objective idealism.

6 Logic and Bivalence

We have seen that Peirce offers an account of the use of vague predicates. He explains how we interpret them by describing their assertibility-conditions, and he stresses their importance for the practice of science. However, Frege's challenge remains: can Peirce respond consistently to the charge that vague language is incoherent because otherwise no logical laws can be laid down. Frege insists that 'the law of excluded middle is really just another form of the requirement that the concept should have a precise boundary.' (*Grundgesetze der Arithmetic*, vol. 2, § 56 in Frege 1970, p. 159): what is Peirce's view of the law of excluded middle?. The question is especially pressing since, as has been mentioned above, Peirce's systems of formal logic are mainly classical.

Peirce's discussion of the example of the skeleton occurs in the course of a critique of some common false logical presumptions. We naturally suppose that any proposition, or its negation, is determinately true: in fact, we assume that the negation of a proposition's being true is the 'same fact' as the proposition's not being true. Vague propositions show that this is incorrect. The fact that it is not destined that 'This skeleton is a man' would occur in the final consensus is compatible with it not being destined that 'This skeleton is not a man' would appear in the final consensus: and, equally, the fact that the former sentence could feature in such an unforced consensus is compatible with the claim that, the facts being as they are, the other could equally legitimately do so. The mistaken presumption rested upon an erroneous conception of *facts* which leads us, mistakenly, to accept the principle of bivalence. We conclude:

P is an ultimately defensible assertion (it will not be successfully challenged), if and only if not-*P* is not an ultimately defensible assertion.

However, when vague predicates are involved, a statement and its negation may both be ultimately defensible. Unless we adopt a convention to sharpen a vague term in one way rather than another, neither is destined to be part of the final consensus.

It is natural to see in this a challenge to accepted logical principles: the law of excluded middle fails, because there is no reason to suppose that either *P* or its negation is actually true. Peirce seems to insist that vagueness is a source of counter examples to the law of excluded middle. Many arguments formulated in everyday language (or, indeed, in scientific language) appear to fail to conform to the 'laws' of classical logic. The common insistence in that case, that some adjustment is required seems irresistible: either we seek an improved formulation of the laws, or we despair of ordinary language and its limitations. The legitimacy of this demand, however, depends upon how the calculi developed by logicians are to be interpreted: how do those who develop systems of deductive logic contribute to the pursuit of truth? It is instructive to note the analogies that Frege and Peirce use to describe the lack of fit between logical 'laws' and the practice of inference employing ordinary vague predicates. While Peirce tells us that vagueness can no more be eliminated from language than 'friction can from physics', Frege insists that for a logician to take vagueness seriously would be like a geometer recognizing 'threads as lines and knots as points'. Both are aware that the laws formulated by logicians idealize the patterns of argument found in ordinary reasoning employing vague expressions: 'external reality' fits the theories only imperfectly. Frege seems to conclude that the theory is really about ideal objects – which fit the laws perfectly – and hence logic deals only with arguments involving precise predicates; he is happy to remark that 'the task of our vernacular languages is essentially fulfilled if people engaged in communication with one another connect the same thought, or approximately the same thought, with the same proposition' (PMC p. 115). He insists that logical laws apply only to sentences in which concepts are expressed and, as we have seen, vague concepts are not really concepts. Peirce is impressed with how we use theoretical idealizations in order to understand less ideal occurrences – a physical theory which abstracts from the effects of friction can provide us with understanding of ordinary physical occurrences, so long as we are careful about how we apply it.

If, as Peirce appears to think, bivalence does not hold in all cases, how can he justify employing a classical logic?

Logic requires us, with reference to each question we have in hand, to hope some definite answer to it may be true. That *hope* with reference to each case as it comes up is, by a *saltus* stated by logicians as a *law* concerning *all* cases, namely the law of excluded middle (NE, iv, xiii).

When I commit myself to investigating a proposition, to determining whether it is true, I assume (or hope) that this is one of those propositions with a determinate truth value. I should not undertake the investigation if I thought that both it and its negation were assertible. Thus, I take it for granted that if it is assertible, its negation is not assertible; I take it for granted that this is one of those propositions for which bivalence holds. I can express the presupposition of my inquiry by saying:

Either this skeleton is a man or it is not.

This reflects my acceptance that a genuine question is at issue on this *occasion*. It does not reflect my acceptance of a general logical law: in general, (1) below is true but (2) is false.

1   (*P*) If I investigate whether *P*, then I hope that if *P* is assertible the negation of *P* is not assertible.
2   I believe that (*P*) if *P* is assertible, then the negation of *P* is not assertible.

Peirce criticizes an illicit move whereby (2) is endorsed by logicians on the basis of a confused awareness of the facts underlying (1). He appears to suggest that I can rely upon any instance of the law which becomes relevant in the course of inquiry although I am not justified in accepting the law as, in general, true.

So long as I am aware of the dangers, I can use classical logic as a tool in my inquiries, for the propositions that I make use of will generally be ones for which I believe bivalence holds. Even if classical logical laws are not in general valid, the instances of them which I actually deal with will normally be true. I use classical logic while sensitive to its limitations. I may occasionally be misled by this, just as my predictions may fail when I apply my elegant physical theory to concrete situations which involve frictional forces not taken into account by my theory. But the risks are worth taking for the elegant simplicity of the framework that is employed. The moral to be drawn from this seems to be that a system of formal logic can answer to our needs – we can interpret its formulae and exploit them in ordering our inquiries – without providing a set of exceptionless laws which apply to all meaningful propositions. We should look at the uses to which logical calculi are put, rather than jumping too rapidly to the claim that they purport to reveal exceptionless laws.

Another example will illustrate the point. One symptom of the curious logical behaviour of vague predicates is the Sorites paradox: so long as we employ classical logical principles, we can 'prove' that evidently red objects are blue, that enormous piles of sand are not heaps, and so on. The argument forms we use are wholly satisfactory when they are not strung together in sequence: thus, given that one object obviously looks the same shade as another plainly red object, we *do* know that it is red. We are deceived by classical logical inferences only if we exploit the transitivity of entailment and construct a lengthy demonstration composed of many such arguments. Insofar as we never have to consider such lengthy proofs, we can retain our elegant classical formalism. If we rarely have to consider arguments which can be undermined by the logical oddities of vagueness, we may once again stay with our classical logic, confident that, if we are led into error, the mistake can be corrected when we check the result of our inference against casual observation. This is wholly parallel to the way in which we might rely, for practical purposes, upon physical theories which abstract from considerations of friction: we know that, in practice, ignoring this complication is unlikely to make much difference; and when this does lead us astray, we have a ready explanation of what has gone wrong, and we allow observation to override the predictions made by our idealized theory. The theory is not *refuted*, because it only offers an idealization, a simplified model, of the physical facts to which it applies.

Sluga has argued that the prevalent nineteenth-century view of formal logic placed it as a branch of applied mathematics: it employed mathematical techniques for the study of argument (1980, ch. 1). This is Peirce's view. Deductive logic is descriptive of our practice of mathematical inference: it may also try to explain it, but has no normative or justificatory role.[6] Formal logic provides an idealized model or diagram of patterns of valid inference. To this end, it can have a heuristic role in avoiding slips or in carrying out inferences a more rigorous fashion. But when an inference that all agree is (in)valid is not certified as such by the logical theory, this indicates the limits of application of the idealized theory rather than a fault in our practice. In wholly analogous fashion, a geometrical theory begins as an idealized modelling of some physical state of affairs (knots and strings). As a mathematical theory it develops autonomously – the mathematician is not constantly thinking of the intended application. But its value lies in its possible applications as iconic representations of other phenomena. So logical laws idealize the structure of ordinary argument and inference: and the application of logical systems must be accompanied by a sense of the limits of application of the formal model as well as a sense of the model's value.

Classical logic does not lead us into error when we employ arguments involving vague predicates because its limitations can be respected: just as experience can teach us where we have failed to take into account the effects of friction in making a predication on the basis of a physical theory, so we can tell that we were wrong to rely upon a classically valid argument. We have a system of checks and balances which alerts us to the limitations of our formalism.

This argument appears to assume that there are no *truths* containing vague predicates which can *only* be known by methods which essentially rely upon possibly suspect logical principles: experiential checks are always available. However, suppose that there was a sphere of reality which dealt with abstract objects which were looked upon as just as real as (for example) ordinary physical objects. We have no experience of them, nor do we enter into any kind of causal interaction with them. In fact, our canonical means of acquiring knowledge of them is through constructing formal proofs, which are not constrained by experience or by other 'checks'. It seems to be common ground between Peirce and Frege that – unless we have an accurate non-classical logic which accounts for the logical behaviour of vague predicates – we can have no reliable knowledge of such objects if our proofs contain propositions involving vague predicates.

Frege's philosophy of mathematics appears to embody just this picture. Logic is not an application of mathematics, but is rather a pre-mathematical discipline with a role in justifying mathematical knowledge. Frege speaks of a distinct 'logical' source of knowledge. Arithmetical knowledge depends upon the proofs that Frege offers in the *Grundgesetze*: unless the laws of logic are exceptionless, we can have no assurance of the truth of arithmetic. The logical source of knowledge can only be a source of *knowledge* if the laws of logic are exceptionless in their application to sentences that genuinely express thoughts. Since such truths are only known through proof, we obtain knowledge of them only through absolutely secure proofs from absolutely secure basic truths.

7   Realism

Peirce often describes himself as a 'realist'. He repudiates nominalist accounts of law and generality. And, especially in his later works, he rejects idealism, holding that we investigate an independent reality whose character is not determined or constituted by our opinions about it. Indeed, one of the tasks of logic is to guide us in conducting our investigations in pursuit of the goal of discovering the truth. Since vagueness is often seen as a problem for realism, I shall close with some comments on Peirce's realism.

Peirce's philosophy of mathematics seems wholly constructivist. Mathematical theories grow out of idealizations of models designed for the solution of 'practical' problems. As idealizations, they are not answerable to the physical 'facts' and are interpreted as autonomous, mathematicians soon losing sight of the practical problems which intially prompted their activities. Since we have no 'logical source of knowledge', it appears to follow that mathematics does not take us to knowledge of an independent reality. Mathematical objects – numbers, points, propositions – lack the independent reality that physical objects have. It accords with this that mathematics is pre-logical: whereas we may be forced to revise methods in the natural science because logic teaches us that they will not lead us to knowledge of reality, there is no scope for comparable logical criticism in mathematics. We can attach no sense to the thought that mathematical reality may be other than we take it to be. Thus, Peirce repudiates realism about mathematics. He denies that it studies an external reality, and insists that mathematics is a pre-logical science which 'needs no foundations'. It is arguable that unless he took this position, his relaxed attitude towards classical logic would be untenable and his use of logical laws which were admitted to be idealizations of the logical relations of everyday beliefs and utterances could not be sustained.

However, he resists a similar constructivism about empirical knowledge: here there is room for logical dispute about the methods of inference and inquiry which are best designed to take us to the truth. Peirce's position is often called 'convergent realism'. The 'investigation-independence' of reality – the fact that its character is independent of what it is taken to be – is supposedly captured by the claim that it is 'fated' or 'destined' that serious, efficient inquiry will eventually arrive at the truth. We now seem to find Peirce claiming that, in the course of inquiry, the meanings of concepts are enriched: vague concepts are replaced by more precise ones: we decide on more precise classifications of things like colours that fall on a continuum. Insofar as it is up to us how we make these adjustments – convention or decision has a role in the development of concepts – it is hard to take seriously the idea that all inquirers will eventually assent to just the same sentences. If it is up to us how we make vague concepts more precise, it must be (at least in part) up to us which propositions would be accepted at the end of inquiry. How can we make sense of Peirce's talk of convergence and destiny?

Consider an investigator, concerned with the pursuit of truth, considering a statement which contains a vague predicate. How are we to account for his understanding of it? One caricature of what occurs would be as follows: he must establish what proposition is expressed by the statement, and his investigation is then directed towards establishing whether that proposition is true. The statement introduces a proposition, a putative candidate for inclusion in the ultimately true account of reality. Since the statement involves vague predicates, it seems highly problematic just which proposition the statement expresses. Yet unless we can account for the identification of this proposition, we have no account of what putative truth is expressed; and he lacks a target for his investigation. If we hold to the 'dyadic' acount of understanding described in section 3, some such picture can seem very attractive. In that case, unless we hold that reality itself is vague, vagueness can appear to be an impediment to the kind of understanding that is required for serious pursuit of the truth.

We can contrast with this the picture of such understanding suggested by pragmatism. The investigator's goal is to contribute to our arriving at an adequate account of the laws that govern the world he encounters through perception. How should he interpret and develop the statement, in the light of this overarching goal? What role have the assertion, criticism and defence of the statement in the broader project of arriving at an adequate account of the laws which comprise reality? He can seek a fuller description of the objects of indexical expressions contained in the statement. He can criticize and enrich the habits of expectation that he links to the predicate expressions. Vagueness can be removed, or unwarranted precision can be mitigated. An account of practices of interpretation which is guided by this overarching goal threatens to bypass the difficulties discussed in the previous paragraph. It is not required that this statement be understood now as expressing a definite candidate for the final consensus. If a statement does not express a 'definite question', it still has a role in the pursuit of truth: it is interpreted as a gesture towards a definite question; or we understand how to recognize that no definite question is raised and to respond accordingly.

There is much more to be said of the details of the views of Peirce and Frege on vagueness, and there are many similarities in their approaches to issues of language and meaning on which I have not touched. My concern has not been to suggest a sharp opposition of approaches to meaning where there is much in common. Rather, I hope to have clarified something of what is distinctive in pragmatist accounts of meaning and understanding, and to have done so in a way which will help us to understand the role of pragmatist ideas in the developments of analytical philosophy which can be traced to the influence of Ramsey and Wittgenstein. The stress upon the practice of interpretation, and upon the respects in which this is senstive to the goals which guide our activities, provides a perspective from which we can understand the role of language in our lives without feeling constrained to search for pristine logical structures which are somehow present in our ordinary assertions.[7,8]

Notes

1   This needs slight qualification. There are a few manuscript pages in which Peirce sketches a three-valued logic, and suggests that this might have application in accounting for the logic of vagueness (Fisch and Turquette, 1966). N. 29, on p. 183 of the reprint of this paper in Fisch, 1986, lists eight papers in which Turquette has extended his study of this system. The fragmentary nature of this material means that the claim made here still stands.

2   In order to prevent misunderstanding by readers who are familiar with the positivists' approach to meaning, two points should be stressed. First, there is no suggestion that the conditionals we arrive at in applying the principle should be *analytic*: they reflect our theoretical understanding of the concept in question; and they will be revised (and

their number grow) as this scientific understanding develops. Second, Peirce is increasingly emphatic that his view would have no plausibility if we lacked a realist understanding of the subjunctive conditionals, (the 'would-bes'), that these formulations contain (see, for example, 5.453, and Hookway, 1985, pp. 239–46).

3 See, for example, Fine, 1975.

4 There are marked similarities between Peirce's approach to quantification and Hintikka's 'game-theoretic semantics': they are discussed by Hilpinen, 1982 and Brock, 1980.

5 Hence, Peirce's 'logic' of vagueness consists in a classification of the different kinds of vagueness and an exploration of how sentences containing vague expressions are interpreted. Brock (1979) discusses some of these claims in more detail, and they are also considered in Nadin, 1980.

6 There is danger of confusion here. Peirce insists that logic is a 'normative science' (see, for example, 1.577). He holds, for example, that deductive logic is a scientific investigation of the norms or standards that govern our practice of mathematical reasoning. It does not purport to criticize that practice. Mathematical reasoning needs no justification. A revision in logic can arise when we arrive at a better characterization of what is involved in deductive validity. But this is answerable to our mathematical or deductive practice: there is no suggestion that logic could be normative in the sense of prescribing a change in our deductive practice (for further discussion, see Hookway, 1985, ch. 6, especially pp. 182–3).

7 There is a further link between Peirce's views on vagueness and his realism which I have not discussed. An important theme in his philosophy is his 'synechism' – a philosophical outlook which stresses continuities in thought and nature. We have already seen that Peirce holds that vagueness is a characteristic of language used to describe phenomena which vary continuously along a dimension such as colours. He also holds that that the reality of continua, and our experience of them, provide the key to a realist account of universals. Discussion of the difficult interpretative issues which this raises would take us beyond the concerns of this paper. There is a brief discussion of them in Hookway, 1985, pp. 172ff.; and see Potter, 1967, passim, and Engel-Tiercelin 1986.

8 I am grateful to David Bell, Neil Cooper and John Skorupski for editorial suggestions, and to Kenneth L. Ketner for his helpful comments on an earlier draft.

References

References to the works of Frege and Peirce use the abbreviations indicated below. References beginning 'R' are to Peirce's manuscripts as catalogued in Robin (1967). Other references are by author and date.

Brock, J. 1979, 'Principal themes in Peirce's logic of vagueness', in *Peirce Studies*, 1. pp. 41–9

Brock, J. 1980, 'Peirce's anticipation of game-theoretic logic and semantics', in *Semiotics 1980*, ed. M. Herzfield and M. D. Lenhart, New York: Plenum Press

Dummett, M. A. E. 1981, *The Interpretation of Frege's Philosophy*, London: Duckworth

Engel-Tiercelin, C. 1986, 'Le vague est-il réel? Sur le réalisme de Peirce', in *Philosophie*, 10, pp. 69–96

Fine, K. 1975, 'Vagueness, truth and logic', in *Synthese*, 30, pp. 265–300

Fisch, M. H. 1986, *Peirce, Semeiotic, and Pragmatism*, Bloomington: Indiana University Press

Fisch, M. H. and Turquette, A. 1966, 'Peirce's triadic logic', *Transactions of the Charles S. Peirce Society*, vol. 2, pp. 71–85, reprinted as ch. 9 of Fisch, 1986

Frege, G. 1970, *Translations from the Philosophical Writings of Gottlob Frege*, eds P. Geach and M. Black, Oxford: Basil Blackwell (TPWF).

Frege, G. 1972, *Conceptual Notation and Related Articles*, Oxford: Oxford University Press (CN).

Frege, G. 1979, *Posthumous Writings*, Oxford: Basil Blackwell (PW)

Frege, G. 1980, *Philosophical and Mathematical Correspondence*, Oxford: Basil Blackwell (PMC)

Frege, G. 1984, *Collected Papers on Mathematics, Logic and Philosophy*, Oxford: Basil Blackwell (CP)

Hilpinen, R. 1982, 'On C. S. Peirce's theory of the proposition: Peirce as a precursor of game-theoretical semantics', *The Monist*, 65, pp. 182–8

Hookway, C. J. 1985, *Peirce*, London: Routledge and Kegan Paul

Nadin, M. 1980, 'The logic of vagueness and the category of synechism', *The Monist*, 63, pp. 351–63

Peirce, C. S. 1923, *Chance, Love and Logic: Philosophical Essays by C. S. Peirce, the Founder of Pragmatism*, ed. M. R. Cohen, New York: Harcourt, Brace and Co. (CLL)

Peirce, C. S. 1931–56, *Collected Writings of Charles Sanders Peirce*, ed. C. Hartshorne, P. Weiss and A. W. Burks (8 vols), Cambridge, MA: Harvard University Press (references give volume and paragraph, e.g. 5.234)

Peirce, C. 1976, *The New Elements of Mathematics* (four volumes in five), ed. C. Eisele, The Hague: Mouton, (referred to as NE, with volume and page)

Peirce, C. 1982, *Writings of Charles S. Peirce: a Chronological Edition*, ed. M.Fisch et al., Bloomington: Indiana University Press, (W, references give volume and page)

Potter, V. 1967, *Charles Peirce on Norms and Ideals*, Amherst: University of Massachusetts Press

Ramsey, F. P. 1931, *The Foundations of Mathematics*, London: Routledge and Kegan Paul

Ramsey, F. P. 1978, *Foundations*, Atlantic Highlands, NJ: Humanities Press

Robin, R. 1967, *Annotated Catalogue of the Papers of Charles S. Peirce*, Amherst: University of Massachusetts Press

Sluga, H. 1980, *Gottlob Frege*, London: Routledge and Kegan Paul

Wittgenstein, L. 1953, *Philosophical Investigations*, Oxford: Basil Blackwell.

Wittgenstein, L. 1967, *Remarks on the Foundations of Mathematics*, Oxford: Basil Blackwell

Wittgenstein, L. 1969, *On Certainty*, Oxford: Basil Blackwell

4

Thought and Perception: the Views of Two Philosophical Innovators

Michael Dummett

Brentano recognized, but notoriously did not so much as attempt to solve, a problem that was therefore left to his followers to resolve. It is unclear how far he really recognized it as a problem, since, in his writing, what promise to be discussions of it always slide off into some other topic, leaving the original problem unresolved. His most famous doctrine was that what distinguishes mental from physical phenomena is their intentionality, although Brentano himself never used precisely that term. This means that they have the characteristic of being directed towards external objects: no one can be simply contemptuous or simply irritated, but only contemptuous *of* something or irritated *at* something.

Mental phenomena are thus, for Brentano, all mental *acts* or attitudes of differing kinds; and this characteristic of being directed towards something was propounded by him as the defining feature of such mental phenomena. The contrast expressly drawn by Brentano is between mental and physical *phenomena*, rather than between mental and physical *acts*. What he understands as 'physical phenomena' appear to be phenomenal qualities, such as colours and auditory tones, and complexes of them; he says:

> Examples of physical phenomena . . . are: a colour; a shape; a panorama which I view; a chord which I hear; warmth; cold; an odour which I smell; and also similar images which appear in the imagination (*Psychology from an Empirical Standpoint*, henceforward *PES*, Book II, ch.1, § 2).

Brentano's distinction between physical and mental phenomena thus differentiates things of a sort that many philosophers have regarded as being among the contents of the mind from those of another sort – mental acts – that are more uncontroversially mental. Brentano explains what he wishes to include among such mental phenomena as follows:

Hearing a sound, seeing a coloured object, feeling warmth or cold, as well as similar states of imagination are examples of what I mean by this term. I also mean by it the thinking of a general concept, provided such a thing actually does occur. Furthermore, every judgement, every recollection, every expectation, every inference, every conviction or opinion, every doubt, is a mental phenomenon. Also to be included under this term is every emotion: joy, sorrow, fear, hope, courage, despair, anger, love, hate, desire, act of will, intention, astonishment, admiration, contempt, etc. (ibid.).

Brentano's celebrated original statement of the thesis of intentionality was as follows:

Every mental phenomenon is characterised by what the Scholastics called the intentional (or mental) inexistence of an object, and what we might call, though not quite unambiguously, reference to a content, direction towards an object (which is not to be understood here as meaning a thing), or immanent objectivity. Every mental phenomenon includes something as object within itself, although they do not all do so in the same way. In a presentation (*Vorstellung*) something is presented, in a judgement something is affirmed or denied, in love something is loved, in hate something is hated, in desire something is desired, and so forth (ibid., § 5).

The doctrine here propounded makes the object intrinsic to the mental act. Brentano insists that what he calls 'physical phenomena' never exhibit anything like the characteristic of 'intentional inexistence', and concludes that we may 'define mental phenomena by saying that they are those phenomena which contain an object intentionally within themselves'. Since his 'physical phenomena' are not acts in even the most general sense, and cannot be referred to by transitive verbs, it would be literally ungrammatical to speak of them as having, and therefore, equally, as lacking, objects; what Brentano means is best seen by contrast with what we should ordinarily call a physical act, for instance that of kicking a football. The object of such a physical act is extrinsic to it *qua* physical act. Up to the point of contact, the act of kicking the football would have been exactly the same if the ball had not been there: it is only to the intention underlying the act that the object is intrinsic, in that I should not have had precisely the same intention if I had meant just to make a kicking motion without impact. In a different terminology, the relation of a physical act to its object is external, that of a mental act to its object internal.

Not only does Brentano's characterization of a mental phenomenon make the object intrinsic to it: it also appears to attribute to the object a special kind of existence, namely intentional inexistence or mental inexistence, as embodied in that act. On such an interpretation, an object may have either or both of two modes of existence: it may exist in the actual world, external to the mind; and it may also exist in the mind, as incorporated in a mental act directed towards it. There would then be no more difficulty in explaining how there could be a mental act directed towards something that had no actual existence than in admitting the actual existence of objects to which no mental act is directed: in the former case, the object would have intentional inexistence but no existence in actuality, while in the latter case it would exist in actuality while lacking any intentional inexistence. To admit the possibility of the latter case is necessary if we are to be realists about the external world; to admit the possibility of the former is necessary if we are to recognize that the mind is not constrained by external reality. It is but a short step from such a position to the thesis that the object of any mental act is always to be considered as enjoying only mental inexistence, but *represents* the external object, if there is one. On this development of Brentano's view, a mental act is always directed towards something that, as an ingredient of the act, is essentially a content of the mind; at this stage, we should be fully entrapped in the bog of empiricism.

But that was not the road down which Brentano travelled. It seems probable that when, in the original edition of *PES*, published in 1874, he originally introduced, or reintroduced, the term 'intentional inexistence', he did mean to ascribe to the objects of mental acts a special kind of existence in the mind, distinguishable from actual existence. But he withdrew from the edge of the bog. He not only declined to take the next step into full-blooded representationalism: he came to repudiate the conception of a shadowy mental existence altogether. He continued to maintain that the object of a mental act is intrinsic to the act, but nevertheless now insisted that it is external to the mind: not merely external in the sense in which one may contrast an external object with the correlate of a cognate accusative, as one might say that the internal object of thinking is a thought, the external object that which is thought about, but external in the full sense of not being a constituent of the subject's consciousness, but a part of the objective world independent of him and of the mental act which he directs towards it. If, for instance, I intend to marry a woman, or promise to marry her, it is *that woman* whom I intend or promise to marry, and who is therefore the object of my mental act, expressed or unexpressed; the object of that act is not my mental representation of the woman, but the woman herself. Thus is 1909 Brentano wrote:

> It is paradoxical in the extreme to say that a man promises to marry an *ens rationis* and fulfils his promise by marrying a real person (letter to Oskar Kraus quoted in Kraus's Introduction to the 3rd edn (1924) of *PES*).

Thus when the object of a mental act exists in actuality, it is that very object, considered as actually existing, that is the object of the mental act. But does this not leave it open that the object also has a different type of existence, as an ingredient of the mental act, and that, when the object of a mental act lacks actual existence, it has only this mental kind of existence? No! Not according to the later Brentano: for, on his later view, there are not, properly speaking, any kinds of existence at all: there is only actual existence, and all other ways of talking, though frequently convenient, are strictly speaking improper:

> All mental references refer to things. In many cases, the things to which we refer do not exist. We are, however, accustomed to say that they then have being as objects [of the mental acts]. This is an improper use of the verb 'to be' which we permit ourselves for the sake of convenience, just as we speak of the Sun's 'rising' or 'setting'. All that it means is that a mentally active subject is referring to those things (supplementary remark V, added to the 2nd edn (1911) of *PES*).

This passage contains another retraction. In the last passage quoted from the 1874 text of *PES*, he went out of his way to assert that the object of a mental act need not be a thing. Brentano used the word 'thing' after the mode generally then current in German philosophical writing, namely, to mean a concrete particular, which, for him, might be either material or spiritual: in effect, a substance in the sense of Descartes. He had originally held that the object of a mental act need not be a thing in this sense; in particular, he had allowed that it might be what he referred to as a 'content', that is, the content of a proposition. His later view was that the object of a mental act could only be something '*real*', that is, not necessarily real in the sense of actually existing, but thing-like: all mental acts must have concrete particulars as their objects. This naturally led him into very involved explanations of the host of apparent counter-examples. His general strategy for such explanations was to admit a large range of different 'modes of presentation' – types of mental act involving different relations to their object. He thus repudiated the entire range of ideal objects admitted by Husserl and Meinong – those objects characterized by Frege as objective but not actual, and whose existence he insisted that we must acknowledge if we are to avoid the twin errors of physicalism and psychologism. Brentano was, in particular, especially scathing about Meinong's 'objectives' – the equivalents of Frege's thoughts.

More germane to the present purpose is the fact, blandly stated by Brentano in the last passage quoted, that 'in many cases the things to which we refer' – the objects of our mental acts – 'do not exist'. As Dagfinn Føllesdal quite rightly observes, in his essay 'Brentano and Husserl on intentional objects and perception', Brentano's insistence that, when the object actually exists, it is that very object, and not any mental representation of it, which is the object of the mental act tallies exactly with Frege's insistence that, when I speak of the Moon, it is the heavenly body itself, and not my idea of the Moon, that is the reference of the phrase I use, and hence is that about which I am talking (in H. L. Dreyfus (ed.), *Husserl, Intentionality and Cognitive Science*, Cambridge, Mass., 1982, p. 32). But all this only provokes the obvious objection that it fails to explain how there can be a genuine mental act, even though there is no object in actuality. There plainly can: someone may be contemptuous of or irritated at something illusory; or, again, he may suffer a hallucination or other sensory delusion. A visual or auditory illusion does not consist in simply seeing or hearing without seeing or hearing anything: the character of intentionality still attaches to mental acts of this kind. To have that character is to be directed towards an object; but, in such a case, there *is* no object.

Brentano seems to have thought it sufficient to observe that:

It someone thinks of something, the one who is thinking must certainly exist, but the object of his thinking need not exist at all (Supplementary Remark I, *PES*).

But this is obviously quite inadequate: for what does the phrase 'the object of his thinking' stand for here? Meinong's answer, 'An object that does not happen to exist', was not available to Brentano, who vehemently denied the admissibility of any notion of being distinct from existence. If, on the other hand, it were answered that the phrase does not stand for anything at all, that would be to equate the statement, 'The object of his thinking does not exist', with the statement, 'His thinking does not have an object': and that would flatly contradict Brentano's salient principle that one who is thinking must be thinking of something, which is difficult to construe otherwise than as meaning that there is something of which he is thinking. Nor was it open to Brentano to say that, in *such* a case, the object of the mental act is, after all, a constituent of the subject's mind; for it would then have been impossible to resist saying the same in a case in which the subject is thinking of an actual object or is having a veridical perception.

This, then, was the problem which Brentano bequeathed to his successors. Husserl's solution was to generalize the distinction between meaning and object (i.e. between sense and reference) from 'expressive' acts (that is, linguistic acts) to mental acts of all kinds. For singular terms, the linguistic distinction lies to hand. The notion of using a singular term to talk about a particular object, or of referring to something by means of such a term, is not a philosopher's invention: it is part of the equipment we already have when we come to the philosophical analysis of language. It has never been necessary to argue that singular terms, in general, have reference: it is a starting-point. The further distinction drawn by Husserl from the time of his *Logische Untersuchungen* onwards, between objective meanings and subjective ideas, parallel to the similar distinction drawn by Frege and, before him, by Bolzano, is not part of everyday modes of thought, however;

the distinction was intrinsic to his recoil from the psychologism of which he had originally been an exponent, but whose implacable enemy he now became.

To complete sentences, and to subsentential expressions other than singular terms, intuition of course demands that we ascribe meanings; but assigning to them anything analogous to reference goes against the grain of common sense: everyone's reaction, on reading Frege for the first time, is therefore to think his extension of *Bedeutung* from singular terms to all significant expressions unwarranted. The problem is thus the opposite of that which arises for singular terms. For them, what requires justification is the ascription to them of a sense distinct from their possessing a particular reference: for expressions of other categories, it is the ascription to them of a reference as well as a sense.

This problem did not trouble Husserl, however. He was at one with Frege in regarding all meaningful expressions as having, or purporting to have, objective correlates, taking this for granted because of his inheritance from Brentano. For a follower of Brentano, all mental acts are characterized by intentionality, and therefore have objects, or at least purport to have them. In itself, of course, an utterance is not a mental act: but its significance is due to its being accompanied by a mental act, called by Husserl the meaning-conferring act, which, as being a mental act, must have, or purport to have, an object.

Husserl was not concerned with convincing anybody that expressions of categories other than singular terms also had objective correlates: the intentionality of mental acts was so axiomatic for him that he saw no need to demonstrate it in particular cases. He therefore paid little attention to the question of what the objective correlates of such expressions should be taken to be, the correct answer to which so exercised Frege. Even if he had attended to it more closely, he would have been perplexed to answer it: for he lacked any general principle for extending the notion of objective reference from singular terms to other categories. Frege had such a principle: namely that the reference of an expression is what is common to every expression which could be substituted for it in any sentence without affecting the truth-value of that sentence. Moreover, on Frege's theory, the reference of an expression constituted its contribution to determining the truth-value of any sentence containing it: the references of the parts jointly formed the mechanism by which the truth-value of the whole was determined. For each logical type that he recognized, Frege appealed to these principles in order to determine what sort of thing we should take the reference of an expression of that type to be. Husserl, by contrast, did not care very much what the objective correlate of an expression is taken to be, as long as it is recognized as having one. He did not identify the reference of a predicate with a concept in Frege's sense; rather, he tended to think of it as the object to which the predicate applies. The most salient instance of his indifference to how we identify the objective correlates of expressions concerns whole sentences, of which he wrote:

If we consider assertoric sentences of the form *S is P*, for example, the object of the statement is normally regarded as being that which constitutes the subject, and thus that *of* which something is asserted. A different conception is, however, also possible, which takes the *whole* state of affairs corresponding to the statement as the analogue of the object denoted by a name and distinguishes it from the meaning of the statement (*First Investigation*, § 12).

He states no preference for either option: he merely records that there are these two ways of ascribing an objective reference to the sentence, and appears indifferent to the choice between them.

Husserl, like Frege, regarded the sense of an expression as being that in virtue of which it has the particular objective reference that it has.

An expression attains an objective reference only through its meaning what it does, so that it can therefore be rightly said that the expression designates (names) the object *in virtue of* its meaning, and that the act of meaning is the particular way in which we refer to the object at a given time (*First Investigation*, § 13).

But since, unlike Frege, he had no systematic theory of the kind of objective reference possessed by expressions of different types, he lacked the basis for any systematic account of how meaning determines reference. This makes a fundamental difference between him and Frege, since Frege's theory of reference is the foundation of his theory of sense. For Frege, the crucial first step towards characterizing the sense of any expression is to decide what kind of thing, and what in particular, constitutes its reference. Its sense is required to take the form of a means by which that reference may be given to one who knows the language, in virtue of his knowing it: hence, while a theory of reference does not yet amount to a theory of sense, it constitutes its indispensable foundation.

For Husserl, as for Frege, the existence of meaningful expressions which miss their mark by lacking any objective correlate is unproblematic in the light of the distinction of meaning from objective reference. We must not confuse lack of reference with meaninglessness, or even logical inconsistency with meaninglessness, for, if we do, we shall be unable to explain how a true denial of existence succeeds in being meaningful. In the period following his *Logische Untersuchungen*, Husserl's fundamental thought was that the notion of sense could be generalized from expressive (linguistic) acts to all mental acts: the notion thus generalized he termed 'noema'. The object of any mental act is given through its noema: since it is intrinsic to the noema to be directed towards an object, it is the noema that imparts intentionality to mental acts, and it is in virtue of it that an act has whatever object it has. It was by introducing this distinction between the object of a mental act and its noema that Husserl believed that Brentano's problem could be resolved. A noema must inform every mental act, giving it the quality of being directed towards an object; but it is no more perplexing that a noema should miss its mark, so that no external object corresponds to it, than that an expression should have a sense that fails to determine any actual objective reference for it. Delusive perceptions are accordingly no longer problematic: they possess the feature of intentionality as well as do veridical ones, but simply happen to lack any actual object.

Husserl insisted that, in the standard case, the meaning of the words employed in a linguistic act is not an object of our thought: 'in the act of meaning, the meaning is not present to consciousness as an object', he said; 'if we perform the act, and live in it, as it were, we naturally refer to its object and not to its meaning' (*First Investigation*, § 34). Frege hardly ever discussed what we are conscious of when we are speaking, regarding this as irrelevant to the objective properties of our words, namely their references and their senses; but he distinguished sharply between speaking of the ordinary referent of an expression, which is the normal case, and the special case in which we are using it to speak of its (ordinary) sense. Husserl likewise maintained that it is the (external) object of any of our acts of perception of which we are aware. Far from its being the noema that we directly apprehend, it does not normally serve as an object of the observer's awareness at all, still less of his perceptions. Just as, in the normal case, a speaker is talking and thinking about the objective referent of his utterance, not about the meaning in virtue of which his words have that reference, so a subject perceives an object in virtue of the noema of the perceptual act, and does not perceive or otherwise apprehend that noema.

Husserl's theory is thus to be distinguished from a sense-datum theory, according to which sense-data are the primary objects of awareness. In the case of perception, Husserl thought that we can, by an act of reflection, make the noema the object of our attention: but he held that this is an extraordinarily difficult thing to do, which only the philosopher can achieve, and that it is the fundamental task of philosophy to fasten attention on noemata and attain a characterization of them.

The only one of Frege's writings to contain any substantial remarks about sense-perception is 'Der Gedanke'. There, using the term 'thing' to mean a material object, he writes as follows:

Sense-impressions on their own do not disclose the external world to us. There are, perhaps, beings who only have sense-impressions, without seeing or feeling things. To have visual impressions is not yet to see things. How does it come about that I see the tree in just that place where I see it? It obviously depends on the visual impressions that I have, and on the particular kind of visual impressions that arise because I see with two eyes. On

each of my two retinas there is formed a particular image, in the physical sense. Someone else sees the tree in the same place. He, too, has two
retinal images, which, however, differ from mine. We must assume that
these retinal images determine our impressions. We thus have visual
impressions that are not only not identical, but markedly divergent from
one another. And yet we move about in the same external world. Having
visual impressions is, indeed, necessary for seeing things, but it is not sufficient. What has still to be added is not anything sensible. And yet it is
precisely this which opens up the external world for us; for without this
non-sensible component each person would remain shut up within his own
inner world. . . . Besides one's inner world, one must distinguish the external world proper of sensible, perceptible things and also the realm of that
which is not sensorily perceptible. To recognize either of these two realms
we stand in need of something non-sensible; but in the sensory perception
of things we have need, in addition, of sense-impressions, and these belong
wholly to the inner world. Thus that on which there primarily rests the distinction between the different manners in which a thing and a thought are
given is something assignable, not to either of the two realms, but to the
inner world.

Frege is here distinguishing between three realms of existence of which we are
each conscious: the inner world, private to each individual and comprising the
contents of his consciousness; the external world of material objects, which we all
inhabit together; and the 'third realm' of thoughts and their constituent senses,
which, like the external world, is accessible to all in common, but whose contents,
though they can be grasped by human minds, are immaterial and immutable,
and do not act on the senses or on each other. At an earlier phase, Frege had
recognized objects of many kinds as being objective, unlike the contents of
consciousness, but causally inert, unlike material objects, and hence not what he
called 'actual': among these were logical objects such as numbers. But, at the time
of writing 'Der Gedanke', he had probably ceased to believe in logical objects: he
could therefore take thoughts and their constituent senses to exhaust the popu-
lation of the third realm. The non-sensible component of perception, converting
it from a sense-impression wholly part of the inner world into the perception of a
material object, thus opening up the external world to us, clearly belongs to the
'third realm'. Frege does not tell us whether it must be a complete thought, say to
the effect that there is a tree in a certain place, or whether it may be a mere
thought-constituent, such as the sense of the concept-word 'tree', involving our
seeing the object *as* a tree, nor whether, if it is a whole thought, the act of perception involves judging that the thought is true, or whether it is sufficient merely to
grasp the thought without advancing from it to the truth-value. Most likely, he
meant that perception involves a judgement as to the truth of a complete thought:

for he accepted sense-perception as a source of knowledge, and knowledge issues in judgement; so at least in the normal case, perception must involve judging some state of affairs to obtain, rather than merely entertaining the thought that it does.

Frege's notion of grasping a sense or a thought requires examination. There is, first, the distinction between grasping a thought as being the sense of a particular sentence, and grasping the thought that happens to be expressed by that sentence, without necessarily recognizing the sentence as having that sense. A second distinction, never drawn by Frege himself, is that between a dispositional and an occurrent grasp of a sense or thought. Consider the opening passage of 'Gedankengefüge':

> It is astonishing what language can do, in that, with a few syllables, it can express unsurveyably many thoughts, so that it can find a clothing even for a thought that has been grasped by an inhabitant of the Earth for the very first time, in which it will be understood by someone else to whom it is entirely new. This would not be possible if we could not distinguish parts in the thought corresponding to the parts of a sentence, so that the structure of the sentence can serve as a picture of the structure of the thought.

Our ability to understand a sentence expressing a thought that is entirely new to us is here explained in terms of our existing grasp of the senses of the constituent parts of that sentence; our grasp of them is surely dispositional. But when Frege speaks of the very first time that an inhabitant of the Earth grasps a given thought, he is, presumably, speaking of grasping a thought in an occurrent sense. The Earth-dweller has long had the *capacity* to frame or understand the thought, as has the one to whom he communicates it: but this is the first time that he, or any other human being, has expressly entertained that thought.

It is the dispositional notion of grasping the sense of an individual word that is primary: what interests us is whether someone will understand the word when he hears it, and whether it will be available to him when he has occasion to use it, rather than whether he has its sense in mind at a particular moment, save when he hears or uses a sentence containing it. Similarly, we are more interested in whether someone does or does not possess a given concept than in whether he is currently exercising his grasp of it. By contrast, what is important about a sentence is not whether someone is capable of understanding it, but whether he understands it on a particular occasion on which he hears it; and what is important about a thought is not whether someone is capable of grasping it, but whether he is currently considering whether it is true or understanding someone else to have asserted it: so it is the occurrent notion of grasping a complete thought that is primary.

Grasping a sense, understood dispositionally, is evidently not a mental act, but a kind of ability: and this tallies with Wittgenstein's dictum that understanding, which he expressly compares to an ability, is not a mental process. But Frege allowed that, while thoughts are not mental contents, grasping a thought is a mental act, although one directed towards something external to the mind; and he must here be construing the notion of grasping a thought in its occurrent sense. Wittgenstein strove to dispel the idea that there is an occurrent sense of 'understand': but it is difficult to see how this can be successfully maintained. We cannot, for instance, simply reduce the conception of understanding an utterance to that of hearing it while possessing a dispositional understanding of the relevant words and constructions: for it is possible to be perplexed by a sentence on first hearing, through a failure to take in its structure, and to achieve an understanding of it on reflection.

Nevertheless, these considerations prompt us to ask exactly what it is to grasp a sense or a thought, according to Frege's conception. For him, it is the sense that is the logical notion: grasping the sense of an expression or of a sentence is a psychological process, irrelevant when our concern is to characterize the sense itself; in consequence, he seldom devotes any attention to the process. One of the few exceptions occurs in his lectures of 1914 on 'Logic in Mathematics'. In *Grundlagen* Frege had insisted that definitions are scientifically fruitful; it would be inconsistent both with his earlier views on content and his later views on sense to dismiss this fruitfulness as a purely psychological matter. In the lectures, he has changed his view in favour of the Russellian one that definitions are no more than abbreviations, and hence logically unimportant. He then comments:

A thought is by no means always present to our consciousness clearly in all its parts. When we use the word 'integral', for example, are we always conscious of everything that belongs to the sense of this word? Only in very rare cases, I think. Usually just the word is present to our consciousness, though associated with a more or less dim knowledge that this word is a sign that has a sense, and that, when we wish, we can recall this sense. . . . We often have need of a sign with which we associate a very complex sense. This sign serves us as a receptacle in which we can, as it were, carry the sense about, in the consciousness that we can always open this receptacle should we have need of what it contains.

Frege even attempts to use these reflections in order to reinforce his distinction between the logical and the psychological:

From this consideration it is apparent that the thought, as I understand the word, in no way concides with a content of my consciousness.

This only proves, however, that my taking a word to have a certain sense does not depend on my bearing that sense continuously in mind: the passage speaks of the sense as sometimes being 'present to the consciousness', and hence supplies no reason for its not being a *content* of my consciousness.

The conception here sketched by Frege differs strongly from Husserl's view that an utterance assumes a meaning by an interior act investing it with that meaning. For Frege a word simply *has* a sense: he does not discuss, here or elsewhere, what confers that sense upon it, but it is clear that he does not think that its bearing that sense in the mouth of a speaker depends upon his performing any mental act of endowing it with that sense. Quite the contrary: even in thinking to himself, he may use the word without adverting to its sense, confident only that he can call the sense to mind when he needs to. When will he need to? When doing so is necessary in order to judge whether a sentence containing it is true, or to decide what follows deductively from that sentence or whether it follows from certain others. This suggests, therefore, that we should interpret his grasp of the sense as an ability which is called into play in determining the truth-value of the sentence, or in attending to particular features of the manner in which its truth-value is determined: the subject employs the word in the confidence that he has this ability, and can recall the contribution the word makes to the truth-conditions of the sentence when it becomes necessary to attend to it.

This interpretation appears in general accord with Frege's explanation of that in which the sense of a word consists. It is nevertheless far from certain that he would have accepted it. He had two modes of writing about sense: the first when he was concerned with the relation between sense and reference, and the second when he was invoking the mythology of the third realm in order to elaborate the ontological status of senses. The interpretation of a grasp of sense as an ability fits very well all that he wrote in the former mode, but not the conception of senses as non-actual but objective and immutable objects. In the latter mode, he thought of the sense of a word or of a sentence as something that we apprehend by an exercise of an intellectual faculty somewhat analogous to sense-perception: so, although it is not a content of consciousness, a sense or thought may be an object of conscious attention. This conception makes awareness of a sense highly disanalogous with awareness of a material object. For, first, there is nothing corresponding to the sense-impression which forms an intergral part of the perception of a physical object: my awareness of the thought, which is *not* a content of my consciouseness, is not mediated by something which *is* a content of my consciousness, namely an impression of that thought. And, second, no *further* sense or thought plays the role which, in sense-perception, Frege believed was played by some constituent of the third realm. In perception, the sense-impression must be accompanied or informed by the sense of some means of referring to or picking out the object, or, more likely, by the thought that such an object is present. When we *refer* to a thought or sense, we do so by means of a further sense, for instance that of the term 'the principle of double effect', whose referent is the first thought or sense: but grasping a sense is something quite different from referring to it or thinking of it. Grasping a sense is immediate. Frege held, with Kant, that an object cannot be given to us save in a particular way; for him, the particular way in which it is given constitutes a sense to which that object corresponds as referent. But there cannot be different ways in which one and the same sense can be given, since everything that goes to determine the referent is part of the sense: more exactly, we ought to say that grasping a sense is not an instance of being *given* an object. The third realm is thus far more directly accessible to us than the external world of physical objects. For all that, the human mind is not capacious enough to be able to attend simultaneously to many senses, or to all the details of a very complex one: but language enables it to handle complicated thoughts, since we can attend to the *words* without, at each moment, attending to all their senses.

This conception is plainly unsatisfactory, precisely because, although it denies that senses are contents of consciousness, it makes adverting to a sense an act of consciousness. Frege's account indeed reflects an experience familiar to anyone who has devised or followed a mathematical proof; a recently defined term may be used for several steps without appeal to its definition: at a crucial point the definition is invoked, but requires a certain effort to recall. The mythology of the third realm gets in the way of a clear account, however. Frege's positive theory, that the sense of an expression consists in the manner in which its referent is determined, as a step in the determination of the truth-value of any sentence containing that expression, is independent of the mythology. The mental processes accompanying the use of the expression on the part of someone who grasps its sense are irrelevant to that sense, according to Frege: they do not enter into the explanation of what it is for it to have that sense. This shows that the psychological has to be distinguished from the logical. What Frege set aside as psychological cannot so easily be dismissed from consideration, however. Sense is distinguished from reference precisely by the fact that it can be grasped – can be apprehended directly, rather than in one or another particular way: were it not so, there would be no place for a notion of sense, as distinct from reference, at all. If, then, we are to have a firm grip on the concept of sense, or to give a clear explanation of it, we need to know exactly what it is to grasp a sense.

Frege was not disposed to explain a grasp of sense as an ability; and this is probably why he paid no attention to the distinction between a dispositional and an occurrent grasp. It was his realism that blocked him from construing a grasp of sense as an ability. A realist interpretation of sense has to link it, not with *our* procedures for deciding the truth-values of sentences, but with their determination as true or as false by the way things objectively are, independently of our knowledge. On such a view, therefore, a grasp of sense must consist, not in the ability to determine the truth-values of sentences, or to recognize them as having one or other truth-value, but in the *knowledge* of what renders them true or false. The notion of sense thus becomes an ineradicably cogitive one: grasping a sense is not a practical skill, but a piece of knowledge. What the mode of that knowledge may be is then a perplexing problem. Thus, in the end, Frege does not supply us with a clear account of what it is to grasp a sense; and, among other reasons, we need to know this in order to assess the thesis that sense-perception involves the grasp of a thought or sense.

The interpretation of a grasp of sense as an ability makes the grasp of sense the primary concept: any account of what sense is must be embedded in the account of a grasp of sense. On such a theory, sense is merely the cognate accusative of the verb 'to understand'; but this does not accord with Frege's mythology, which takes a sense to be an independently existing object with which the mind somehow makes contact. A further obstacle to Frege's interpreting a grasp of sense as an ability, had he considered doing so, was that this would have conflicted with his conception of the relative priority of thought and language, which viewed senses as intrinsically capable of being, but not intrinsically being, the senses *of* linguistic expressions. He held, namely, that it is not intrinsic to thoughts to be expressed in language, and that there is no contradiction in supposing beings who can grasp them in their nakedness, divested of linguistic clothing; but he added that 'it is necessary for us men that a thought of which we are conscious is connected in our consciousness with one or another sentence' ('Erkenntnisquellen').

This latter difficulty does not relate only to the notion of grasping a sense, but is intrinsic to Frege's various doctrines concerning sense itself: on it turns the question whether his two modes of discussing sense can be reconciled. On the interpretation of a grasp of sense as an ability, to grasp that a word has a certain sense is to apprehend how its presence contributes to determining the sentence in which it occurs as true or as false. If another word, in the same or another language, makes the same contribution, it has the same sense, and anyone who understands it may be allowed to have grasped the sense of the original word, considered independently of its being the sense of any particular word: but that leaves it unexplained what it would be to grasp that sense, but not *as* the sense of any actual or even hypothetical word. *We* cannot do that, according to Frege: but we ought to be able to explain what it would be to do it.

It might be suspected that the context principle was generated by overlooking the occurrent–dispositional distinction. Dispositionally construed, grasping the sense of a word does not have a context. The sense of the word may provide for its occurrence in certain contexts and not in others: but the word itself is understood in isolation, in that, if someone understands it at all, he thereby grasps its contribution to the sense of any larger context in which it can intelligibly occur. Nevertheless, we cannot quite dispense with an occurrent conception of the grasp of the sense of a word: for one may be quite familiar with the fact that a particular word has two distinct senses, and yet, when someone utters a sentence containing it, take it (perhaps wrongly) in just one of those senses. A disposition must be capable of being actuated or realized; the context principle may thus be understood as saying that the dispositional grasp of a sense can be activated only in the occurrent grasp of a thought of which that sense is constituent. That is why the appeal to sense which is involved in sense-perception must consist in the grasp of a complete thought.

Frege's ground for holding that sense-perception involves the grasp of a sense is, persumably, that sense-perception normally requires the awareness of one or more objects, whereas an object can only be given to us in one or another particular way. This thesis means that we cannot ever simply be aware of an object, in the sense that our state of awareness can be completely described by indicating the object of which we are aware: the way in which the object is given is always a sense which can be a thought-constituent. A sense-impression may be an impression of some particular object, but, being a mere content of consciousness, does not point beyond itself to that object: only a sense – a thought-constituent – has that capacity to point to something as its referent.

Despite its considerable plausibility, the theory fits rather badly with Frege's view of the relation between thought and language. We saw that to conceive of a grasp of sense as an ability conflicts with his thesis that there is no intrinsic impossibility in grasping a thought in its nakedness, without a verbal clothing: but his account of perception jars, conversely, with his further thesis that human beings can grasp only those thoughts which they attach to sentences as their senses. This thesis cannot be reduced to the contention that none of us can have a thought which he is incapable of expressing; rather, he says, in effect, that we can think only in words or symbols. Plainly, the notion that sense-perception involves the grasping of a thought or the making of a judgement wars powerfully with this view, for it is far from plausible that sensory perception always involves, or is even often accompanied by, any conscious linguistic operation.

In the First *Logical Investigation*, Husserl came close to Frege's view of perception, saying that 'if we imagine a consciousness prior to all experiences, it is a possibility that it has the same *sensations* as we do. But it will see no things and no events involving things, it will perceive no trees or houses, no flight of birds or barking of dogs.' But in the Sixth *Investigation* he expressed a wholly contrary view, construing our recognizing what we see as, say, a dog as an *accompaniment* rather than an ingredient of the act of perception, a judgement *prompted* by, but not inseparable from, it. It was in *Ideen* that he introduced his notion of noema, and developed a new account of sense-perception as informed by a noema. This new account is not to be equated with that given by Frege in 'Der Gedanke', since Husserl explicitly characterizes his notion of noema as a *generalization* of that of sense: thus in the posthumous third volume of *Ideen* he says, 'The noema is nothing but a generalization of the idea of sense to the field of all acts.' The remark rules out the possibility of Husserl's consistently explaining sense in the same way as Frege: for Frege's explanation does not allow for any generalization. For him, a sense is conceivable only as a constituent of thoughts, and, as he remarks in 'Der Gedanke', 'thoughts stand in the closest connection with truth.' On Frege's view, a sense is, as it were, an instruction for taking a step towards determining a thought as true or as false; such a step can be represented as the determination of a referent of the appropriate logical type, and the instruction as a particular means of determining it. Thoughts are *sui generis*: every thought may intelligibly be characterized as true or as false, and whatever can intelligibly be so characterized is a thought. The constituents of a thought are therefore likewise *sui generis*. Whatever serves the purpose of a sense – whatever constitutes a particular means of determining an object or a function – *is* a sense, forming a part of various thoughts; whatever does not serve that purpose cannot in any respect resemble a sense. Sense must be conceived quite differently if it is to be a notion capable of generalization, as Husserl wished to generalize it to the wider notion of noema.

It might be thought that Husserl's generalization consists solely in stripping the sense from its connection with any linguistic expression, and that it therefore does not follow that his conception of sense must have differed radically from Frege's. This interpretation appears to accord with some of Husserl's explanations, as when he says in *Ideen*:

The words 'mean' and 'meaning' relate in the first instance only to the linguistic sphere, of 'expressing'. It is, however, almost inevitable, and, at the same time, an important advance, to extend the meanings of these words, and to modify them appropriately, so that they become applicable in a certain manner ... to all acts, whether they are connected with expressive acts or not (*Ideen*, vol. I, § 124).

The interpretation cannot be sustained, however. Husserl distinguishes between two ingredients of the noema of a mental act: that which is capable of being expressed in words, which he sometimes calls 'the noematic sense', and which forms what he terms the 'central nucleus' of the noema; and that which is not so expressible, and forms the outer layer of the full noema. Thus he says:

'Within' each of these experiences there 'dwells' a noematic meaning; and, however closely related, and, indeed, as regards a central nucleus, in essence identical, this remains in different experiences, it nevertheless differs in kind when the experiences differ in kind... Thus within the *complete* noema ... we must separate out *as essentially different* certain *strata* which group themselves around a *central 'nucleus'*, the sheer *'objective meaning'* which ... can be described in purely identical objective terms (ibid., § 91).

He further specifies that:

> Every intention in the noematic sense, as the noematic nucleus, of any act
> whatever can be expressed by meanings.... 'Expression' is a remarkable
> form, which allows itself to be adapted to every sense (to the noematic
> nucleus), raising it to the realm of Logos (ibid., § 124).

It is plain that by 'meanings' Husserl intends 'linguistic meanings'. A noema thus
consists, in its central part, of a sense that can be attached to a linguistic
expression, but may inform a mental act without being so attached, and, in
addition, of further layers not linguistically expressible. The noematic sense
represents a generalization of linguistic meaning only in that it is detached from
language; but the other layers constitute a more radical generalization.

What, then, is the noema of an act of sense-perception? It would be a complete
mistake to equate it with the sense-impressions incorporated in the perceptual
act, collectively called 'hyle' by Husserl. His view of them is the same as Frege's:
having sensations does not in itself amount to seeing things or events involving
things. The noema is what endows the perceptual act with an object; like a sense,
therefore, it points beyond itself to an object in the external world. Sense-
impressions, on the other hand, do not, in themselves, point to anything beyond—
we simply *have* them; and here 'in themselves' does not mean 'when they occur
in isolation', but merely 'considered as such'.

The noema must, then, have the following properties:

1 it is that which renders the perception the perception *of* an object;
2 it may be a common ingredient of different acts of perception, just as a sense
   may be the sense of different utterances;
3 and it may vary while the object remains the same, just as there may be
   different senses with the same reference.

It therefore consists, in the first instance, in our interpreting our sense-
impressions as representations of external objects.

Surprisingly, Husserl makes little effort to use the notion of noema in order to
explain what makes a particular object that towards which a given act of perception is directed. His concern, when discussing the noema of such an act, is wholly
concentrated upon the perceiver's apprehension of the object, not merely as an
external object, but as having certain gereral characteristics. The principal consequence, for him, of the fact that every act of perception is informed by a noema
was that we always perceive an object as having such characteristics: as being of a
certain kind, say, or as having a certain three-dimensional shape or again as
disposed to behave in certain ways.

For all that, if the notion of noema is truly a generalization of that of sense, it
must also explain what makes one object, rather than another similar to it, the

one which is, at a given time, perceived by a particular subject. Nowadays we are inclined to explain it in causal terms: the object perceived is that which gives rise to our sense-impressions. The theory of noema must deny this, holding that what determines the object of perception, or of any other mental act, is internal to the act, because intrinsic to the noema which informs it, just as what determines the object that is being spoken of or thought about is, on Frege's account, internal to the thought expressed or entertained. The object of discussion is the referent of the sense associated with the singular term used; the object under consideration is the referent of the sense constitutive of the thought; and the object of perception must likewise be the objective correlate of the noema.

It would be possible to reconcile the causal theory with that of noema, by holding that the noema informing any act of perception always involves reference to a particular object via the notion of causality, namely as being the cause of the subject's sense-impressions, as when I think of someone as the person my noticing whom initiated my present train of thought. Since Husserl leaves the question unexplored, there is no way of saying whether or not he would favour such a solution. As remarked, he discusses the noema of a perceptual act largely in terms of the general characteristics of the perceived object; and, in some passages, he carries this very far:

> The factual world of experience is experienced as a *typified world*. Things are experienced as trees, bushes, animals, snakes, birds; specifically, as pine, lime-tree, lilac, dog, viper, swallow, sparrow and so on. The table is characterized as being familiar and yet new (from the posthumously published *Erfahrung und Urteil*).

Husserl presumably here means that the table is new, inasmuch as that particular table has not been seen before, but familiar in being a *table*. He continues:

> What is given in experience as a new individual is first known in terms of what has been genuinely perceived; it calls to mind the like (the similar). But what is apprehended *according to type* also has a horizon of possible experience with corresponding prescriptions of familiarity and has, therefore, *types* of attributes not yet experienced but expected. When we see a dog, we immediately anticipate its additional modes of behaviour: its typical ways of eating, playing, running, jumping and so on. We do not actually see its teeth: but we know in advance how its teeth will look – not in their individual determination but *according to type*, inasmuch as we have already had previous and frequent experience with similar animals, with dogs, that they have such things as teeth and of this typical kind (English translation by J. Churchill and K. Ameriks, Evanston, 1973, p. 331; cited from H. L. Dreyfus (ed.), ibid., introduction, pp. 18–19).

According to Husserl, then, the noema of a visual perception of a dog renders the perception intrinsically that *of a dog*, in that, even if it were illusory, a characterization of the perceptual experience would have to include its being of a dog. In such a case, it is therefore embodied in the noema that informs the perceptual act that what I am seeing is a dog. A possible first reaction to this passage is that Husserl's earlier account of perception is truer to the facts of such a case. However much of a unity may be formed, in experience, by our recognition of the animal as a dog, or of the object as an animal, and our perception of it, the two are, on this view, distinguishable acts: registering what is seen as a dog accompanies the act of perception, and is not a component of it.

I believe this reaction to be mistaken, but shall not here pursue the point. What plainly cannot be detached, even conceptually, from the perception is the percipient's apprehension, relative to himself, of the region of three-dimensional space occupied by the object: its rough distance from him, its orientation and its shape, including, of course, that part of it not actually presently accessible to the senses. Equally integral to the perception is his impression of the rigidity and cohesion of the object seen: whether he takes it to be something that will disperse, like a puff of smoke, flow, like water or treacle, droop, like a piece of string, move of itself, like an animal or a functioning machine, or retain its present shape and position. Such characters as these all have to do, as Husserl says, with the expectations generated by our perception of the object. In particular, the shape the object is seen as having governs not only our expectations of its appearance from other viewpoints, but also of its behaviour, such as whether (if it is solid) it will rest, topple, roll or slide. Our apprehension of the world as revealed to us in sense-perception is guided, from a very early stage of our lives, by a rudimentary terrestrial physics and geometry, backed by a basic classification of types of substance according to their behaviour. At least this much may be reckoned as belonging to the noema.

Frege and Husserl's accounts of perception both approach what must be the truth of the matter, but neither is acceptable as it stands. What shows this more sharply than their internal weaknesses is the impossibility of adapting them to explain the perceptual processes of animals or of infants not yet in possession of language. We cannot say that animals are locked into their inner worlds of sensation and are unable to attain an awareness of physical reality: yet there are strong objections to ascribing to them thoughts of the kind that are expressible in language. Frege himself voiced such an objection when he pointed out that we cannot attribute to a dog such a thought as, 'There is only one dog barring my way', since he does not have the concept 'one'. He nevertheless admits that the dog may well be able to distinguish between being attacked by one hostile dog and by several. The dog's awareness cannot accurately be expressed in language, because any sentence that suggests itself is conceptually too rich for the purpose. Human thought-processes differ radically from the analogous processes in animals, and, in particular, by their capacity to be detached from present activity and circumstances. Our thoughts may float free of the environment: we may follow a train of thought quite irrelevant to our surroundings or what we are engaged in doing. An adult human being may be suddenly struck by a thought as he is walking along. He may have hit on the key to solving a mathematical problem, or he may suddenly have remembered that he has left his spectacles at home; in the latter case, he may turn round and go back for them. An animal, or, equally, an infant, cannot act in such a way. An animal may solve quite complex problems, by a process that may reasonably be called thinking, as was illustrated by Köhler's chimpanzees: but its thought-processes cannot float free, but can occur only as integrated with current activity.

The proper characterization of the mental processes of animals is thus an exceedingly delicate task; but without accomplishing it, we can hardly attain an adequate account of our own. It is surely a mistake to suppose that, because, by means of language, we can engage in thought-processes both far richer and more precise than those of which animals are capable, we do not also engage in ones very similar to theirs. A cat can perceive a dog just as a human being can: there is no good reason to suppose that utterly different accounts should be given of feline and of human perceptions of such an object. Frege and Husserl were obviously right to hold that perception is not simply a matter of sensation, but that it has a further component at least analogous to thought. Frege simply identified it with thought, whereas Husserl wanted it to be a generalization of thought; but the one failed to show how thought could be fused with sensation, while the other failed to explain how the notion of thought was capable of generalization.

Husserl was the founder of phenomenology, Frege the grandfather of analytical philosophy, two schools which today are generally regarded as utterly diverse and barely capable of communicating with one another. Yet the analogy between the ideas of Frege and those of Bolzano has frequently been remarked on, and Bolzano was the salient influence on Husserl's *Logische Untersuchungen*. Just after the publication of that book, Frege and Husserl would have appeared, to anyone who knew the work of both, remarkably close in their philosophical views: what was it in the thought of each that set their followers on such divergent paths? Frege was the first philosopher in history to achieve anything resembling a plausible account of the nature of thoughts and of their inner structure. His account depended upon his conviction of the parallelism between thought and language. His interest was in thought, not in language for its own sake: he was concerned with those features of language irrelevant to the expression of thought only in order to set them aside. Nevertheless, his strategy for analysing thought was to analyse the forms of its linguistic or symbolic expression; and this strategy became the characteristic mark of the analytical school. Although he continued to reiterate that it is inessential to thoughts and thought-constituents that we grasp them as the senses of sentences and their parts, it is quite unclear that his account of the senses of linguistic expressions is capable of being transposed into an account of thoughts considered independently of their verbal expression.

For this reason, Frege's theories are of little assistance towards an explanation of unverbalized thought. Unverbalized thought is of importance to an account of human psychology because it is involved in perception and in our manipulation of objects, for example in driving a car, when it can be a highly active process. It also bears upon the philosophical analysis of language itself, since the problem of correctly characterizing a speaker's knowledge of his mother-tongue, unsolved by Frege, remains unsolved. Even if we reject realism, it cannot be classified as a practical skill like the ability to swim, since it is not a technique for doing something of which we know in advance what it is to do it; and yet it plainly cannot wholly consist of verbalized knowledge. Husserl's ideas, however, do not supply the guidance in this matter that we fail to derive from those of Frege. It is of little use to propose a generalization of the notion of meaning unless we first have a clear conception of what meaning is and can then see in which direction it is possible to generalize it. Frege's notion of sense seems incapable of generalization, and Husserl provided no clear alternative notion: his proposal was therefore purely programmatic. It was just at this point that the philosophical heritage of each diverged. That of Frege prompted an exclusive concentration on language, yielding rich dividends but rendering adequate accounts of various important concepts impossible; that of Husserl turned philosophical attention away from language, but left an essential vagueness at its centre.

Where both failed was in demarcating logical notions too strictly from psychological ones. Together, they quite rightly attacked the psychologism of their day, from which no genuine progress could be expected: but, by setting up too rigid a barrier between the logical and the psychological, they deprived themselves of the means to explain what it is to grasp a thought. That is a notion that cannot be relegated to psychology, but of which any adequate philosophical account of thought owes an explanation. These failings have left philosophy open to a renewed incursion from psychology, under the banner of 'cognitive science'. The strategies of defence employed by Husserl and Frege will no longer serve: the invaders can be repelled only by correcting the failings of the positive theories of those two pioneers, and of the many toilers in the vineyards which they planted.

5

The Nature of Acts: Moore on Husserl

Wolfgang Künne

I

In those happy years before the 'Analytic – Continental Split' Bertrand Russell, as is well known, commented extensively and for the most part very favourably on several treatises of Meinong, and Meinong in turn tried to defuse Russell's objections. What is less well known is that, in 1903, when G. E. Moore proudly announced the refutation of idealism, he wrote in praise of Meinong's teacher Franz Brentano.[1] What seems to be hardly known at all is that Moore (if somewhat indirectly) discussed the masterpiece of the Brentanist school, Edmund Husserl's *Logical Investigations* (*LI*). This discussion is the topic of my paper.

Incidentally I hope to provide an explanation for an entry in the diary, written by Boyce Gibson (the translator of Husserl's *Ideen*) when he visited Husserl in Freiburg in 1928: 'Moore admired the *Logische Untersuchungen* but could not swallow the *Ideen*.' Herbert Spiegelberg (the chronicler of the phenomenological movement and editor of this diary) confesses: 'This information is at best puzzling.'[2] The data I shall present make it likely that Boyce Gibson correctly describes Moore's attitude to the *LI*.

Moore's indirect comments to Husserl's *LI* are contained in a long 'Critical Notice' (Crit.) which appeared in *Mind* July, 1910. Here is the opening passage:

This seems to me to be an extraordinarily good book. It is an attempt to classify all the kinds of elements which may occur as constituents of mental phenomena, and to point out the most important respects in which different mental phenomena may differ from one another. And it seems to me to make the main outlines of the subject most unusually plain. It is written beautifully simply and clearly, and is very well arranged; and Dr Messer is wonderfully successful in making plain, by means of examples, exactly what it is that he is talking about (Crit., p. 395).

The extraordinarily good book Moore is talking about is August Messer's *Empfindung und Denken* (*Sensation and Thought*), published in Leipzig, 1908. Who on earth was August Messer? Messer was professor of philosophy at the University of Giessen from 1910 to 1933. He defended a sort of Critical Realism that he had originally adopted from Oswald Külpe's works. In the Weimar Republic he was widely read. His *Psychologie* and his *Geschichte der Philosophie* went through many editions. In his later years he worked mainly on ethics and the philosophy of value. A third edition of the book Moore reviewed appeared in 1928.

Now in many respects, and in almost all those respects discussed by Moore, this book is nothing but a rather faithful summary of Husserl's *Logical Investigations*, especially of the fifth investigation entitled 'On Intentional Experiences and their "Contents" '[3] Moore's review is a sort of companion piece to another brilliant but forgotten paper of his which he read to the Aristotelian Society on 6, December 1909: 'The subject-matter of psychology' (Psych.). By the way, and contrary to what Alan White and A. J. Ayer say in their books on Moore, it is in those two articles that Moore first introduces the term 'sense datum'.[4] What is more important for my intentions, as far as I know these two articles contain the entire reaction of the first Cambridge generation of analytic philosophers to what turned out to be, for some decades, the most influential philosophical movement on the continent.

On the whole the reception of Husserl's most closely argued book in the English speaking world was a rather sad affair. The first translation appeared only in 1970.[5] And it is symptomatic that in *Mind* neither the first (1900) edition nor the second (1913) edition of the *Logical Investigations* was reviewed. The explanation of the second fact is not without interest. In 1920 Bertrand Russell wrote a letter to Husserl:

> 70 Overstrand Mansions
> Prince of Wales Rd
> Battersea SW
> 19. 4. 20

Dear Sir,
 Mr Bosanquet has sent me your letter of March 25, with its most kind postscript about myself. I am very glad indeed that any writings of mine should have had such an effect as you mention; all the more as I have, of course, followed your work with interest and sympathy for many years. Indeed, the new edition of your *Logische Untersuchungen* was one of the books I had with me in prison.

> Yours sincerely
> Bertrand Russell[6]

I do not know whether Russell actually ever *read* the *LI* but I think I know why in the summer of 1918 he had the book with him in prison. Some letters Russell then wrote to his brother Frank show that he had promised G. F. Stout a review of the *LI* for *Mind*.[7] It is a pity that Russell did not keep his promise, but then writing the *Introduction to Mathematical Philosophy* in prison was quite a remarkable achievement.

II

I shall now summarize and evaluate the most interesting of Moore's indirect comments on the *LI*.

Following Husserl Messer claims that all mental phenomena (Moore's translation of *'Erlebnisse'*) 'belong to one or other of two very different classes, which may be called the class of 'sensations' (*Empfindungen*) and the class of 'acts' (*Akte*)' (Crit., p. 396). Let us for the time being put aside Moore's comments on what he takes to be the Husserlian conception of sensations, and turn at once to Moore's question: 'What exactly is *the nature of acts?*' (p. 399). 'Dr Messer tries to express the most fundamental characteristic that is common and peculiar to them all by saying that 'in' all of them we are 'directed towards' (*gerichtet auf*) some object (*Gegenstand*); and he accepts Husserl's name for acts, *Intentionen*, as expressing this characteristic' (Crit., p. 400). Moore first asks what it is that is primarily directed towards an object: Is it the ego, or is it the act itself? He complains that Messer does not give a clear answer to this question, and then declares that he is inclined to adopt the latter alternative. The author of the first edition of the *LI* was not only inclined to adopt it, he clearly did adopt it. As to the ego Moore feels uncertain whether an ego is a Humean collection of mental events *or* a further mental entity distinct from such a collection and from every one of its members *or* a human body (Psych., pp. 51–5). Husserl, in *LI*, distinguishes between an ego, which is nothing but a collection of *Erlebnisse*, and an ego, which is a Strawsonian person, and he explicitly denies that there is any further entity which deserves to be called an ego.[8] Later on he believes himself to have discovered such a further entity,[9] whereas Moore, as far as I can see, at *one* other place repeats his doubts (*PS*, p. 174ff.) and then never returns to the topic. I shall drop it here, since Husserl himself claims that his alleged discovery of a *Transzendentales Ich* is 'irrelevant' to the substantial content of his *LI*.[10]

III

Now Moore himself thinks his gravest objection to Messer's book is that it fails to recognize that there are two fundamentally different kinds of cognitive acts:

acts in which we are 'directly' conscious of an object, and acts in which we are 'indirectly' conscious of an object. What Moore here calls 'direct consciousness' he will soon start calling 'direct apprehension' (*SMPP*, p. 46ff.; *PS*, p. 173ff.). Now the trouble with this objection is that Moore's paradigm for direct apprehension is the relation which I am supposed to have to a visual sense datum at the moment, and only at the monent, when I am seeing it. This is unfortunate because it is doubtful, to say the least, whether we ever have such a relation to such an entity. What Moore calls Dr Messer's most serious mistake, his tendency, that is, 'to identify Acts with those among Acts which do not consist merely in a direct consciousness of sense-data' (Crit., p. 403), is not a mistake at all, of course, if there just are no such acts. Once again let me postpone this issue until I briefly sketch the Husserlian view of sensations.

IV

Acts can differ as to their objects, but, Moore adds, 'this kind of difference does not seem to me *itself* a mental difference' (Psych., p. 47). Moore frankly confesses that the cannot tell why. Let me try to offer what seems to me a good reason for Moore calls a relational property (PS, 281f.). From the fact that Socrates loses points to a book lying in front of him and observes at t_1: That is my copy of the *Logical Investigations*. Whilst his back is turned for a moment somebody exchanges John's copy for another that very closely resembles it. At t_2 John still insists: That is my copy of the *LI*. But the copy he points to now is not the copy he pointed to previously, although he notices no difference between the two, Clearly John thinks at t_2 of a different book than at t_1 that it is his copy of the *LI*. Does it follow that John *himself* has undergone a change? What has changed is rather his environment, one feels inclined to say.

Plato and Aristotle ran up against a structurally similar problem in their discussions of the category of change (*metabole*).[11] Socrates is, to begin with, as tall as Theaetetus; then Theaetetus but not Socrates grows; thus it ceases to be the case that Socrates is as tall as Theaetetus. Does it follow that *Socrates* has changed? No – answers Aristotle, and the answer seems to me to be plausible. Having the same size is a relation; having the same size as Theaetetus is what Moore calls a relational property (PS, 281f.). From the fact that Socrates loses this relational property it follows only that one of the relata of the relation has changed. It remains an open question just which one of the relata has changed.

To think of some given thing that it is thus or so is also a relational property of the thinker. From the fact that a person first has this property and then no longer has it, it follows only that one of the relata has changed, but not which one: the thinker or the thing of which he thinks that it is thus or so. But then this relational property is not a genuine mental property. For of such a property it is true that if a person first has it and then loses it then the person himself has changed. (This follows immediately from two premises both of which I am convinced are true. The first premise runs: if the mental state of a person at t_2 differs from his state at t_1 then his internal physical state at t_2 differs from that at t_1. The second premise runs: if the internal physical state of a person at t_2 differs from his state at t_1 then the person himself has undergone a change.) Here we have a good reason, I think, for accepting Moore's point: The difference between John's relational properties in t_1 and t_2 is not a *mental* difference.

V

Husserl tries to show that acts which are directed towards the same object (thing, event, state of affairs) can vary in different dimensions. He calls these dimensions of variation:

Qualität
Materie
Empfindungsmaterial

The acts of being pleased that p and of asking oneself whether it is the case that p may be directed towards one and the same state of affairs, and they differ in respect of their *Qualität*.[12] Moore agrees: 'Even when there is no difference in the object, there may be a difference in the mode of consciousness' (Psych., p. 49).[13] But when Moore suggests that every difference in what he calls the mode of consciousness is a difference in what Husserl calls an *Aktqualität*, he is not quite right. Being pleased that p and being sorry that p would be examples of acts which differ in their mode. Do they also differ in their *Qualität*? Some of the things Husserl says suggest an affirmative answer. But on the whole, his notion of *Qualität* seems to be rather this: There are just two *Aktqualitäten*, being positing (*setzend*) and being non-positing (*nicht-setzend*).[14] An act is positing iff it involves the belief that its intentional object really exists/occurs/obtains or the belief that this is not the case. But then the difference between being pleased that p and being sorry that p is not a difference in *Qualität*, since both acts are positing. Modes, one might say, are those properties of acts in virtue of which they have either of the two *Aktqualitäten*.

VI

Both Husserl and Moore apply the label 'act' not only to mental events, but also to mental states. The dangers of blurring this distinction become manifest when one considers their disagreement about the question whether non-propositional ('nominal') acts can be positing. Following Husserl Messer gives an affirmative answer.[15] Moore disagrees:

> In this, however, I cannot help thinking he is wrong ... Dr Messer only gives as an instance of the cases where, according to him, a 'positing' nominal Act occurs, what happens when we believe such a proposition as 'The Emperor Charles conquered the Saxons.' When we 'posit' this proposition, we also, he thinks, 'posit' its subject, the Emperor Charles. But surely there is a confusion here. When we believe such a proposition as this, it is, I think, generally true that we believe also in the existence of the subject ... But ... beliefs in the existence ... of a subject are 'propositional' Acts ... I am inclined to think, therefore, that Dr Messer only thinks that 'nominal' Acts can be positing, because he mistakes for a nominal Act, in these instances, what is, in reality, a 'propositional' Act (Crit., p. 407).

Now if one assumes that a Russellian account of the truth-conditions of 'The F is G' mirrors the internal structure of those (episodic) Acts of judgement which can be expressed by such sentences, then it is tempting to think that one cannot judge that the F is G without *judging* that *there is* an F. But Husserl would not accept this (quasi-) Russellian account of the structure of such judgements. Their complexity does not consist in their having parts which are themselves judgements. Rather they contain a *thinking of* something as the F.[16] This contained episodic act is positing if it involves the belief that there really is an F. Beliefs are propositional, but they are states rather than episodes.

Moore seems to think that judgements that the F is G always involve a belief in the existence of the subject. The judgement I express by 'The winged horse called "Pegasus" has often been depicted' is a counterexample, since it does not involve a belief in the existence of winged horses.

VII

According to Husserl's theory of intentionality two acts having the same object (and the same mode) can differ in what he calls their *Materie* (matter) or their *Auffassungssinn* (interpretive sense), whereas any two acts which have different objects must also have different 'matters'.[17] (Put 'expression' for 'act', *Sinn* for 'matter' and *Bedeutung* for 'object', and you obtain a central Fregean claim.) Moore suggests, reasonably enough, that Husserl 'means by the "matter" of an act what is often called its "content" (*Inhalt*) as opposed to its object' (Crit., p. 403).[18] He then goes on to attack both parts of Husserl's thesis on the role of contents.

As far as Moore's published work is concerned, Russell can only have this attack (in Crit. and Psych.) in mind when he writes in 1919:

Many analytic psychologists – Meinong, for example – distinguish three elements in presentation [*Vorstellung*], namely the act . . ., the content, and the object. Realists such as Dr Moore and myself have been in the habit of rejecting the content, while retaining the act and the object . . . Idealists, in effect if not in words, have rejected the object and kept [the act and] the content.[19]

Notice, incidentally, that Russell here uses the adjective 'analytic' to describe the *Brentanist* way of doing things.

VIII

The second conjunct of the Husserlian conception of content was this: Difference of object entails difference of content, or, by contraposition, sameness of content entails sameness of object. Why does Moore find this unacceptable? 'There seems to me to be one very strong argument against it, namely that it is impossible to verify by observation the existence of any internal qualitative difference between every pair of Acts which have different objects' (Crit., pp. 403–4; cp. Psych., p. 55).[20] The strength of this objection becomes manifest as soon as one thinks of cognitive situations like John's where somebody takes himself to be perceiving, and referring to, what is numerically and qualitatively the same object as before, although in fact it is a different object: John is 'quite unable, by introspection, to discover' any 'internal qualitative difference' between his two acts. In this respect acts are in the same boat as pictures: This picture might show John's copy of the *LI*, whereas that picture shows someone else's copy; but it is quite possible that even the closest inspection of both pictures fails to reveal any 'internal qualitative difference' between them.

IX

Now even if contents cannot do everything Husserl wants them to do, they may still achieve something. The first conjunct of the Husserlian conception of content was this: Two acts which have the same object may yet have different contents. Here is an example taken from Messer's book and discussed by Moore. In one act, he thinks of Berlin as the capital of Prussia, and, in another, he thinks of it as the biggest town in Germany. (Thus Berlin does for Messer what Venus did for Frege.) Moore comments on this: 'In all such cases, though the two Acts do have the same object, it is also true that they contain Acts with different objects . . .' (Crit., p. 404). So far there is nothing Husserl would want to deny. On the contrary, he supplies, among other things, a useful terminology for describing such cases.[21] If an act directed towards an object x contains an act directed towards an object y Husserl calls x the primary and y the secondary object of the containing act. (Husserl also points out that sometimes the object of the contained act is identical with the object of the containing act. Take Kaiser Wilhelm thinking of his *Vaterland* as the only country which is not afraid of the German Empire.) But according to Moore the so-called difference in content of two acts with the same primary object is 'in reality' the difference between their secondary objects. And this Husserl would not accept. Now one might expect that Moore takes *Prussia* to be the relevant secondary object when somebody is thinking of Berlin as the capital of Prussia. But this is not Moore's point. He says: 'for instance, in the case quoted, the one Act contains an Act which has for its direct object the universal "capital" while the other [in which Berlin is thought of as the biggest town in Germany] contains an Act which has for its direct object the universal "biggest town"' (Crit., p. 404).[22] Now if Moore wants to show that any alleged difference in content between co-referential acts is nothing but a difference between their secondary objects, this kind of move will certainly not always do. If in thinking of Berlin as the capital of Prussia the universal in question is 'capital', then the same universal is involved in thinking of Berlin as the capital of the German Empire, and what Husserl calls difference of content remains unaccounted for. In *this* case the relevant secondary objects seem to be particulars rather than universals. But on the other hand, in *some* cases the relevant secondary objects cannot be particulars. Take a thought of Berlin as the capital of Prussia and a thought of Berlin as the biggest town in Prussia. Thus in order to give a unified account for all such cases in terms of intentional objects Moore can neither rely on particulars nor on universals which are relations. But perhaps relational properties would fit the bill. However, any attempt to account for what is, according to Moore, misdescribed as difference of content by recourse to difference between secondary intentional objects which are non-particulars threatens to become circular, by Husserl's lights, if it cannot justify identity claims concerning these abstract objects otherwise than by appeal to sameness of *meaning* of the abstract terms designating those objects.

X

But, of course, Husserl too owes us a criterion of identity for contents. Here, I am afraid, we shall only find a relatively clear answer to the less demanding question: What does *not* suffice for sameness of content? I will stick to one kind of examples: acts of judging. Let us call those philosophers *intensionalists* who deny that sameness of truth-value is a sufficient condition for sameness of judgement-content, and distinguish between two kinds of intensionalists. The *soft* intensionalist claims that *a priori* provability of sameness of truth-value suffices for sameness of content, whereas the *hard* intensionalist denies this. Does an act of judging that equiangular triangles are sometimes used as religious symbols have the same content as an act of judging that equilateral triangles are sometimes used as religious symbols? No, Husserl answers.[23] Thus he is a hard intensionalist.

'*Äquivalenz*' is Husserl's title for *a priori* provability of sameness of truth-value, and he takes it to be a sufficient condition only for sameness of contingent states of affairs (*Sachverhalt*), – states of affairs being in his theory the primary intentional *objects* of judgings.

Now there are degrees of hardness. Let us call philosophers who even deny that immediate self-evidence of sameness of truth-value suffices for sameness of content *very hard* intensionalists. Does an act of judging that the Sun is larger than the Moon have the same content as an act of judging that the Moon is smaller than the Sun? Husserl's answer is: no.[24] Thus he is a very hard intensionalist: Not even *unmittelbare Äquivalenz* (immediate equivalence) guarantees identity of content.[25]

Moore, in a paper first published in 1944 in the Schilpp volume on Russell, adopts an analogous position as regards sentence-meaning. Using the same example as Husserl, he argues that the sentences 'The Sun is larger than the Moon' and 'The Moon is smaller than the Sun', according to one meaning of 'meaning', do not have the same meaning. After all, 'if we had to translate '*Le soleil est plus grand que la lune*' into English, it would be definitely incorrect to translate it by the second of these two sentences instead of by the first' (*PP*, p. 182). (To this extent Moore as well as Husserl are harder hard intensionalists than Frege.)[26]

Husserl hints at the criterion of identity he has in mind when he says: *A* is the same judgement-content as *B* iff *A* and *B* are *congruent*. This hint is to be found in a review article he sent to Frege.[27] In a letter to Husserl Frege complains that he cannot see what would settle questions concerning the congruence of contents.[28] Husserl's answer, we are told, referred to Bolzano.[29] So I presume that 'congruent', as applied to judgement-contents, means something like this: built in the same way out of the same sub-judgemental contents.[30] But then we need, of course, a criterion of identity for these smaller units. Perhaps we can now rely on the idea of 'immediate equivalence': *a* is the same sub-judgemental content as *b* iff for every judgement-content which contains *a* it is immediately self-evident that it has the same truth-value as the corresponding judgement-content comprising *b*.

XI

Before concluding, let me sketch Husserl's conception of the third dimension in which acts which have the same object can differ from each other. This will enable me to locate the one fundamental misunderstanding in Moore's discussion of Husserl's theory of intentionality.

Suppose you gradually move towards or away from a loudspeaker producing for some time a sound of constant volume. Then something within your experience changes. But this does not imply that you hear a crescendo or diminuendo. It is very well possible that you hear the sound as of constant volume. What changes in you experience when you hear the sound first from this place and then from that place is what Husserl calls (auditory) *Empfindungen* (sensations).[31]

It is also possible that our sensations remain constant while the content of our perception changes. We may see the same notorious picture alternately as representing a duck and as representing a rabbit while having the same visual sensations.

Husserl's theory of perception makes use of an Aristotelian model. Husserl describes our sensations as the sensory material (*sensuelle Hyle*) of our acts of perception, and the content of these acts (together with their character of being positing) as their intentional form (*Intentionale Morphe*).[32] Several features of the Aristotelian model have interesting analogues in the case of perception. I have just mentioned two of them. For one thing, you can make changes in the material from which an artefact was originally built and keep the form constant. Secondly, you can keep the material constant and transform what was an artefact of kind *A* into an artefact of kind *B*. There is still another interesting analogy: from a given material you cannot make just anything you please. E.g., as Aristotle says, you cannot make a saw out of wool.[33] Similarly, as Husserl says, 'it is not entirely up to us' (*es steht uns nicht ganz frei*)[34] how to organize our sensations; they provide, as Føllesdal has put it, boundary conditions for our perceptions.[35]

We perceive external objects by dint of having sensations. From this it does not follow that sensations are the objects, let alone the 'real or ultimate' objects, of our acts of perception. Husserl would diagnose the opposite view as a counterpart to the use-mention confusion. That we refer to objects by using words does not imply either that the real or ultimate objects of reference are words. Of course, we may on occasion refer to our words, and sensations, likewise, occasionally become intentional objects, in acts of introspection.[36]

Now all this is entirely misunderstood by Moore when he says: 'I think there is no doubt at all that the [the phenomenologist] means by "sensations" what I should prefer to call sense-data, never our direct consciousness of these sense-data' (Crit., p. 397). No, what the phenomenologist means by '*Empfindung*' is neither the one nor the other.

XII

Let me end as I began: with a historical note. In June 1922 Husserl delivered four lectures on *Phänomenologische Methode und Phänomenologische Philosophie* at University College, London.[37] When Husserl gave his last lecture Moore was chairman. Like many of Husserl's writings after the *LI*, those lectures were devoted to the profitless task of promising epoch-making results to be obtained by applying the one True Method of Philosophy, and they suffered from an excess of grandiose and very unperspicuous terminology. Moore could not possibly compliment this German professor for being 'wonderfully successful in making plain, by means of examples, exactly what it is that he is talking about' (Crit., p. 395). On the contrary, I am sure he could not swallow these lectures. The days where Moore and Husserl could have had a philosophically exciting discussion were definitely over. The London meeting already belongs to the history of what has been called the 'Analytic – Continental Split'.[38]

Notes

1 Review of Brentano, *The Origin and the Knowledge of Right and Wrong*, *International Journal of Ethics* xiv (1903), pp. 115–23.
   Hereafter I will employ the following abbreviations for Moore's works:

   Psych.: 'The subject-matter of psychology', *Proceedings of the Aristotelian Society* x (1900–10), pp. 36–62
   Crit.:   Review of Messer, *Empfindung und Denken*, *Mind* 19 (1910), pp. 395–409
   SMPP: *Some Main Problems of Philosophy*, Lectures 1910–11 (George Allen and Unwin, London, 1953)
   PS: *Philosophical Studies* (Routledge and Kegan Paul, London, 1922)
   PP: *Philosophical Papers* (George Allen and Unwin, London, 1959)

2 Spiegelberg, 'Husserl in England: facts and lessons', *The Journal of the British Society for Phenomenology* I/1 (1970), p. 15 (cp. the edition of the diary in the same journal: II/2 (1971), p. 71)

3 Husserl's critical remarks on Messer (cp. *Husserliana* (Nijhoff, Dordrecht, 1950 vol. III, 1, p. 177; vol. XXV, pp. 226–52) are not concerned with this book but with two articles which appeared several years later. Husserl complains that Messer did not properly grasp the differences in *method* between eidetic phenomenology and empirical psychology. This alleged misunderstanding is not relevant to the topics which Moore finds interesting in Messer's earlier book.

4 Alan R. White, *G. E. Moore: A critical Exposition* (Basil Blackwell, Oxford, 1969). p. 153, and A. J. Ayer, *Russell and Moore: The Analytical Heritage* (Macmillan, London, 1971), p. 233, both claim that Moore introduced the term in his lectures SMPP (p. 30) which were delivered in the winter of 1910–11 (p. xi).

5 *Logical Investigations*, revised 2nd edn, trans. lated by J. N. Findlay (Humanities Press, New York).

6 Louvain Husserl Archives, R II Russell B.

7 Cp. Spiegelberg, 'Husserl in England', p. 14, n. 7.

8 *LI*, V, §§ 2–4, 8.

9 Cp. the following footnotes added to the 2nd edn. of the *LI*: v, § 6 n., § 8 n.

10   *LI*, V, § 8, postscript to the 2nd edn.
11   Plato, *Theaetetus*, 155 B–C; Aristotle, *Metaphysics* 1088 a 34–5.
12   *LI*. V, § 20.
13   Cp. John Searle, *Intentionality* (Cambridge University Press, 1983), p. 6.
14   See, for example, *LI*, VI, § 16, first paragraph.
15   *LI*, V, § 34f., 38.
16   There are obvious affinities between Husserl's view and one strand in Strawson's
      criticism of Russell's theory of descriptions: cp. P. F. Strawson, 'On Referring', esp.
      section III, in his *Logico-Linguistic Papers* (Methuen, London, 1971).
17   LI, V, § 20.
18   Moore was already acquainted, I presume, through Russell's (first) article on
      'Meinong's theory of complexes and assumptions' (*Mind* 13 (1904)), with another
      Brentanist version of the three-fold act–content–object distinction. Husserl's use of
      Materie bears especially close affinities to Bolzano's use of *Stoff* (as opposed to
      Inhalt): cp. Bernard Bolzano, *Wissenschaftslehre* (Seidel, Sulzbach, 1837), § 56, p. 271.
19   B. Russell, 'On propositions: what they are and how they mean', in *Logic and Knowl-
      edge*, ed. Marsh (George Allen and Unwin, London, 1956), p. 305.
20   There is an echo of this objection in Russell, 'On the nature of acquaintance' (1914),
      in *Logic and Knowledge*, p. 173, or in *Theory of Knowledge: The 1913 Manuscript*
      (George Allen and Unwin, London, 1984), p. 43.
21   *LI*, V, § 17.
22   Moore claims that his argument 'applies to all cases where we think of objects by
      means of what Mr Russell calls "denoting concepts" (Crit., p. 404). Now although
      the terminology points to Russell's 'Principles of mathematics' the doctrine alluded to
      seems to be rather that of 'On denoting' (1905). Our knowledge about a particular
      with which we have no acquaintance depends, according to Russell, on an acquaint-
      ance with a universal of which the particular in question is an instance (*Logic and
      Knowledge*, p. 41f., 55f.). Cp. also Russell, 'Knowledge by acquaintance and knowl-
      edge by description' (1910–11), in *Mysticism and Logic* (George Allen and Unwin,
      London, 1963), p. 166: 'We have descriptive knowledge of an object when we
      know that it is the object having some property of properties with which we are
      acquainted.'
23   *LI*, V, § 20.
24   *LI*, V, § 23.
25   Cp. Künne, 'Edmund Husserl: Intentionalität', § 4, in J. Speck (ed.), *Grundprobleme
      der grossen Philosophen, Philosophie der Neuzeit IV* (Vandenhoeck and Ruprecht, Gö-
      ttingen, 1986).
26   According to Frege's *Logical Investigations* '*p*' and 'It is true that *p*', '*p* and *p*', 'not-
      not-*p*', express the same sense. Concerning the first pair cp. Moore, *SMPP*, p. 275f.
      and *PP*, p. 82.
27   Husserl, Aufsätze und Rezensionen, 1890–1910, Husserliana vol. 22 (M. Nijhoff, The
      Hague, 1979), p. 255.
28   Frege to Husserl, 1 November 1906, in Frege, *Philosophical and Mathematical
      Correspondence* (Basil Blackwell, Oxford, 1980), p. 70.
29   Husserl to Frege, 10 November 1906 (a letter unfortunately not preserved), ibid.

30 Cp. Bernard Bolzano, *Wissenschaftslehre*, § 32, 92 (1). A comparison with Rudolf Carnap's use of the notion 'isomorphism' would be illuminating: see *Meaning and Necessity* (University of Chicago Press, 1947), § 14.

31 *LI*, I, § 23; V, § 14, 21, VI, § 14 b, 22–7.

32 He introduces this terminology in *Ideas: General Introduction to Pure Phenomenology*, trans. Boyce Gibson (Macmillan, New York), § 85. But the framework is already present in the *LI*.

33 Aristotle, *Metaphysics*, 1044 a 29.

34 *LI*, VI, § 26.

35 Dagfinn Føllesdal, 'Husserl's theory of perception', in Hubert Dreyfus (ed.), *Husserl, Intentionality and Cognitive Science* (MIT Press, Cambridge, Mass., 1982), pp. 93–6.

36 Cp. Colin McGinn, *The Character of Mind* (Oxford University Press, 1982), p. 45.

37 See Spiegelberg, idid., p. 6.

38 I am indebted to Thomas Baldwin, Dagfinn Føllesdal and Kevin Mulligan for valuable suggestions.

6
Moore and Philosophical Scepticism

Thomas Baldwin

I

I am at present, as you can all see, in a room and not in the open air; I am standing up, and not either sitting or lying down; I have clothes on, and am not absolutely naked; I am speaking in a fairly loud voice, and am not either singing or whispering or keeping quite silent; I have in my hand some sheets of paper with writing on them; three are a good many other people in the same room in which I am . . . (p. 227).

I here repeat Moore, in the his 1941 paper 'Certainty';[1] and I am happy to continue to do so, in affirming that 'I do not think that I can be justly accused of dogmatism or over-confidence for having asserted these things positively in the way I did'; rather 'I should have been guilty of absurdity if, under the circumstances, I had not spoken positively about these things, if I spoke of them at all' (C, p. 227). There is much more of the same kind in this paper – many more of Moore's characteristic affirmations of certain knowledge. Yet, notoriously, when Moore turns at the end of the paper to confront the dream sceptic, the fragility of his certainty becomes only too apparent: to know the truth of his opening affirmations, he concedes, he needs to know that he is not dreaming. But how can he know this when, in his opinion, there is nothing in his present sensory experiences to rule out the possibility that he is dreaming? Moore says that perhaps the dream possibility can be ruled out, on logical grounds, by the conjunction of his present sensory experiences and his memories of his immediate past. But this response has never convinced anyone, including apparently Moore himself (see the footnote to C, p. 251). So the paper, Moore's last substantive treatment of the issue of scepticism, ends up by undermining the certainties with which it starts.

One thing I want to try to elucidate in this paper is why this was so, why

Moore the philosopher failed in the end to substantiate the assertions of his plain self. But I shall also try to explain how we should respond to Moore's assertions of knowledge; for, reverting to my initial quotation, there is surely something right in what Moore says about it (C, p. 228): 'if *now* I am not guilty of dogmatism in asserting positively that I'm not naked, certainly I was not guilty of dogmatism when I asserted it positively in one of those sentences with which I began this lecture. I knew then that I had clothes on, just as I know now that I have.'

II

On one level it is easy to see why Moore's final treatment of scepticism in 'Certainty' is a failure. He combines the assumption that his knowledge requires that he be able to eliminate the possibility that he is dreaming with the belief that his current sensory experiences do not enable him to do so. But it is less easy to understand why, after all those affirmations of certain knowledge, he did not just affirm that he was certain that he was not then dreaming. In his 'Proof of an External World' of 1939 he had, indeed, allowed that he could not prove that he was not then dreaming (PEW, p. 149); but he did not then suppose that this inability undermined his claim to know what he asserted when he uttered 'Here is one hand.' On the contrary, as he put it, 'How absurd it would be to suggest that I did not know it, but only believed it... You might as well suggest that I do not know that I am now standing up and talking' (PEW, p. 146).

Part of the explanation for Moore's position in 'Certainty' lies, I think, in his foundationalist conception of knowledge. This is not explicit in 'Certainty', but it is manifest in his contemporary paper 'Four Forms of Scepticism'. For he here maintains that he has 'immediate knowledge' of his own sensory experiences and personal memories, but not of such things as that 'This is a pencil' (4FS, p. 225), his knowledge of which is, rather, founded upon things of which he has immediate knowledge. This is a position which is notoriously vulnerable to sceptical arguments, and Moore here allows that he is unable to eliminate on logical grounds the possibility that a malicious demon is producing his present sensory experiences, a possibility which, he implies, he does need to be able to eliminate if he is to know that 'This is a pencil.' However, he allows here that it suffices if he can eliminate this possibility 'on the basis of an analogical or inductive argument'; and although he does not specify just what arguments he has in mind, he implies that such arguments are available in standard cases. So his position here does not so obviously collapse into scepticism; on the other hand, once one introduces inductive scepticism, the position does threaten to collapse into that to which he is driven in 'Certainty'.

Foundationalist conceptions of knowledge are often associated with representative theories of perception. For if one is looking for cases of immediate knowledge, then knowledge of the ways in which things appear to one is a natural candidate for such knowledge, and one can choose to regard this as knowledge of the qualities of the appearances that are given to one, of the qualities of the 'sense-data' one 'apprehends directly'. Obviously much here is disputable, but in Moore's case this association is present, and the difficulties Moore encountered in articulating a tenable account of perceptual knowledge serve to underline his vulnerability to sceptical arguments.

In ascribing a representative theory of perception to Moore one needs to acknowledge that he did not regard his sense-datum analysis of perceptual judgements as by itself committing him to such a theory. For his sense-datum analysis was supposed to leave the ontological status of sense-data *vis-à-vis* material objects undetermined, and Moore was notoriously attracted by the hypothesis that visual sense-data are the visible surfaces of material objects (cf. SJP). But he had to admit that the balance of arguments did not support this view (e.g. cf. DCS, pp. 56–7), and his predominant view was that material objects are never 'directly' apprehended in the way that sense-data are – which is the position of a representative theorist. Once direct apprehension is given cognitive significance, as giving rise to immediate knowledge of existence, it follows that sense experience is such that the existence of material objects is never in that way known immediately; and since there is no alternative to sense experience as a means of obtaining this knowledge, it follows that the knowledge must be at best indirect, which as I have indicated, is indeed Moore's position in 'Four Forms of Scepticism'.

Although he acknowledges the vulnerability of this position to Cartesian scepticism, he here thinks that inductive considerations provide as adequate response to such scepticism. We may well have doubts on this score, but rather than pursue them I want to consider Moore's reaction to a Humean sceptical argument which brings out sharply the problematic nature of his account of knowledge of an external world in the light of this theory of perception. In his 1910–11 lectures *Some Main Problems of Philosophy*, Moore presents his sense-datum theory and argues that we never directly apprehend material objects. He then introduces two principles which he takes from Hume's critique of Locke (*SMPP* pp. 109–10): (i) 'nobody can ever know of the existence of anything which he has not directly apprehended unless he knows that something he has directly apprehended is a *sign* of its existence': (ii) 'nobody can ever know that existence of any one thing A is *sign of the existence* of another thing B, unless he himself (or, under certain conditions, somebody else) has experienced a *general conjunction* between *things like* A and *things like* B. And the important thing to remember about this second rule is that nobody can be said to have *experienced a conjunction* between any two things, unless he has *directly apprehended* both the things.' Moore now argues that, given these principles and the premise that we never directly apprehend material objects, it follows that we can never know of the existence of a material object; and this is surely correct.

Moore, of course, did not accept the sceptical conclusion of this argument, and I shall consider below the way in which he invokes *modus tollens* in *SMPP* in order to turn the argument on its head. But I want now to ask which of the premises of the argument Moore rejects. In the lectures it seems that it must be the first principle that is rejected, though Moore never explicitly says so. For, having set out the sceptical argument, he introduces a distinction between immediate knowledge and direct apprehension, and insists that he can have immediate knowledge of the existence of a material object – e.g. the pencil he is holding up – even though he does not directly apprehend it. This conflicts with 'Hume's' first principle, because that principle entails that any knowledge of the existence of things not directly apprehended must be inferential, and therefore not immediate. The resulting position is, therefore, one in which Moore refuses to attach any epistemological significance to the distinction between direct and indirect perceptual apprehension, and this induces a potential divorce between his epistemology and philosophy of perception.

It is not going to be easy on this view to explain why we have immediate knowledge only of the existence of things we currently perceive or remember perceiving (which is Moore's implicit position in *SMPP*), since the content of our perceptions is elucidated in terms of the direct apprehension of sense-data and this is denied any special epistemological significance. Nonetheless the position has some merits if one really wants to combine a sense-datum philosophy of perception with a non-sceptical conclusion. What is puzzling about Moore is that having set out this position in *SMPP*, and briefly hinted at it in the closing sentences of his 1913 paper 'The Status of Sense-Data' (p. 196), he then drops it. Thus in his 1925 paper 'A Defence of Common Sense' he states that his knowledge that he is perceiving a human hand is a deduction from a pair of propositions ('I am perceiving *this*' and '*This* is a human hand') of both of which a sense-datum is 'in a certain sense, the principal or ultimate subject' (pp. 53–4). But how, then, is the sceptical conclusion of his earlier lectures to be avoided? Moore, infuriatingly, never confronts the issue head on. It looks as though he will have to reject 'Hume's' second principle and allow that sense-data can be evidence for the existence of material objects without experience of appropriate conjunctions between them. This seems to be the position he advances in his lectures notes of 1928–9 (*Lectures on Philosophy* pp. 102–3). But he does not attempt to confront the objections to it and confesses 'I own I myself feel very uncomfortable about it' (p. 102; cf. DCS, p. 57). Another option here might be phenomenalism; but Moore held that it did not offer an adequate account of the content of our beliefs about the external world (e.g. DCS, p. 58).

The fact is that Moore never provided an account of perceptual knowledge which yields a satisfactory response to the Humean sceptical argument which he presented in *Some Main Problems of Philosophy*. This is symptomatic of his general failure to explain how knowledge of an external world is possible. He was always vulnerable in this area, and this is part of the explanation of the final collapse of his anti-sceptical position in 'Certainty'.

III

But it is only part of the explanation; for it does not explain why, in these late papers, Moore does not rely on the anti-sceptical strategy he employs in *SMPP* and elsewhere. Before discussing this, however, I need to say something about this strategy itself. Central to it is Moore's insistence that we are more certain that we know such things as that 'this is a pencil' than we are of any premise of the sceptical argument, and thus that it cannot be rational for us to accept the conclusion of the sceptical argument; for in doing so, we would assent to a proposition of whose negation we are more certain than we are of our reasons for assenting to it.

It will be useful to have a brief statement of this argument by Moore himself; here is a passage from his 1918 lecture 'Some Judgments of Perception':

> For some philosophers seem to me to have denied that we ever do in fact know such things as these [that this is a finger], and others not only that we ever know them but also that they are ever true... But it seems to me a sufficient refutation of such views as these, simply to point to cases in which we do know such things. This after all, you know, really is a finger: there is no doubt about it: I know it, and you all know it. And I think we may safely challenge any philosopher to bring forward any argument in favour either of the proposition that we do not know it, or of the proposition that it is not true, which does not rest upon some premise which is, beyond comparison, less certain than is the proposition which it is designed to attack (pp. 227–8).

The confidence which this passage manifests explains why Moore did not feel it necessary to spell out in detail which of the premises of the sceptical argument which I discussed above are mistaken; according to Moore, we can be confident that there is a mistake in such sceptical arguments even if we are not confident about just what the mistake is. Equally, although Moore accepted that there was some intimate relation between his philosophy of perception and his epistemology, it was not necessary, at least for the purpose of refuting scepticism, to make it clear what the relation was. For even if our knowledge that 'this is a finger' is not immediate, we are more certain that we have such knowledge than we are of any philosophical theory which explains how we have it, so the philosophical theory is not necessary in order to legitimate our claim to such knowledge. Although the resulting situation is unsatisfactory in the way I explained above, it was fortunate in one respect: since it enabled Moore to present his 'defence of common sense' without any close commitment to his sense-datum theory, it is possible to assess important aspects of the former without reference to the latter. Thus the situation is in practice somewhat as if Moore had stuck with the divorce between epistemology and philosophy of perception which he briefly adopted but then abandoned.

Yet does Moore's anti-sceptical argument really warrant the confidence which he placed in it? Moore does not here simply contrapose and in that way 'beg the question' against the sceptic, as is sometimes alleged.[2] It certainly does not refute the sceptic to observe that he must be wrong if Moore knows that he has a finger; but that is not Moore's argument. Rather, Moore's appeal is to the fact that we are much more certain that we know such things as that 'this is a finger' than we are of the premises of the sceptic's argument. But, as Moore later noted in 'Certainty' (pp. 238–9), we need to distinguish between subjective certainty ('I feel certain that ...') and objective certainty ('It is established as certain that ...'); and once we ask which kind of certainty he is appealing to in his anti-sceptical argument, an unattractive dilemma opens up for Moore. If we say that Moore is appealing to differences in objective certainty, then the anti-sceptical conclusion follows; but we can surely ask Moore where, and how, it is established as certain that he does know that 'this is a finger'. Without an answer to this question, the sceptic's question has indeed been begged. If then we try the subjective interpretation instead, which fits well with the rhetorical appeal in Moore's text, we get premises which are doubtless true, for most people anyway, and whose acceptance does not beg any questions. But now the difficulty is to detach an anti-sceptical conclusion from them; for the sceptic will suggest that it is not proper for us to feel as certain as we do feel that we know that 'this is a finger', and until his arguments have been laid to rest we cannot place any rational reliance on the fact of our pre-reflective certainty.

In *Some Main Problems of Philosophy* Moore makes a further move which in one way offers help. He here maintains that he knows immediately that he knows that 'this is a pencil' (p. 125). Clearly if this were right it would establish the objective certainty of his knowledge that 'this is a pencil'; and he could now legitimately draw the anti-sceptical conclusion, since if you know the conclusion of an argument to be mistaken, and the grounds for your knowledge are not called into question by the premises of the argument (a condition obviously satisfied by immediate knowledge), you can contrapose without begging any questions. But this new argument is only as good as its new premise; which means that it is no good at all. For whatever one thinks about the possibility of any immediate knowledge, it is clear that there cannot be immediate knowledge of knowledge; claims to knowledge require a justification that is not immediately (self-evidently) apparent. Moore's new premise seems to arise from the conception of knowledge as an introspectible inner state of which Wittgenstein accused him in *On Certainty* (section 178): 'The wrong use made by Moore of the proposition "I know" lies in his regarding it as an utterance as little subject to doubt as "I am in pain"' (in Moore's defence, I should add that I do not believe that Moore employs this conception in his 'A Defence of Common Sense', to which Wittgenstein is here actually referring.)

There is a different line of argument in *Some Main Problems of Philosophy*, however, which has *prima facie* a greater chance of success. This rests on the thought that Moore does not need to establish the absolute certainty of his claim to knowledge, but only that it has a greater degree of objective certainty than the sceptic's premises. Moore's argument for this conclusion is just that the sceptic's general premises about the limits of human knowledge can only be grounded in particular facts about what is, or is not, known. So 'it follows that no such general principle can have greater certainty than the particular instances upon the observation of which it is based. Unless it is obvious that, in fact, I do not know of the existence of a material object in any particular instance, no principle which asserts that I cannot know of the existence of anything except under conditions which are not fulfilled in the case of material objects, can be regarded as established' (*SMPP*, p. 143).

This is a line of thought which does have considerable weight. For example, when Moore suggested in *Ethics* that voluntary actions are those which are performed as the result of choices which we have chosen to choose, it is a legitimate objection to this general principle that it implies that few, if any, human actions are voluntary. Nonetheless Moore's argument does not establish more than a presumption against the sceptic, and this for two reasons. First, a sceptic can argue for some general principles concerning knowledge from its application within one domain (e.g. mathematics) and then show that the result of applying these principles strictly in other domains (e.g. beliefs concerning matters of fact) has sceptical implications. The possibility of limited sceptical arguments which depend upon critical comparisons between different domains is one that Moore's argument does not eliminate. Not all particular cases of putative knowledge are of the same kind. Second, and more importantly, Moore's argument fails to take account of the *normative* character of the concept of knowledge. This is connected with Moore's tendency to treat cases of knowledge as matters of fact to be observed and enumerated. But when we think of knowledge as 'justified' or 'warranted' belief, or of a claim to knowledge as a claim to the 'right to be sure', we use normative concepts; indeed the expression 'claim to knowledge' itself employs such vocabulary (we do not need to 'claim to believe').

General normative or evaluative principles are not grounded in particular cases in the way in which general truths concerning matters of empirical fact are. In moral cases, there is a complex interaction between our recognition of what is appropriate in a particular case and our assent to a general principle. Neither the Kantian priority of universal law, nor the Prichardian priority of particular intuition, seems adequate to the situation. Fortunately it is not necessary here to attempt to elucidate what is required. But one has only to think of the moral case to recognize that our assent to normative principles concerning what we can know is not just a matter of generalizing from particular cases. Furthermore, to a considerable extent, sceptical claims are to be understood by reference to the normative aspect of the concept of knowledge: the sceptic about the external world thinks that our beliefs about the objective existence of material objects are unwarranted, and it is no good trying to confront him with paradigm cases of such knowledge, since he thinks there are none. His position is comparable to that of a moral reformer, say a vegetarian, who thinks that no killing of animals for the purpose of eating them is warranted: one can invite such a person to think through the application of their principle to difficult particular cases, but one cannot just confront them with particular paradigm cases of the justified killing of animals for the purpose of eating them.

Although this last point establishes that Moore's argument from differential certainty does not have the conclusiveness that Moore attributed to it, there is a rejoinder to it. Granted, it may be said, that the concept of knowledge is normative, yet where do we get our standards for assessing claims to knowledge from if not from our actual practices – from the judgements concerning knowledge we unhesitatingly accept, the retrospective criticisms of knowledge claims we allow, the arguments in support of them we advance, and so on? The situation here, it will be urged, is no different from that which obtains in the moral case, where we take our standards from reflection upon the values already inherent in social and private life. In both cases we bring to our critical reflections requirements of consistency and rationality which ensure that the standards adopted are not just descriptions of actual practice; but these reflections are necessarily grounded in our practices and cannot totally repudiate them. So, in the cognitive case, although recognition of the normative character of the concept of knowledge legitimates the critical assessment of claims to knowledge, one cannot justify standards for knowledge which would overturn such central knowledge claims as Moore's knowledge that 'this is a hand.' There is a core of 'common sense' propositions concerning knowledge which an account of the standards for knowledge has to respect, not controvert.

This is a line of argument which a sceptic does not have to accept without more discussion. And even if the general line of argument is accepted, the sceptic may still object to the singling out of Moore's knowledge claims as essential to the concept of knowledge, which he has to respect; instead, he may say, it is certain familiar lines of argument for and against claims to knowledge which are central to the concept, and his sceptical conclusions can be regarded as just the outcome of pressing those lines of argument to the limit. So it is unfair to represent his sceptical conclusions as the result of the imposition of alien standards upon our claims to knowledge; they are instead just the outcome of the kind of critical reflection which this line of thought explicitly permits.

If one were directly concerned with the topic of philosophical scepticism, I think one would have to acknowledge that this response cannot be easily rejected. But, returning now to the issue of Moore's response to philosophical scepticism, I want to ask only whether one can properly attribute the anti-sceptical argument sketched above to him. For despite the fact that I have presented it as a development of his argument from differential certainty, one may feel that it is not really a Moorean rejoinder to the sceptic at all, that it owes more to Wittgenstein's *On Certainty* than to Moore's 'A Defence of Common Sense'. In particular, since the strategy involved is one in which the primary values of critical reflection are consistency and rationality, which are the values of a coherence theorist, to attribute this position to Moore is to treat him as a coherence theorist in respect of cognitive claims. It is no surprise to find Wittgenstein expressing this point of view in *On Certainty* (e.g. section 191); but surely one should not ascribe any such position to that Moore?

If one thinks in general terms of Moore's metaphysics, this seems right; the way in which he writes in *Some Main Problems of Philosophy* of 'observing' particular cases of knowledge (*SMPP*, p. 143) is indicative of a realist conception of knowledge that is incompatible with that of a coherence theorist. Furthermore, as I indicated in the previous section, Moore typically employs a foundationalist conception of knowledge which a coherence theorist will want to repudiate; for the coherence theorist will call into question the status of any claim to knowledge, however apparently self-evident or 'immediate'. Yet there is a strain of thought in his work which points in another direction. This is the view that propositions such as 'This is a chair' cannot be *proved* – a view propounded equally in *Principia Ethica* of 1903 (p. 75) and in 'Proof of an External World' of 1939 (pp. 149–50). What lies behind these remarks is the view that there is nothing that we can bring forward in support of these propositions which both establishes their truth and is more certain than they are themselves; and they further suggest that if these things cannot be proved, then the best we can do is to form as coherent a picture of the world and our place within it as we can in the light of our (subjectively) certain beliefs about the world and what we know of it. Moore draws this implication in *Principia Ethica* (pp. 75–6), but does not attempt to integrate it into the realist metaphysics and intuitionist epistemology he also here presents; nor does he address this issue in his later writings. Thus although my formulation of the argument from differential certainty connects with one of Moore's characteristic theses, it has to be acknowledged that it does not sit happily with the bulk of his writings on this topic.

IV

So far I have concentrated on Moore's argument from differential certainty. I have suggested that although it is by no means the knock-down argument Moore presents it as, it is not just a dogmatic denial of scepticism; there lie behind it further arguments which raise challenging questions for the sceptic although their development threatens to take one away from Moore's philosophy. Moore advances other anti-sceptical arguments, typically to the effect that there is a pragmatic incoherence in the secptic's presentation of his scepticism (cf. e.g. DCS, pp. 42–3). But, partly for reasons which he himself had expressed in an early paper (HP, esp. p. 159), these arguments are of little force, and I shall not discuss them here. Instead, I want to address an important interpretative issue concerning Moore's response to philosophical scepticism – the characterization of Moore as the philosopher's 'plain' man, employing his appeal to common sense in an ineffectual attempt to refute the philosophical sceptic. For if this interpretation is correct, then my own discussion so far has been a misguided attempt to impute to Moore arguments of a kind which he never really sought to advance.

This account of Moore's position was made famous by Thompson Clarke in his influential paper 'The Legacy of Scepticism',[3] and has recently been set out in detail by Barry Stroud in chapter 3 of *The Significance of Philosophical Scepticism*,[4] and I shall concentrate on Stroud's presentation of it. Stroud brings to his discussion of Moore a distinction between what he calls 'internal' and external' reactions to claims to knowledge: an 'internal' reaction is supposed to be one which does not question the accepted criteria by which such claims are assessed; an 'external' reaction is to be one which embodies 'a certain withdrawal or detachment from the whole body of knowledge of the world' (*SPS*, p. 117), and thus does not permit reliance upon accepted criteria. Moore, as portrayed by Stroud, never gets beyond the internal reaction, and always interprets the sceptic as raising an internal doubt. This, then, is why he appeals to common sense: for if one judges solely by internal criteria, then of course Moore knows that 'this is a finger', and a sceptic who raises doubts about this can be as brusquely dismissed as Moore dismisses him in the passage cited earlier from 'Some Judgments of Perception'. But the philosophical sceptic as represented by Stroud does not accept the internal criteria; for he is reacting 'externally' to a claim to knowledge. Hence, Stroud proposes, Moore did not so much beg the question as miss the point. But this presupposes that there is a point to be missed, and for Stroud Moore's importance is that his work (if not the man himself) raises the issue whether we can really make sense of there being an external reaction to claims to knowledge, a reaction which Moore, through some 'philosophical lobotomy',[5] cannot hear. Indeed, at the end of the book Stroud, following, but not altogether endorsing, Clarke, suggests that perhaps after all Moore was right, though without knowing that he was, in that 'the fully "external" or "philosophical" conception of our relation to the world, when pressed, is really an illusion' (*SPS*, pp. 273–4).

Before assessing Stroud's approach, there is an important vacillation in his response to Moore which needs to be brought out. At several points (*SPS*, pp. 99–100, 114, 117) Stroud implies that we can judge that Moore's claims to knowledge are correct, even though they are assessed only from an internal point of view. Such a judgement assumes that we can detach the external reaction to a claim to knowledge from an internal one in such a way that we can forget about the former and employ the latter as a self-sufficient condition of knowledge 'from the internal point of view'. This indeed is what he takes Moore's practice to be; the implication is, therefore, that Stroud accepts that Moore's putative common sense knowledge is indeed knowledge, and when the situation is presented in this way one can see why Stroud suggests that Moore might after all be right (if the external point of view turns out to be an illusion). But when he later faces the issue of this detachment head on (*SPS*, pp. 126–7), Stroud confesses that he does not after all think it possible, because the truth of claims to knowledge 'from the internal point of view' presupposes the refutation of external scepticism – a thesis Stroud has indeed argued for at length in an earlier chapter (*SPS*, chapter 2). This confession makes quite a difference to Stroud's account of Moore; for if Moore's claims to knowledge conflict with the sceptic's thesis, then the Clarke-Stroud picture of Moore as 'lord of the plain', the internal point of view, gives him no territory at all until the sceptic has been refuted. And with this the supposed merit of Moore's position, as interpreted by Clarke and Stroud, has largely disappeared.

This point is important not only for its bearing on the significance which Clarke and Stroud attach to Moore, but also because of the general issue of the significance of philosophical scepticism which it raises. I shall return to this below, but I want first to cast some doubt on Stroud's 'external – internal' distinction and his application of it to Moore. For it seems to me absurd to suppose that Moore was as insensitive to philosophical scepticism as Stroud suggests. The Humean argument which Moore discussed in *Some Main Problems of Philosophy* (and which I discussed in section II above) has as its aim precisely the denial of all ordinary claims to perceptual knowledge of an external world, and I do not see what more Moore needed to say to show that he understood that all ordinary criteria for the assessment of claims to perceptual knowledge were being rejected by the sceptic, that the sceptic was advancing an 'external' reaction to such claims.

It may nonetheless be felt that Moore's reaction to that sceptical argument, his argument from differential certainty, manifests only an 'internal' reaction to the argument. If an internal reaction is simply one that invokes uncritically the accepted criteria, then that judgement is certainly unfair; for, as I have been at pains to stress, Moore's argument is not a simple, quesiton-begging, *modus tollens*. Nonetheless it is right to say that Moore's argument appeals in some way to our actual practice, to our actual conviction that we do know such things as that 'this is a hand', and in the previous section I have tried to explore the nature of this appeal and its effectiveness as a response to sceptical arguments. One implication of that discussion, however, is that there are pefectly respectable, and familiar, sceptical arguments which can be represented as embodying an 'internal' reaction to claims to knowledge in so far as they base themselves upon features of our actual use of the concept and seek to show that if we take seriously the requirements implicit in these features, then we should reject many claims to knowledge – e.g. perceptual knowledge of an external world. So it is just not true, as Stroud claims, that philosophical scepticism can always be represented as requiring the adoption of a point of view wholly external to our practice. Certainly there are sceptical positions, such as that of Moore's Humean sceptic, which can be thus represented, but they are not the only ones. There are quite sufficient strains within our cognitive practices for sceptical arguments to proceed solely on the basis of 'internal' criteria and requirements of consistency and rationality.

Indeed, once one realizes that not all philosophical scepticism requires the adoption of a point of view 'external' to a type of knowledge claim (though it must entail a detachment of some kind from the knowledge claims called into doubt), then one's confidence in the 'external – internal' distinction itself as a useful way of thinking about scepticism and Moore's response to it is much diminished. It is not even clear that Stroud's paradigm case of scepticism from an external point of view, dream-scepticism, has to be so regarded; for, as Stroud himself makes admirably clear, the dream sceptic starts from facts and lines of argument that are familiar features of our actual treatment of claims to knowledge and just pushes them to the limit. So the dream sceptic certainly starts by accepting ordinary criteria for assessing claims to knowledge, and thus, one would think, from within the internal point of view; what he then argues is that judged by those criteria, all claims to perceptual knowledge are false, and thus he certainly ends up by rejecting much of what we take ourselves to know. But since this rejection is not motivated by anything outside our ordinary conception of the world and of our knowledge of it, it seems to differ only in degree, and not kind, from the ordinary critical assessment of claims to knowledge. Thus we seem to end up with the thought that because the philosophical sceptic raises general doubts, his doubt is external, whereas because Moore's anti-sceptical affirmations are particular, they are internal. But if this is all the distinction boils down to, it does not explain why Moore fails to refute the sceptic; the 'external' proposition 'No one knows anything about the external world' is inconsistent with the 'internal' one 'I know one fact about the external world – that this is a hand.'

In rejecting Stroud's 'external – internal' distinction, and thus his approach to

Moore's treatment of scepticism, I do not dispute that there is something special about philosophical scepticism. But it seems to me that Descartes put the requisite distinction better than Stroud when, in his reply to Gassendi, he distinguished between practical and theoretical doubt:

We must note the distinction emphasized by me in various passages between the practical activities of our life and an inquiry into truth; for, when it is a case of regulating our life, it would assuredly be stupid not to trust the senses, and those sceptics were quite ridiculous who so neglected human affairs that they had to be preserved by their friends from tumbling down precipices. It was for this reason that somewhere I announced that no one in his right mind seriously doubted such matters; but when we raise an enquiry into what is the surest knowledge which the human mind can obtain, it is clearly unreasonable to refuse to treat them as doubtful.[6]

It is valuable to compare this passage, with its distinction between what we doubt and what we treat as doubtful, with the following passage from Moore's paper 'Four Forms of Scepticism', which, incidentally, shows that Moore did recognize the special nature of philosophical scepticism:

And also, curiously enough, a man who denies that we ever know for certain things of a certain sort, need not necessarily feel any doubt whatever about *particular* things of the sort in question. A man who, like Bertrand Russell, believes with the utmost confidence that he never knows for certain such a thing as that he is sittting down, may nonetheless feel perfectly sure, without a shadow of doubt, on thousands of occasions that he is sitting down ... I think that the common opinion that doubt is essential to scepticism arises from the mistaken opinion that if a man sincerely believes that a thing is doubtful he must doubt it. In the case of sincere philosophical opinions this seems to me certainly not the case ... There is, therefore, a sort of scepticism which is *compatible* with a complete absence of doubt on any subject whatever (pp. 198–9).

Is Moore's distinction the same as that of Descartes? Certainly they agree that it is one thing to doubt a proposition and another thing to regard it as doubtful. It might seem from the passage quoted that Moore, unlike Descartes, would want to apply this distinction only to propositions about particular cases (e.g. 'I am now sitting down'), but I think he is just here arguing, in his characteristic way, from the particular to the general, and would want to insist that even if Russell believes it to be doubtful that there is an external world, this is still not a conclusive reason for taking him to doubt that there is. Yet there is, I think, a difference between Moore and Descartes. Moore makes it clear that in his view philosophical scepticism is essentially a second-order doubt – doubt whether one knows; despite the distinction Descartes draws in the passage quoted between what we treat as doubtful and what we doubt, it is difficult to suppose that Descartes takes a similar view of philosophical doubt. There is, for example, no suggestion to this effect in his first Meditation, whose subtitle is simply 'of what we may doubt'.

In practice Moore's paradox ensures that there is no apparent difference, from the first-person perspective of the thinker, between Moore and Descartes on this issue. The Moorean philosopher cannot coherently frame the thought 'I believe that I don't know whether I am sitting down, but I do know that I am sitting down.' But this does not ensure that there is no difference here – only that one will not be able to tell who is right by considering the sceptic's presentation of his project. Rather, the point at issue between Moore and Descartes here is similar to that which Stroud discussed in terms of the relation between internal and external reactions to claims to knowledge. As I mentioned, although Stroud vacillates a bit, he ends up affirming that even if a claim to knowledge satisfies internal criteria, we cannot regard it as knowledge unless it also satisfies whatever further external conditions upon knowledge there are. In this Stroud follows Descartes: philosophical doubt, being first-order, is not compatible with knowledge; whereas the Moorean position is that philosophical doubt is second-order, and is therefore compatible with first-order knowledge.

Who is right here? I am inclined to think that Moore is. The main reason for this is implied by Descartes's insistence that philosophical scepticism has no practical significance for the conduct of life: for if one takes a pragmatist view of belief and doubt, there is then no ground for ascribing a doubt whether p to one who has a philosophical doubt whether p. Descartes may insist that there can still be a theoretical doubt whether p; but it is very unclear what the content of this doubt is, if it is not the Moorean second-order doubt. I think that this can be confirmed by reflecting on our reaction to a situation in which a philosophical sceptic has advanced an argument for some sceptical position (e.g. concerning the external world) which we take to be a bad argument. Certainly, we will take it that the sceptic believed that he did not know that there is an external world; but will his scepticism, which we take to be ill-founded, lead us to think that he did not know that there is an external world because he doubted its existence? I think not; we will retrospectively interpret his doubt as only second-order (though of course that is not how it can appear to the sceptic at the time). It seems to me, therefore, that Moore is right about this: philosophical doubt, being second-order, is compatible with first-order knowledge. It does not of course follow from this that one who doubts philosophically does not call first-order knowledge into question; the sceptical project is not undermined by this conception of sceptical doubt. For even if sceptical doubt is compatible with knowledge, it coheres better with its absence.

V

So far I have said little about Moore's 'Proof of an External World', and this may seem to be evasion on my part, since it is widely held that Moore does here attempt to refute scepticism by waving his hands at his audience and persuading them that he knows that 'Here is one hand, and here is another.' This is certainly how Stroud and others have interpreted Moore's 'Proof' (*SPS*, p. 107). But let us see what Moore himself has to say about it in his reply to his critics :

I have sometimes distinguished between two different propositions, each of which has been made by some philosophers, namely (1) the proposition 'There are no material things' and (2) the proposition 'Nobody knows for certain that there are any material things'. And in my latest published writing, my British Academy lecture called 'Proof of an External World' ... I implied with regard to the first of these propositions that it could be *proved* to be false in such a way as this; namely, by holding up one of your hands and saying 'This hand is a material thing'. But with regard to the second of these two propositions.... I do not think I have ever implied that *it* could be *proved* to be false in any such simple way; e.g. by holding up one of your hands and saying 'I know that this hand is a material thing; therefore at least one person knows that there is at least one material thing' (PGEM, p. 668).

This seems on the face of it a pretty unequivocal statement, written in 1942. One might object that in the passage from his 1917 lecture 'Some Judgments of Perception', which I quoted earlier, he does propound exactly the argument which he here denies having ever propounded. But although in that passage he comes close to the line of argument he here outlines, any such interpretation would omit the argument from differential certainty which I regard as the main point of it. But even if I am wrong about this, and Moore's 1917 argument does falsify the claim made in his reply, that would be an error of memory over 25 years, and for that reason quite understandable. What is not understandable is that Moore should in 1942 fail to recall what he was trying to show in 1939. But this is what Stroud (*SPS*, p. 107 n. 15) and Burnyeat accuse him of;[7] for they both note this passage in Moore's reply, but then insist that he did not know what he was talking about.

Why do Stroud and Burnyeat take up this *prima facie* implausible position? Basically, because they cannot see what Moore is seeking to accomplish in his 'Proof' if not to refute scepticism: and, surely, if Moore does there prove that there is an external world, then he must take himself to know that there is one – so what more is needed to refute the sceptic?

Now I want to concede at the start that Moore's 'Proof' is a puzzling paper, and one central puzzle is just what Moore thinks he is there accomplishing. But it also seems to me that we have to accept Moore's comment in his reply as a constraint on admissable interpretations. In outline, the way to satisfy this constraint is fairly straightforward: one has to distinguish between proving that p and proving that one knows that p. If one switches to the third person case, the distinction is obvious – between proving that p and proving that someone else knows that p: the latter, but not the former, requires a proof that the belief that p of the person concerned is appropriately related to the fact that p (e.g. that it is a reliable indicator of it). The delicate point is that, despite Moore's paradox, this distinction still obtains when one switches back to the first person case: if I take myself to prove that p, then although I thereby take myself to know that p, I do not necessarily take myself to have proved that I know that p. For to prove that I know that p, I should have to prove that my proof is a good one; and that I do not prove in simply giving my proof. A mathematician who uses the law of excluded middle in a non-constructive proof that p will have proved that p if non-constructive proofs are good proofs; but he will not have proved this in his proof that p.

If one applies this line of thought to Moore's 'Proof', one takes Moore to be here seeking to prove that there is an external world, but not seeking to prove that his proof is a good one, and thus not proving that he knows that there is an external world. We can recall here Moore's characterization of sceptical doubt as doubt whether one knows; scepticism thus characterized is a higher-order attitude, and its refutation therefore requires a proof that one knows, or, at any rate, an undermining of the sceptic's reasons for thinking that one does not know. Thus Moore's 'Proof' and the refutation of philosophical scepticism operate on different levels.

Yet this is not the end of the matter. For Moore does not only state his proof; he also sets out to show that it is a good one, that 'it is perhaps impossible to give a better or more rigorous proof of anything whatever' (PEW, p. 146), and he takes it to be a requirement of this that he should know the premises of his proof to be true. How can he show this to be so, we may well ask, without proving that he knows that there are external things? Moore asserts with characteristic forcefulness that he has the requisite knowledge – 'I certainly did at the moment *know* that which I expressed by the combination of certain gestures with saying the words "There is one hand and here is another"' (PEW, p. 146). But what does he say to show that this is true? He just appeals to our ordinary convictions – 'How absurd it would be to suggest that I did not know it, but only believed it, and that perhaps it was not the case. You might as well suggest that I do not know that I am now standing up and talking – that perhaps after all I'm not, and that it's not quite certain that I am' (PEW, pp. 146–7). It is here that it looks as though Moore is attempting a dogmatic refutation of scepticism. But this interpretation, I suggest, misunderstands Moore's intent; he wants to show that his original proof is a good one, and he accepts that it will be such only if he knew its premises to be true. So he accepts that he has to show that he knows these premises to be true, and his appeal to our convictions is intended to achieve this. But it is not intended to prove that he knows these premises to be true.

This interpretation rests on a distinction between showing that one knows something and proving that one does. The distinction is perhaps a rather tenuous one, but the important point is that whereas a proof of knowledge would require a refutation of sceptical doubts, an exhibition of knowledge does not, and can proceed by means of an appeal to the audience's beliefs. Yet there is a price to be paid; for if Moore is not attempting a dogmatic refutation of secepticism, then his argument will have no significance for those who have sceptical doubts about whether Moore does know the things that he says he knows. They have therefore been given no reason for supposing that Moore's proof is a good one; thus even if it is a good proof (because Moore does know the things he claims to know), the sceptic, who has been given no reason for thinking this, can continue to doubt whether there is an external world. But if Moore's proof is not addressed to sceptics, then to whom is it addressed? It can only be directed to those who accept that we do know such things as that 'this is a hand', but still doubt whether there is an external world. Perhaps there have been philosophers who have held this combination of views, as Moore insists in his reply, but it is not easy to think of an interesting way of combining them. The result of depriving Moore's 'proof' of anti-sceptical significance, therefore, seems to be that one deprives it of most of its philosophical significance. And this is why, as I said at the outset, there is a puzzle about what Moore thinks he is here accomplishing.

VI

Although I have accepted Moore's denial that his 'proof' is intended to have an anti-sceptical conclusion, it seems to me no accident that it was followed closely by two papers in which Moore explicitly discusses scepticism – 'Four Forms of Scepticism' and 'Certainty'. Moore, perhaps conscious of the widespread mis-understanding of the purport of his 'Proof', wanted to substantiate the claims to knowledge which he there makes by undermining sceptical doubts concerning them: success in this project would enable him to address his proof to sceptics and non-sceptics alike, thereby actually giving it the significance that Kant attached to the project of giving a proof of the external world.

But how is the philosophical sceptic, who doubts whether he knows, to be refuted? Moore says in his 'Reply' (*PGEM*, p. 669) that we cannot prove that we know that there are external things in the way in which, according to him, we can prove that there are external things – i.e. by holding up one of our hands and saying 'I know that this is a hand.' So not only is Moore's 'Proof' not an attempt at a refutation of scepticism, but actually on his own admission the strategy he employs there would not be appropriate to the refutation of scepticism. This is surely the last nail in the coffin for the Clarke-Stroud interpretation of Moore. How then are we to proceed? Moore is not very helpful in his 'Reply': he just says that 'In the case of the proposition "Nobody knows that there are any material things" it does seem to me obvious that some further argument is called for, if one is to talk of having *proved* it to be false, than in the case of "There *are* no material things"; this difference is, I think, connected with the fact that an immensely greater number of philosophers have held that *nobody knows*, than have held that *there are none*' (*PGEM*, p. 669).

The implication of this last remark is that a proof of the falsity of scepticism requires a refutation of the arguments propounded by sceptical philosophers. This is certainly the way Moore proceeds in 'Four Forms of Scepticism' and 'Certainty'. In each case the bulk of the paper is devoted to the refutation of possible, but implausible, sceptical arguments which hinge on confusions concerning different kinds of possibility. Moore's discussions, although not without insights into our concepts of possibility, only address serious sceptical arguments (in both cases those characteristic of Cartesian scepticism) until he has left himself with too little time to deal adequately with the topic. But one striking feature of both papers, at least in the light of his earlier discussions of scepticism, is the fact that he does not rely on the argument from differential certainty. The argument is indeed mentioned in 'Four Forms of Scepticism', right at the end of the paper, but Moore's presentation of it has none of his earlier assurance. He writes:

> Russell's view that I do not know for certain that this is a pencil ... rests, if I am right, on no less than four distinct assumptions ... what I can't help asking myself is this: Is it, in fact, as certain that all these four assumptions are true, as that I *do* know that this is a pencil? I cannot help answering: It seems to me *more* certain that I do know that this is a pencil ... than that any single one of these four assumptions is true, let alone all four. Nay more: I do not think that it is *rational* to be as certain of any one of these four propositions, as of the proposition that I do know that this is a pencil. And how on earth is it to be decided which of the two things it is more rational to be certain of? (4FS, p. 226).

This last question, with which the paper ends, is not rhetorical. It represents Moore's recognition that the bald statement of the argument from differential certainty needs to be buttressed by further arguments which show that it is more 'rational' to be certain that one knows that 'this is a pencil' than of the assumptions about knowledge which lead to Russell's sceptical conclusion. And it is perhaps for this reason that the argument is simply not mentioned at all in 'Certainty'.

I suggested earlier, in section III of this paper, that the argument can be taken further, along lines consistent with Moore's defence of common sense, if one is prepared to take a coherence view of the truth of claims to knowledge. An important implication of this was that the foundationalist conception of knowledge associated with Moore's representative theory of perception which I discussed in section II must be called into question. Moore, however, having earlier failed to think through in detail an account of perceptual knowledge that is not vulnerable to the Humean sceptical argument, shows no sign of wanting to do so now. The resulting situation is one in which he lacks the arguments to substantiate his anti-sceptical convictions. A good way to reflect on his position is by considering his attitude to the cognitive status of 'This is a hand.' When thinking in terms of his defence of common sense, Moore regards it as certain and unprovable: when thinking in terms of his foundationalist theory of perceptual knowledge, he regards it as only known indirectly, and therefore to be justified by reference to things which are known immediately. Which of these attitudes, we may wonder, is his guide in his last anti-sceptical discussions? Despite the sentiments with which he opens 'Certainty', quoted at the start of this paper, it is quite clear that it is the latter. In this final discussion Moore felt that in order to vindicate perceptual knowledge he had to be able to prove solely on the basis of his present sensory experience and memory of the immediate past (all that he 'knew immediately') that he was not dreaming. This he was unsurprisingly unable to do. If I am right, however, his failure was due to a loss of philosophical nerve, to an unwillingness to pursue the implications of the appeal to common sense manifest in his argument from differential certainty. So it was Wittgenstein, in *On Certainty*, who grasped the significance of Moore's defence of common sense better than Moore himself. Nonetheless, Moore deserves some credit for having opened up lines of thought which Wittgenstein pursued further; he certainly does not deserve to be represented as a 'plain man' who has overheard a discussion about philosophical scepticism and systematically misunderstands what the participants are driving at.

Notes

This is a revised version of a peper presented in Munich in April 1986. I am much indebted to those present at the conference for helpful comments, and also to Myles Burnyeat and Marie McGinn for their help.
1   Page references are to the paper as published in Moore's *Philosophical Papers* (Allen and Unwin, London, 1959). Throughout my page references are to Moore's papers as published in that collection and in his earlier *Philosophical Studies* (Routledge and Kegan Paul. London, 1922). I also use the following abbreviations of the titles of Moore's works in giving references to them in the text of the paper:

HP – 'Hume's Philosophy' in *Philosophical Studies*
SJP – 'Some Judgments of Perception' in *Philosophical Studies*
DCS – 'A Defence of Common Sense' in *Philosophical Papers*
PEW – 'Proof of an External World' in *Philosophical Papers*
4FS – 'Four Forms of Scepticism' in *Philosophical Papers*
C – 'Certainty' in *Philosophical Papers*
SMPP – Some Main Problems of Philosophy, Allen and Unwin, London, 1953
PGEM – The Philosophy of G. E. Moore ed. P. A. Schilpp, Open Court, Lasalle, 1942.

2   This charge is made by Barry Stroud in *The Significance of Philosophical Scepticism* (pp. 104–13). A generation ago it was made by three of Moore's critics in *PGEM* – Malcolm (p. 352), Lazerowitz (pp. 382–3) and Ambrose (p. 399).

3   T. Clarke 'The legacy of scepticism' *The Journal of Philosophy*, 1972, pp. 754–69.

4   Clarendon Press, Oxford, 1984. In the text I abbreviate this title as *SPS* when giving references to it.

5   Clarke, ibid., n. 3, p. 757.

6   *The Philosophical Works of Descartes* vol. II, trans. E. Haldane and G. Ross, Cambridge University Press, Cambridge, 1911, p. 206.

7   M. Burnyeat 'Examples in epistemology: Socrates, Theaetetus, and G. E. Moore' *Philosophy*, 1977, p. 395.

7

Logic in Russell's Logicism

Peter Hylton

Russell, as is well known, was a logicist.[1] He believed, and attempted to demonstrate, that mathematics is reducible to logic. What is perhaps less clear is *why* Russell was a logicist – what philosophical purpose was served by his belief in this doctrine, what motive lay behind his attempt to reduce mathematics to logic. An investigation of this point will, I think, enable us to see more clearly what logicism amounts to in Russell's hands. Russell's logicism was originally intended as part of some kind of argument against Kant, and post-Kantian idealism, but how exactly does this argument go? Russell, unlike the logical positivists, does not seek to use logicism to show that mathematics is analytic; his use of logicism against Kant is quite different from that of the positivists. But how, then, does Russell think that logicism is anti-Kantian? A fairly clear answer to this question emerges from an examination of the earliest phase of Russell's logicism (i.e. that dominated by *The Principles of Mathematics*).[2] In section I, I attempt to articulate this answer. My discussion of the motivation of Russell's early logicism is intended as the starting point of a discussion of Russell's conception of logic, and this is the subject of section II. The significance of the reduction of mathematics to logic depends, of course, upon the conception of logic that is in play. An understanding of the significance that Russell attributed to logicism in the early years of this century will therefore provide us with insight into the conception of logic that he held at that period, and into his reasons for holding it. Russell's conception of logic is antithetical to one crucial element, at least, in the modern view of logic. I shall call this element the model-theoretic conception. I shall try to show that the differences between Russell's conception of logic and this modern conception are closely connected with his use of logicism as an argument against Kant (as he interpreted Kant) and against idealism. In particular, if Russell's conception of logic were the model-theoretic one, his argument against Kant would not have the force that he took it to have. Both the motivation that I attribute to Russell's early logicism, and the conception of logic upon which it relies, are threatened by the paradox which bears Russell's name. The theory of types, which was Russell's response to the paradox, undermines logicism as Russell had originally conceived it. These very complex issues will be briefly discussed in section III.

I

Russell thought of logicism as anti-Kantian. This is clear both from his discussion at the time (see *Principles, passim*) and from his later statements. Thus he says, in *My Philosophical Development*:

> The primary aim of *Principia Mathematica* was to show that all pure mathematics follows from purely logical premisses and uses only concepts definable in logical terms. This was, of course, an antithesis to the doctrines of Kant, and initially I thought of the work as a parenthesis in the refutation of [Kant].[3]

(A similar passage, repeating the phrase 'a parenthesis in the refutation of Kant', is to be found in Russell's 'Autobiography', in the Schilpp volume on Russell.)[4] But how, exactly, did Russell take logicism to be part of an argument against Kant? Most fundamentally, Russell's logicism was intended as a refutation of Kant's view of mathematics. Russell, as we shall see, does not deny the Kantian claim that mathematics is synthetic *a priori*. He does, however, deny the claim that mathematics is based on what Kant had called the forms of our intuition, forms which impose spatiality and temporality upon the objects which we intuit. Russell insists that mathematics is wholly independent of space and time. Logicism was to constitute a basis for this insistence in the following way. If one accepts, as Kant did, that *logic* is independent of space and time (and of our forms of intuition), then logicism will show that the same is true of mathematics. One crucial property which logicism shows to be transferable from logic to mathematics is thus the property of being independent of space, time and the forms of intuition.[5]

Kant, according to Russell, held the opposite opinion only because of his ignorance of mathematics and, in particular, of the new logic.[6] The logic available to Kant was syllogistic logic, which lacks even the full power of monadic quantification theory. Given this logic, the theorems of Euclid, say, do not follow from Euclid's axioms by logic alone. As Russell sees the matter, this fact is at the basis of Kant's theory of mathematics:

> There was, until recently, a special difficulty in the principles of mathematics. It seemed plain that mathematics consists of deductions, and yet

the orthodox accounts of deduction were largely or wholly inapplicable to
existing mathematics. Not only the Aristotelian syllogistic theory, but also
the modern doctrines of Symbolic Logic ... In this fact lay the strength of
the Kantian view, which asserted that mathematical reasoning is not strictly
formal, but always uses intuitions, i.e. the *a priori* knowledge of space and
time. Thanks to the progress of Symbolic Logic, especially as treated by
Professor Peano, this part of the Kantian philosophy is now capable of a
final and irrevocable refutation (*Principles*, section 4).

A decisive advance here was Russell's development of polyadic quantification
theory, and the associated understanding of quantifier dependence.[7] One result of
this was a logic which, unlike syllogistic logic, could handle the reasoning which
is involved in mathematics, for example, in deriving theorems from axioms. A
second result concerns the understanding of the calculus. The work of Dedekind,
Cantor and Weierstrass allowed the crucial notions of the calculus to be given
precise definitions. These definitions require the use of nested quantifiers if they
are to be put in rigorous form; quantifier dependence is crucial here. These
definitions make no appeal to space, time or motion; nor do they rely upon the
notion of an infinitely small quantity, or infinitesimal.[8] This second point too
Russell sees as an advance which undermines Kant's theory of mathematics:

> It was formerly supposed – and herein lay the real strength of Kant's
> mathematical philosophy – that continuity had an essential reference to
> space and time, and that the Calculus (as the word *fluxion* suggests) in some
> way presupposed motion or at least change. In this view, the philosophy of
> space and time was prior to that of continuity, the Transcendental Aes-
> thetic preceeded the Transcendental Dialectic, and the antinomies (at least
> the mathematics ones) were essentially spatio-temporal. All this has been
> changed by modern mathematics (*Principles*, section 249).

These results of polyadic quantification theory are impressive, especially to
a mathematician educated to think that logic means syllogistic logic. Impressive
as they are, however, these results do not amount to logicism. They may show
that modern logic is necessary for a (non-Kantian) understanding of mathematics, but they do not show that it is sufficient; they do not amount to a
reduction of mathematics to logic. For this we need to take into account the fact
that logic, for Russell, is not (what we call) first-order logic but is, rather,
higher-order logic, as powerful as set theory. This fact is something that I shall
discuss later. The present point is that it makes possible the full reduction of
mathematics to logic. Two issues in particular are worth emphasizing. First,
given the Russellian analogue of set theory, the arithmetic of the real numbers
can be understood in terms of the natural numbers. Second, it appears to be

possible to reduce the arithmetic of the natural numbers, in turn, to logic – given Russell's generous conception of what is to count as logic. This is in contrast to the view that the natural numbers are special entities, governed by their own laws, laws which might admit of, or even require, explanation in terms of the form of our intuition. From Russell's point of view, then, modern logic and mathematics show that the reliance upon spatio-temporal notions, which is characteristic of Kant's theory of mathematics, is not required at any point for an understanding of geometry or of the calculus, or of any part of mathematics.[9] Kant's theory of mathematics is thus refuted by logicism, the view that mathematics is reducible to logic.

The use of logicism against Kant's view of mathematics may seem to be a relatively narrow point. It is not clear, on the face of it, why the success of this claim of Russell's should carry any weight as a general argument against Kantianism, or as an argument against Kant's idealist successors, most of whom were far less concerned with mathematics than was Kant himself. But in Russell's hands the refutation of Kant's view of mathematics served as the basis for a more general attack on Kantianism and on post-Kantian idealism. The attack is against what Russell at least took to be a single doctrine, crucial to both Kantianism and post-Kantian idealism. We can formulate this doctrine as follows: our ordinary knowledge (of science, history, mathematics, etc.) is, at best, true in a conditioned and non-absolute sense of truth. This formulation obscures several points, having to do in particular with the differences between Kant and the idealists, and with idealist (and Russellian) interpretations of Kant. More subtly, perhaps, the idea that this doctrine is objectionable suggests that there is an absolute or unconditioned sense of truth which can be contrasted with conditioned truth. These matters will require some discussion.

Kant held that our knowledge is not unconditioned. It is confined to the world of appearances, which cannot be thought of as ultimately real and independent of us. One important basis for this claim is embodied in the argument of the antinomies, that if the world is taken to be 'a whole existing in itself', i.e. as independent of our representations of it, then contradictions can be derived. Kant's conclusion is that the world is not such a whole. This is the doctrine of transcendental idealism, that the world is empirically real but transcendentally ideal. All of our knowledge thus has this status: it is knowledge only of the world as it appears to us, and if construed more strongly than this is contradictory. The idea of the unconditioned, or of a world of things-in-themselves, plays a purely negative role here; our knowledge is *not* unconditioned, is *not* of things-in-themselves. (This is not to deny that these ideas may play a positive role in other parts of Kant's philosophy.)

The post-Kantian idealists rejected Kant's distinction between the phenomenal world, or world of appearances, and the noumenal world, or world of things-in-themselves. This distinction is closely connected with other Kantian dualisms which the idealists rejected: that between sensibility and the under-standing, and that between the analytic and the synthetic (one of the con-nections, at least, will emerge in our later discussion; see note 29). The fact that the idealists rejected the distinction between the phenomenal world and the noumenal world meant that they drew un-Kantian conclusions from Kant's arguments against the consistency of regarding the world we know as a thing-in-itself. The idealists claimed that these arguments (and others) show that the ways in which we ordinarily think of the world are inconsistent. Ordinary 'knowledge', if thought through with full rigour, leads to contradictions. For the idealists, these contradictions do not result from a special metaphysical way of construing our ordinary knowledge, as if it were about things-in-themselves rather than about appearances. For the idealists the contradictions simply are implicit in (what we take to be) our ordinary knowledge. For this reason, they do not infer from the contradictions that we should eschew metaphysics. They infer, rather, that the categories of thought used in ordinary 'knowledge' are inadequate, and that we must attempt to find categories of thought that are not vulnerable to such inconsistencies. The only truly consistent way of thinking – that which yields 'absolute knowledge' – is to be found in the metaphysical conception of the world as a single organic whole, every part of which is internally related to every other. (This idealist position is perhaps most obviously articulated in the Heglian dia-lectic; but something like this is, I think, a distinguishing characteristic of post-Kantian idealism in general.) The idea of absolute knowledge affords the idealists a perspective from which all of our ordinary (i.e. non-metaphysical) claims to knowledge can be judged and found to be at best relatively or conditionally true.

For the idealists, then, real truth is absolute truth, which in turn means unconditioned truth. This makes it natural for the idealists to read Kant as if he too held that conditioned truth is second-rate, somehow not real truth – even though for Kant there is no other sense of true than the sense in which it refers to conditioned truth. Now the important point, from our perspective, is that Russell more or less took for granted this idealist reading of Kant. Given the idealist orthodoxy in which he was educated, this is hardly surprising. The point, how-ever, goes deeper than Russell's reading of Kant. Russell also took for granted the conception of truth from which this reading stems. Truth, for Russell, was absol-ute and unconditioned. Like the idealists, but unlike Kant, he held that there is an absolute sense of truth, and that it is to this that human knowledge should aspire. Unlike the idealists, however, Russell held this to be the only sense of truth, anything else being just a polite word for falsehood. From Russell's point of view, then, the crucial doctrine common to Kant and to his successors is the claim that all of our ordinary knowledge is true in a second-rate sense. What we call 'knowledge' is only relatively true, not absolutely true, true only from an empirical point of view, not from a transcendental point of view. (From this point I shall, where convenient, ignore the fact that this claim cannot be straightforwardly attributed to Kant. Equally, I shall sometimes speak of Kant as an idealist, as Russell does without hesitation.) Russell objects to this claim because he thinks it tantamount to saying that all of what we ordinarily take as knowledge (including mathematics) is false.

Russell uses logicism to argue against the crucial idealist and Kantian claim that our ordinary knowledge cannot be absolutely or transcendentally true. There are, I think, two rather different arguments that connect logicism to the refutation of this claim, though only one of them is explicit in Russell's texts. The first, and explicit, connection has to do with the arguments that Kant, and to some extend other idealists, used as a basis for the claim that the world as we ordinarily understand it is not wholly consistent. (I am here presupposing an idealist interpretation of Kant – in particular that for Kant it is our ordinary understanding of the world, and not only a metaphysical construal of that understanding, which is inconsistent.) For Kant, as I have already said, one important basis for this idea is to be found in the antinomies. The first two antinomies are spatio-temporal, and claim to show that if space and time are taken as real – as features of the world as it really is, rather than merely of the world as it appears to us – then contradictions follow. This claim, if accepted, seems immediately to show that the world as we take it to be cannot be fully real, for the world as we take it to be is spatial and temporal, and these features, it seems, give rise to contradictions. This point seems to have been more or less taken for granted by many of Kant's idealist successors. Hegel, for example, says:

> These Kantian Antinomies will always remain an important part of the critical philosophy; they, more than anything else, brought about the downfall of previous metaphysics and can be regarded as a main transition into more recent philosophy.[10]

More striking than this, perhaps, are the flattering terms in which Hegel refers to Zeno, calling him, for example, 'the originator of the dialectic' (*der Anfähnger der Dialektik*).[11] For one post-Kantian idealist, in particular, the supposed contradictions in the notion of space were of the highest importance. This was Russell himself, who argued, in the late 1890s, that space, if considered as devoid of matter, gives rise to contradictions: '... empty space ... gives rise to the antinomy in question; for empty space is a bare possibility of relations, undifferentiated and homogeneous, and thus wholly destitute of parts or of thinghood.'[12] This claim, which was elaborated in his *Foundations of Geometry*, was intended to be the first step in an elaborate 'dialectic of the sciences', which would take scientific knowledge as the subject of a Hegelian-style dialectic.[13] The result of this dialectic would be to show that all such knowledge is merely relative, i.e. not fully true as it stands. So when, a few years later, Russell argues against (what he took to be) Kant's claims of the inadequacy of the notions of space and time, it is perhaps with the fervour that is said to characterize recent converts.

In *Principles*, in any case, Russell's claim is that space and time are consistent, and that modern (i.e. nineteenth-century) mathematics demonstrates this beyond doubt. More accurately, perhaps, he claims that modern mathematics makes available consistent theories which may represent the truth about space and time; whether they in fact do so is a matter on which he is willing to remain agnostic. The crucial point is that mathematics makes consistent theories of space and time possible.[14] The importance of this point to Russell can be gathered from the fact that the notion of space, which is hardly an obvious subject for a book on the foundation of mathematics, is the subject of Part VI of *The Principles of Mathematics*, and occupies nearly 100 pages of that book. This part of the book concludes with a discussion of Kant's antinomies, and claims that they are 'disproved by the modern realization of Leibniz's universal characteristic' (section 436). Russell's claim that there are consistent mathematical theories of space and time draws, as one would expect, upon the treatment of real numbers and of continuity made available by Cantor, Dedekind and (especially) Weierstrass. It is important, however, to see that it also depends upon the central claim of Russell's logicism, that mathematics is wholly independent of the Kantian forms of intuition. It is only if mathematics is in this way independent of space and time that it can be used, in non-circular fashion, as an argument for the consistency of the latter notions. Russell thus takes the central claim of logicism, and the claim of the consistency of space and time, as crucial to his opposition to Kant:

> The questions of chief importance to us, as regards the Kantian theory, are two, namely, (1) are the reasonings in mathematics in any way different from those of Formal Logic? (2) are there any contradictions in the notions of space and time? If these two pillars of the Kantian edifice can be pulled down, we shall have successfully played the part of Samson towards his disciples (*Principles*, section 433).

This, then, is the first and most explicit way in which Russell takes logicism as part of a general argument against Kant and post-Kantian idealism. Logicism shows that consistent theories of space and time are available; the spatio-temporal world need not be written off as contradictory and not fully real.

Less explicit in the text of Russell's work, but hardly less important, I think, is the idea that mathematics functions as a particularly clear counterexample to the crucial idealist claim about knowledge which I briefly discussed earlier. A direct consequence of the Kantian version of the claim is that our knowledge is confined to what can be given in intuition, i.e. to actual or possible objects of sensible experience. Since these objects are partially constituted by our minds, a second consequence of the Kantian view is that our knowledge is conditioned by the nature of our cognitive faculties. The post-Kantian idealist analogue of this general claim is that all of our ordinary, non-metaphysical knowledge is at best relatively true. As against these very general idealist claims as to the inadequacy of our ordinary (non-metaphysical) knowledge, Russell sets out, in *Principles*, to show that mathematics is true – not true just as one stage in the dialectic, or more or less true, but true absolutely and unconditionally; not just true if put in a wider context, or if seen as part of a larger whole, but true just as it stands; not, to revert to the Kantian idiom, true from the empirical standpoint but false from the transcendental standpoint, but simple TRUE, with no distinctions of standpoint accepted. Mathematics, for Russell, is thus to function as a counterexample to a claim which he sees as crucial to any form of idealism, Kantian or post-Kantian.[15] The claim that mathematics is independent of space and time is again important, here for two reasons. First of all, as before, space and time were themselves held by the idealists to be inconsistent or only 'relatively true'. If mathematics were based on these notions it would be subject to the same doubts. Second, if mathematics were based on space and time, it would not be *unconditionally* true; its truth would be confined to the sphere of the spatio-temporal.[16]

For Russell in the early years of this century, then, logicism was the basis for a complex argument against idealism, of both the Kantian and the non-Kantian varieties. It is worth contrasting this argument with that of the logical positivists,[17] for whom logicism also formed part of an argument against Kant, but an argument of a very different sort. For the positivists, the essential claim about logic was that it was analytic, in the sense of being true by meaning or true by convention; they held that truths which are analytic in this sense were empty of content, and made no claim on reality. Logicism, on this account, enables one to maintain the *a priori* and non-empirical status of mathematics while denying that there is any genuine *a priori* knowledge. Because mathematics is logic it is analytic, and because it is analytic it is empty of content; so one can insist that it is not genuine knowledge. This, in turn, enables one to maintain the empiricist claim that sense experience is the source of all genuine knowledge. Mathematics, which threatened to provide a counterexample to this principle, is shown by logicism not to do so. All of these points can be seen in, for example, Carnap's discussion of the impact that Wittgenstein's *Tractatus* had on the Vienna Circle.[18] Given this account of logicism and its philosophical significance, it is clear why logicism can be thought of as an anti-Kantian doctrine. Kant held that our knowledge of mathematics is *a priori* even though the truths of mathematics are synthetic rather than analytic. One of the motives of his philosophy as a whole was to explain the possibility of this (supposed) kind of knowledge – to answer the question which he at one stage described as 'the proper problem of pure reason', namely: 'How are synthetic *a priori* judgments possible?'[19] If logicism shows that mathematics is analytic, then it shows that at least in one clear case, perhaps the clearest, Kant's motivating question is simply based upon a mistake. More generally, as way indicated above, logicism seems to clear the way for the anti-Kantian view that all knowledge is straightforwardly based on a single source, and that source is sense experience.

For the positivists, then, the point at which logicism told against the Kantian view had to do with the issue of the sources of knowledge – in particular, whether knowledge must be thought of as having the mind as one of its sources. Given the Kantian assumption that knowledge is correlative with what is known, the issue is at the same time the issue of whether the world that is known must be thought of as partially constituted by the mind. Russell's use of logicism against Kant is quite different. One sign of this is the fact that he does not hold that mathematics is empty of content or analytic or tautologous. It is clearly Russell's view that mathematics is genuine knowledge, and this is essential to the use that he makes of logicism. A deeper sign of the difference between Russell and the positivists is that for the former the terms 'analytic' and 'synthetic' bear no real philosophical weight. He does say that mathematics (and logic) are synthetic,[20] but these remarks function simply as a denial of what he sees as the absurd view that the propositions of mathematics follow from the law of contradiction, and nothing else.[21] The claim that mathematics is synthetic is not, in Russell's hands, part of a theory of mathematics. Nor is it part of a theory of analytic and synthetic knowledge. Russell has no such theory, and no concern at all with the distinction between the analytic and the synthetic except to reject it as philosophically unimportant. The fundamental point here is that Russell in *The Principles of Mathematics* completely rejects the Kantian concerns with the sources of knowledge, and with anything recognizable as epistemology at all. Underlying the arguments against Kant and the idealists is a shift of focus, due as much to Moore as to Russell, from epistemology to ontology, from knowledge to truth.[22] He believes, or writes as if he believes, that in favourable cases the mind has direct and unmediated contact with abstract objects: we simply perceive them, in some non-sensuous sense of 'perceive' which is held to be unproblematic and presuppositionless. Metaphysics is no longer subservient to epistemology; knowledge now appears as merely our access to what we know, not as constitutive of it. (We can perhaps recognize in this the sort of view that Kant found objectionable in Leibniz and Wolff; certainly it has the same results, that metaphysics proceeds without epistemological constraints, and threatens to run riot.)

First and foremost among the things with which the mind has direct contact, in Russell's view, are *propositions*. These are abstract entities, neither linguistic nor mental. The notions of truth and ontology (being) are very closely connected with that of a proposition. Propositions are the bearers of truth and falsehood; the absoluteness and objectivity of truth requires the objectivity and independence of propositions. Propositions have constituents; everything that is, is a constituent of propositions, and everything that can be a constituent of a proposition must have some sort of ontological status (in Russell's words, it *is*, even if it does not exist). The notion of a proposition is thus central to Russell's philosophy. Elsewhere I have discussed its general role in his break with idealism,[23] and I shall not repeat this discussion here. In the next section, however, we shall see that this notion plays a role both in the use that Russell wishes to make of logicism and in his conception of logic.

II

Given that Russell's use of logicism as part of an argument against Kant and the idealists is as I have described it, what does this imply about Russell's conception of logic? To play the philosophical role that Russell had in mind, logic must, above all, be *true*. Its truth must be absolute, unconditioned and unrestricted. These features may appear to be uncontroversial, even trivial, but in fact they mark a crucial difference between Russell's conception of logic and what I have called the model-theoretic conception. Logic, for Russell, was a universal language, a *lingua characteristica*, not a mere calculus which can be thought of as set up within a more inclusive language.[24] He thus conceives of logic as universal and all-inclusive. I shall endeavour to explain both this conception of logic and its connection with Russell's use of logicism against the idealists.

The idea of logic as made up of truths already marks a difference between Russell's conception and the model-theoretic conceptpion. According to the latter, logic is made up of a formal system which contains schemata which are subject to interpretations, where each schema has a truth-value in each interpretation. The crucial notion in thus *truth in all interpretations* or validity. For Russell, by contrast, the crucial notion is imply truth. Logic on his conception does not consist of schemata whose truth-values wait upon the specification of an interpretation; it consists of propositions which have a content and a truth-value on their own account.[25] Propositions, as we have already said, are taken to be objective non-linguistic and non-mental entities; they have their truth-values independently of our language, of our acts of synthesis or of any interpretation. The propositions of logic, as Russell constantly implies, contain variables and logical constants, and nothing else (see e.g. *Principles*, ch. I); this implies, and Russell clearly accepts, that variables and logical constants are themselves non-linguistic entities.

The notion of an interpretation, and the correlative idea of an uninterpreted formalism, are wholly alien to Russell's thought at this period. He simply never mentions such ideas; the conception of logic as universal is not something that Russell articulates and defends, but something that he seems to take entirely for granted. He does, however, defend one feature of his conception. On Russell's conception of logic, there is no question of our specifying what the variables are to range over; they range over everything. It is thus a part of his conception that there is no room for the specification of a universe of discourse. (We might say that the only universe of discourse, on Russell's conception of logic, is *the* universe, the actual universe, comprising everything that there is. To say this, however, is to reject the notion of a universe of discourse within which the range of the variables is confined.) Thus the propositions of logic are wholly general: they contain variables, and the variables range over everything. Russell's argument against the idea of (restricted) universes of discourse is revealing, and I shall examine it at some length.

The basic argument is one that Russell repeats several times in his work in the first decade of the century. One version goes as follows:

> it is quite essential that we should have some meaning of *always* which does not have to be expressed in a restrictive hypothesis as to x. For suppose 'always' means 'whenever x belongs to class i'. Then 'all men are mortal' becomes 'whenever x belongs to the class i, then, if x is a man, x is mortal; i.e. 'it is always true that if x belongs to the class i, then, if x is a man, x is mortal' . But what is our new *always* to mean? There seems no more reason for restricting x, in this new proposition, to the class i, than there was before for restricting it to the class *men*. Thus we shall be led on to a new wider universe, and so on *ad infinitum*....[26]

The point of this argument is that if we are to have a restricted universe of discourse (i.e. something other than simply *the* universe), then we must establish this universe of discourse by means of a statment which says what the variable is to range over. But in *that* statement there is no reason to suppose that we are using a restricted universe of discourse. Nor, indeed, can we be doing so unless there is yet another statement in which the restrictions on the first statement are made explicit; and then, of course, exactly the same point will apply to the second statement. Thus it is, on this view, possible to use restricted variables, but the use of such variables presupposes the use of unrestricted variables, which simply range over everything that there is. Thus we can conclude that it is the unrestricted variable which is fundamental. We can also conclude that only propositions using such variables should be thought of as propositions of logic, at least by Russell's standards of what is to count as logic. A proposition which uses a restricted variable is made within the context of some other statement which establishes the universe of discourse. Its meaning, and its truth if it is true, are thus conditional upon that other statement. To say this, however, is to say that it is not unconditionally true. By Russell's standards it thus has no right to be thought of as a proposition of logic; such propositions must be unconditionally true, and this in turn require that they contain all their conditions within themselves.

This argument of Russell's takes it for granted that the statement which establishes the universe of discourse is on the same level as the assertion which is made once the universe of discourse is established. Thus the former can be taken as antecedent and the latter as consequent in a single conditional statement. Russell, that is, assumes that all statements are on the same level; this contrasts with the model-theoretic view that we must distinguish some as object-language statements and some as metalanguage statements. Intrinsic to Russell's conception of the universality of logic is the denial of the metalinguistic perspective which is essential to the model-theoretic conception of logic. This makes a crucial difference to the way in which one thinks of logic. Consider, for example, the question of the completeness of a system of logic, which is so natural for us. This question relies upon the idea that we have, independently of the logical system, a criterion of what the system ought to be able to do, so that it relies upon the essentially meta-theoretic notion of an interpretation, and of truth in all interpretations. These meta-theoretic ideas, however, are foreign to Russell's conception of logic; the question of the completeness of a system in the modern sense simply could not arise for him.[27] Logic for him was not a system, or a formalism, which might or might not capture what we take to be the logically valid body of schemata; logic for him was, rather, the body of wholly general truths.

The fact that Russell does not see logic as something on which one can take a meta-theoretical perspective thus constitutes a crucial difference between his conception of logic and the model-theoretic one. Logic, for Russell, is a systematization of reasoning in general, of reasoning as such. If we have a correct systematization, it will comprehend all correct principles of reasoning. Given such a conception of logic there can be no external perspective. *Any* reasoning will, simply in virtue of being reasoning, fall within logic; any proposition that we might wish to advance is subject to the rules of logic. This is perhaps a natural, if naive, way of thinking about logic. In Russell's case, however, we can say more than this to explain why he should have held such a conception. Given the philosophical use that Russell wishes to make of logicism, no other conception is available to him. If logic is to be unconditionally and unrestrictedly true, in the sense that Russell must require it to be, then it must be universally applicable. This in turn implies that statements about logic must themselves fall within the scope of logic, so the notion of a meta-theoretical perspective falls away. If this were not so, if logic were thought of as set up within a more inclusive metalanguage, then by the standards which Russell and the idealists share, it would appear that logic is not absolutely and unconditionally true. Logic, on this modern picture, is not unrestricted, for it is set up in a more inclusive language which must fall outside its scope. Nor can the truth of logic, conceived of in this way, be thought of as absolute and unconditioned, for it is dependent upon the metalanguage within which it is set up. There is no reason to believe that Russell ever considered anything like the model-theoretic conception of logic – at least as a conception of *logic* – but if he had done so, the use he wishes to make of logicism would have given him reason to reject it in favour of the conception of logic as universal.

My claim here, of course, is a claim about Russell and about the argumentative stituation that he found himself in. Given that situation, I want to say, he would have found this view of logic necessary to sustain his attack on the idealists.[28] We can reinforce this idea by seeing that the conception of logic as universal, and some arguments for it, have analogues in certain idealist lines of thought. What I have particularly in mind here is the argument which the post-Kantian idealists used against the Kantian notion of the thing-in-itself. The Kantian thing-in-itself, as the idealists understood the notion, provides a contrast with all knowledge that is possible for us. What we know are appearances, which are conditioned by our forms of sensibility and by the (schematized) categories of the understanding. The thing-in-itself is, by definition, that which is independent of us and our cognitive faculties; it is therefore something of which we can have no knowledge. Kant's claim, of course, is that although we can – almost by definition – have no knowledge about things-in-themselves, we can nevertheless think of them, and may, indeed, have rational grounds for belief about them. He does, moreover, presuppose that we can at least know that there are things-in-themselves, even though we can have no (other) knowledge about them. These views of Kant's were widely attacked by his idealist successors; it is the basis of the attack that is of concern to us. If things-in-themselves are really wholly beyond the reach of our knowledge, how could we know even that there are such things? More broadly, since the categories of the understanding are surely conditions of *thought* as well as of knowledge, how can we even have thoughts or beliefs about things-in-themselves?[29] These objections are clearly expressed by McTaggart:

> The thing-in-itself as conceived by Kant, behind and apart from the phenomena which alone enter into experience, is a contradiction. We cannot, we are told, know what it is, but only that it is. But this is itself an important piece of knowledge relating to the thing. It involves a judgment, and a judgment involves categories, and we are thus forced to surrender the idea that we can be aware of anything which is not subject to the laws governing experience.[30]

McTaggart is attacking Kant for being insufficiently serious and literal about the idea of generality. If the categories really are the categories, then they must apply to everything. There is nothing that we can conceive of as being exempt from them, and no position from which we think without employing them. In particular, they must apply to the critical philosophy, and thereby to the very statement of the categories themselves.

Russell, I wish to suggest, might have accepted similar arguments against the idea of a perspective external to logic, from which we can establish logic. On

Russell's conception, logic applies to everything – including the very statements which establish logic. This point can be very clearly seen in certain passages in *Principles*. Russell denies that we can prove the independence of a truth-functional axiom by finding an interpretation for the negation of that axiom together with the other axioms. The general technique is clearly well-known to him, but he argues that it is not available in this specific case. If we deny an axiom of this sort, reasoning itself becomes impossible:

> it should be observed that the method of supposing an axiom false, and deducing the consequences of this assumption, which has been found admirable in such cases as the axiom of parallels, is here not universally available. For all our axioms are principles of deduction; and if they are true, the consequences which appear to follow from the employment of an opposite principle will not really follow, so that arguments from the supposition of the falsity of an axiom are here subject to special fallacies, *Principles*, (section 17).

This view, moreover, seems to be one that Russell held not only in *Principles* but also later, at the time when he was completing *Principia*.[31]

Russell's conception of logic as universal is connected with another crucial feature of his view of the subject. For Russell, logic has direct and immediate metaphysical or ontological implications. If the propositions of logic are indeed general truths, then certain things follow from them about what the world must be like. To put it another way: logic has metaphysical implications, which must be correct if logic is true. This is suggested by an important passage in the Preface of *Principles*, where Russell acknowledges his indebtedness, in metaphysical issues, to G. E. Moore:

> On fundamental questions of philosophy, my position, in all its chief features, is derived from Mr G. E. Moore. I have accepted from him the non-existential nature of propositions (except such as happen to assert existence) and their independence of any knowing mind; also the pluralism which regards the world, both that of existents and that of entities, as composed of an infinite number of mutually independent entities, with relations between them which are ultimate, and not reducible to adjectives of their terms or of the whole which these compose. Before learning these views from him, I found myself unable to construct any philosophy of arithmetic, whereas their acceptance brought about an immediate liberation from a large number of difficultes which I believe to be otherwise insuperable. The doctrines just mentioned are, in my opinion, quite indispensable to any even tolerably satisfactory philosophy of mathematics . . . Formally my premises are simply assumed; but the fact that they allow mathematics

to be true, which most current philosophies do not, is surely a powerful argument in their favour (*Principles*, p. xviii).

The 'philosophy of arithmetic' which Russell found himself able to construct after (but only after) accepting certain metaphysical views from Moore is of course logicism; logicism has these presuppositions because they are presuppositions of logic itself.

Russell, then, sees logic as requiring the existence of propositions as non-spatio-temporal and non-mental entities; the existence of infinitely many distinct and independent entities; and the existence of non-reducible relations holding among these entities. These claims are fundamental to a whole metaphysics, which is sketched by Russell and Moore in conscious opposition to idealism. Why should logic have any such implications? This question can be approached through the technical considerations that we have already touched on. The propositions of logic, for Russell, contain only variables and logical constants; and the variables range over everything in the (actual) universe. So the letter 'p' in (say) '$p \vee q$' and the letter 'F' in 'Fx' are treated as free variables, in the same way as 'x' is treated as a free variable in 'Fx'. This has the immediate implication that the propositions of logic assert not merely that there are objects over which the objectual variables range, but also that there are propositions over which the propositional variables range, and predicates or their analogues over which the predicate variables range. The truth-functional part of logic requires that each proposition be determinately true or false; if the truth of logic is to be absolute, objective and completely general, then all true propositions must be objectively and absolutely true. Russell, I think, took this to imply that propositions themselves must be non-mental entities, which exist independently of any mind.[32] The quantificational part of logic, similarly, requires that there are predicates which are determinately true or false of objects (and never both); if logic is to be wholly general, each predicate must be determinately true or false of *each* object. These implications are, as Russell fully realized, claims which would be rejected by his idealist opponents. His position is that the power of logic, and the insight that it affords us into mathematics, ought to persuade us to accept the metaphysical presuppositions on which logic rests.

Russell's position here is closely connected with another issue which I have mentioned in passing: the fact that for him logic is (what we would call) higher-order logic, and first-order logic not even a natural fragment of logic. To put the point a different way: for Russell, higher-order logic is implicit in first-order logic, and involves nothing new in principle. In its mature form, in *Principia Mathematica*[33] or in 'Mathematical Logic as Based on the Theory of Types', Russell's logic quantifies over propositional functions as well as over individuals. It is, of course, because of this fact that Russell is able to achieve the power of set theory without assuming that there are sets; it is also because of this fact that some commentators have claimed that Russell's mature logic is not more logic properly so-called than is set theory.[34] From the present perspective, the question is whether the universality of logic is compatible with, or even implies, the idea that we can, as a part of logic, quantify over propositional functions. Such quantification involves us in existential claims; do such claims introduce a new and special subject matter (the theory of propositional functions)? My claim is that from Russell's point of view the introduction of quantification over propositional functions into logic is, in itself, quite compatible with the universality of logic, and arguably even implied by it. The necessity for avoiding the paradoxes, however, leads as we shall see in section III, to steps which are not compatible with the universality of logic. My emphasis here, however, will be on the first and positive claim, that if one grant Russell the conception of logic as universal, and waive the issues raised by the paradoxes, then one can argue that the theory of propositional functions is indeed part of logic whereas set theory, say, is not. In the end Russell may be wrong to think that he has a coherent conception of logic according to which *Principia* is logic, for in the end the paradoxes cannot be ignored. But there is, I think, more to be said for this Russellian view than most of his critics acknowledge.

Let us begin by taking it for granted that what we call first-order logic is indeed logic. Presupposing the Russellian notion of a proposition, we can say that first-order logic requires that we analyse propositions in a certain way. We must show that there is something shared by the propositions that Caesar killed Caesar and that Brutus killed Brutus, which is not shared by the proposition that Caesar killed Brutus. This much is necessary to show e.g. that the first two imply '($\exists\, x$) (x killed x)' whereas the third does not (although all three imply '($\exists\, x$) ($\exists\, y$) (x killed y'). But what is this 'something shared'? Given the non-linguistic nature of a Russellian proposition, it can hardly be a merely linguistic entity (an open sentence); it is, rather, what Russell calls a propositional function.[35] What the first two propositions have in common, which the third does not, is that they are values or instances of the propositional function $\hat{x}$ *killed* $\hat{x}$. It is for these sorts of reasons, not simply because of a need for an analogue of set theory, that Russell's logic requires that there be propositional functions. The crucial point is that even doing first-order logic requires that we accept that there are propositional functions. The formal reflection of this fact is that the primitive proposition (axiom) of *Principia* which assures us of the existence of propositional functions is laid down as part of the transition from truth-functional logic to quantification theory. (The primitive proposition states: 'If, for some a, there is a proposition ϕa, then there is a [propositional] function $\phi\hat{x}$, and vice versa. Pp.' Since the transition from truth-functional logic to quantification theory is done twice over, in different ways, this proposition has two different numbers: *9.15 and *10.122.) The transition from first-order logic to higher-order logic in *12,

by contrast, requires no primitive propositions concerning the existence of propositional functions, and, indeed, no new primitive propositions at all. (The axiom
of reducibility does occur in *12 but, as we shall see in section III, it is not
required for Russell's higher-order logic; the need for it arises from the project
of reducing mathematics to this logic). Hence from Russell's point of view the
distinction between first-order and higher-order logic is of no particular significance. Since quantification over objects of any sort requires that we accept that
there are propositional functions, introducing quantification over these latter
entities does not, by Russell's lights, involve any new principle; higher-order
logic merely makes explicit what is in fact implicit in first-order logic.[36]

Let us contrast this Russellian view with that of a modern logician, who
thinks that the distinction between first-order and higher-order logic is an important distinction of principle. Quine sees the schemata of first-order logic as
made up of schematic predicate letters and quantified (or quantifiable) variables. The latter have true generality. When the schema is interpreted, they
become variables ranging over some specified domain of entities (the universe of discourse of the interpretation in question). The former, however, do
not have this sort of generality. When the schema is interpreted, each predicate
letter is replaced by a particular predicate. The generality which seems to attach
to a predicate letter, unlike that of a genuine variable, is simply a matter of the
multiplicity of possible interpretations which are available; within any given
interpretation, however, the predicate letter is simply interpreted as a particular
predicate, which is in turn thought of as a linguistic entity. Quine has emphasized the importance of the contrast between a schematic letter and a true variable in a passage which deprecates the use of the notation of higher-order logic,
rather than that of set theory:

> This notation has the fault ... of diverting attention from major cleavages
> between logic and set theory. It encourages us to see the general theory of
> classes and relations as mere prolongations of quantification theory, in
> which hitherto schematic letters are newly admitted into quantifiers and
> other positions that were hitherto reserved for 'x' and 'y' etc.... The exis-
> tence assumptions, vast though they are, can become strangely inconspi-
> cuous; they come to be implicit simply in the ordinary rule of substitution
> for predicate letters in quantification theory, once we have promoted
> these letters to the status of genuine quantifiable variables ... along with
> somewhat muffling the existence assumptions of the theory of types,
> [the notation] fostered a notion that quantification theory itself, in its
> 'F' and 'G', was already a theory about classes or attributes and relations.
> *It slighted the vital contrast between schematic letters and quantifiable
> variables.*[37]

The contrast which is crucial to Quine's position is, however, not available to Russell. The notion of a schematic letter is an essentially meta-theoretic one, which relies upon the idea that logic consists of schemata which are subject to interpretation. Given Russell's conception of logic as universal, and as consisting of propositions which have a meaning and a truth-value just as they stand, the notion can make no sense to him. To understand Russell's position we therefore have to invert all of Quine's points. Given Russell's conception of logic, higher-order quantification theory – and thus the Russellian analogue of set theory – really *is* a mere prolongation of quantification theory, and the existence assumptions of this theory really *are* implicit in the ordinary rules for quantification theory. Quine's remarks occur in the context of a discussion of Russell's use, in *Principia* and elsewhere, of propositional functions rather than classes as fundamental entities. Quine's position is that it would be on every score preferable to assume classes or sets as fundamental, rather than to define them in terms of propositional functions. From the perspective afforded by a Russellian conception of logic, however, Quine's implicit attack on Russell is misdirected. Given this conception, the ontology of propositional functions (or at least of some entities corresponding to predicate variables) really is implicit in ordinary quantification theory and, indeed, in all ordinary propositions. The ontological assumptions here may indeed be vast, but they are not special assumptions about some special subject matter, as the assumption of the existence of classes would be. This, from a Russellian point of view, provides a reason to think that the theory of propositional functions is logic, as the theory of classes would not be.

This contrast between Russell and Quine enables us to see more clearly what is involved in Russell's conception of logic. Russell's conception of logic cannot be characterized simply in terms of the rejection of what I have called the model-theoretic conception of logic, for Quine's position does not depend upon his holding that conception. Quine, indeed, does not appear to hold this conception; he does not, that is to say, accept that logic consists of a formalism which is subject to various interpretations.[38] One salient feature of Russell's conception of logic is thus not merely its rejection of the view of logic as formalism and interpretation, but its insistence upon the unconditional and presuppositionless character of logic. For Russell, anything whose existence must be presupposed in order to establish or state logic is itself a part of logic. If logic demands that there be propositions, or relations, then as a matter of logic there are; so also for propositional functions.[39] In discussing Russell's use of logicism against idealism we saw something of the basis for this idea of presuppositionlessness. It is, perhaps, a matter of indifference whether one thinks of this as intrinsic to the universalist conception of logic, or as merely a feature of Russell's universal conception of logic. A second salient feature of Russell's conception of logic is that he takes it for granted that our concern is not with language. The 'entities corresponding to predicate variables', on Russell's account, are not linguistic entities. This assumption stems form Russell's general attitude that it is propositions which are of real concern, and that the study of language (as distinct from the propositions which it expresses) is of no intrinsic philosophical significance. (This attitude is seen most clearly in *Principles*. It is somewhat modified by the rejection of the *Principles* theory of denoting, which leads to the view that certain expressions must be understood as incomplete *symbols*; and by the theory of types, according to which certain *symbols* lack significance. Even in *Principia*, however, this attitude survives. It is manifest in the explicitness and emphasis with which Russell says he is talking about symbols when he is, as if he sees talking about symbols as an odd thing to do. See e.g. vol. I, pp. 11, 48 n. and 66–7.) This Russellian attitude is connected with a further feature of his early logic, to which I now turn.

Logic, for Russell, is not a subject to be studied syntactically. Russell, indeed, shows no sign of having a conception of syntax as a tool which might be used for this task. There is, of course, a contrast here with what I have called the model-theoretic conception of logic. According to that conception, logic consists of a formalism subject to various interpretations, and a formalism is an object defined and studied by syntactic means. One does not, however, have to hold the model-theoretic conception of logic in order to think that logic can be studied syntactically, Even on something like a universalist conception, one might think that at any rate certain significant fragments of logic could be set up and studied by syntactic means, and results proved which would show something about logic in the universal sense. This suggests that the contrast between the universalist conception of logic and the model-theoretic conception is too crude. Many philosophers, I suspect, hold both and are more or less conscious of the differences and the connections between them. Certainly it seems reasonable to attribute something like this two-fold attitude to Quine. The use of syntactic methods in the way that I have suggested appears, moreover, seems to be compatible with the view that in the fundamental sense logic is universal and presuppositionless. A philosopher who comes close to exemplifying this two-fold approach is Frege, and at this point it will be helpful briefly to compare Frege's view of logic with that of Russell.

Much of what I have said of Russell's conception of logic as universal could also, I think, be said of Frege's conception of logic (although the motivation of Frege's logicism is, as I have already remarked, quite different from Russell's). What I have said of Russell's propositional functions, for example, could equally well be said of Fregean *Begriffe*. (There is of course a difference arising from the presence, within Frege's system, of a sharp distinction between *Begriffe* and *Gegenstände*. This has the consequence that no analogue of set theory, and hence also no danger of paradox, arises for Frege until we add to his system the statement that to every *Begriff* there is a corresponding *Gegenstand* – axiom V of *Grundgesetze*. For Russell, by contrast, no such axiom is necessary.) There is, however, one general difference between Russell's conception of logic and

Frege's. Russell's conception of logic is based on a metaphysical view which could be, and to some extent was, articulated quite independently of logic. Russell, as we have seen, held himself to be indebted to Moore for the metaphysics of propositions and their constituents, of being and truth. This metaphysics is independent of the logic which Russell erected upon it (which is not to say that it has any plausibility when considered apart from Russell's logic). For Russell, then, the metaphysics was independent of and prior to the logic. For Frege, at least according to the interpretation that I find most compelling,[40] the opposite is true. For Frege, logic, in the sense of the inferences that we do in fact acknowledge as correct, is primary; metaphysics is secondary, and articulated in terms which presuppose logic.

What is the significance of this difference for the conceptions of logic held by Frege and by Russell? Since Frege took logic, the body of correct inferences, as prior to metaphysics, he was bound to be concerned to delimit this body in terms which made no metaphysical presuppositions. It is for these reasons, I think, that Frege gives something very like a modern syntactic account of logic. Frege's standards of formal rigour approach those of the more rigorous of modern logicians. For this reason the notion of a formal system seems to be at least implicit in Frege's work. (If one takes this notion to imply a meta-theoretic perspective, then of course Frege does not have it. His concern with rigour was an internal concern, an object-language concern: he wanted to do deductions and assure himself that they were gap-free.) For these reasons too it is easy to suppose that Frege holds something like the modern conception of logic, implying at least the possibility of a meta-theoretic approach. This, I think, is a mistake. Frege's use of syntax has a different origin from that of a modern logician; although his work seems to exhibit similar standards of rigour, the reason for the rigour is different.

To look at Russell's work with the expectation of finding anything like syntactic rigour, however, is to be disappointed. As Gödel has said of *Principia*:

> It is to be regretted that this first comprehensive and thoroughgoing presentation of mathematical logic . . . is so greatly lacking in formal precision in the foundations . . . that it presents [*sic*] in this respect a considerable step backwards as compared with Frege. What is missing, above all, is a precise statement of the syntax of the formalism. Syntactical considerations are omitted even in cases where they are necessary for the cogency of the proofs, in particular in connection with the 'incomplete symbols'.[41]

Our earlier discussions suggest that Russell's lack of concern with syntactic rigour is not a matter of carelessness. Why should Russell have any concern with syntax? Not in order to define an uninterpreted formalism which can then be subject to various interpretations, or to be able to treat a system of logic meta-theoretically, as itself the object of mathematical study. Both of these reasons are ruled out, for Russell, by his lack of a genuinely meta-theoretical perspective. Nor, on the other hand, does Russell have a reason of Frege's sort. Russell's philosophical-logical views do not need to be based on a neutral, and therefore syntactic, notion of correct logical inference, for Russell's metaphysics is independent of logic and therefore available for use in defining the notion of logic. The definition is given in terms of the notion of a proposition, of the constituents of a proposition, and of truth. These notions are, as we have already seen, ones to which we have direct and immediate access, through a non-sensuous analogue of perception. Thus there is no need for a a syntactic approach, from Russell's point of view. This is not to say that anything in Russell's conception of logic in fact rules out such an approach, though this conception of logic does show something about the significance of the results which can be obtained in this way. What it does indicate is that the syntactic approach is not a natural one for someone with Russell's conception of logic; there is no particular reason why it should have occurred to Russell. Nor, indeed, do I think that it did. From Russell's point of view, therefore, there is no reason that the proofs of *Principia* should obey standards of rigour at all different from those of any ordinary working mathematician. By these standards the proofs of *Principia* can be faulted, but the faults are confined. The view of *Principia* as pervasively lacking in rigour stems from the assumption that the appropriate standards of rigour are syntactic. But this is not the authors' view of the matter – otherwise it would be wholly inexplicable that they should claim that their proofs are in fact unusually rigorous.[42] The fact that Whitehead and Russell employ standards of rigour which are not those of either Frege or of the modern logician is not something that we have to accept as inexplicable (or explicable only by the dubious supposition of Russell's carelessness). Once we have a correct understanding of Russell's conception of logic we shall also understand what his standards of rigour are, and why they are not those of Frege, or of the modern logician.

What I have said above about Russell's standards of rigour in logic can, I think, be generalized. Much of what Russell says about logic differs from what a modern logician would say. But we do Russell an injustice, and impede our own understanding, if we do not see that these differences are explicable in terms of a coherent (if perhaps ultimately untenable) conception of logic which is quite different from the modern one. This conception of logic, in turn, is directly connected with the philosophical motivation of Russell's logicism. When we see why logicism mattered so much to Russell, we see also that his conception of logic *must* have been quite different from ours.

III

Although I have, in the preceding sections, drawn to some extent on *Principia Mathematica*, what I have said of Russell's conception of logic, and especially of the motivation of his logicism, is clearly more inspired by *Principles* than by *Principia*. How does the picture change when we focus on the later work? One important general shift is that the anti-idealist motivation ceases to play any overt role. Russell was as much of an anti-idealist in 1910 as in 1902, but the issue no longer seems urgent to him; he looks on that battle as long since won. A second change is philosophically more interesting. In *Principia* Russell expounds, and relies upon, the theory of types; this alters the picture suggested by *Principles* in ways that are extremely complex. In what follows I shall simply attempt to indicate some of the changes most relevant to the present perspective.

The theory of types has two effects which are worth distinguishing. First, it threatens the conception of logic that I have attributed to Russell; here the crucial facts are that Russell's logic after 1907 has to contain explicit type restrictions, and the axiom of reducibility. Second, it makes it dubious, at best, whether what Russell attempts to reduce to logic is indeed mathematics; here the chief difficulty is the necessity, in *Principia*, for what Russell calls (misleadingly, as we shall see) the axiom of infinity and the axiom of choice (I shall largely confine my discussion to the former.)[43]

Let me begin with the axiom of reducibility. There is a clear contrast here between *Principles* and *Principia*; in the earlier work no such axiom is mentioned. In *Principles* there is no need for the axiom of reducibility or any analogue of it. The axiom of reducibility is required in *Principia* because of two features of that work, which conflict if the axiom is not assumed. First, propositional functions are employed to do the work of classes, whose existence need not be presupposed (in this respect *Principia* is unlike *Principles*). Second, to avoid the threat of paradox, there are complex distinctions of category among propositional functions; in particular, these distinctions prevent us from generalizing over all the propositional functions which are true or false of a given entity. The two features threaten to conflict because if propositional functions are to play the role of classes, it is essential that we be able to generalize over all propositional functions which are true or false of a given entity; otherwise the reduction of mathematics to logic (including the theory of propositional functions) becomes quite impossible. The axiom of reducibility removes this difficulty, more or less by stipulation. The crucial consequence of the axiom is that distinctions of ontological category among propositional functions true or false of a given object – i.e. distinctions of order – can be ignored for mathematical purposes.[44] The axiom achieves this effect by stipulating that for every propositional function, of whatever order, there is a *co-extensive* propositional function of the lowest order.[45] Thus in mathematics, where only the extensions of propositional functions concern us, we can achieve the effect of generalizing over all propositional functions true or false of a given object simply by generalizing over those of the lowest order. By this method, the needs of mathematics are reconciled with Russell's type theory.

If *Principia* is to count as a reduction of mathematics to *logic* then the axiom of reducibility must, of course, be a logical truth. It is, however, very far from clear that counting this axiom as logically true is consistent with the conception of logic that I have attributed to Russell. In one sense the axiom is so consistent: it can be stated using only logical expressions. It is, however, very hard to see how the sort of rationale that I gave for thinking that the theory of propositional functions is part of logic could be extended to show that this axiom is a truth of logic. That rationale was, roughly, that the assumption that there are propositional functions is required to make sense of logical relations in which any proposition stands, whatever its subject matter; thus this assumption is required not to explain some special class of statements – those about classes, say – but to explain the possibility of propositions and their logical relations in general, regardless of their subject matter. Clearly, however, no such rationale will justify the idea that the axiom of reducibility is a truth of logic. The truth of the axiom is not required to explain the possibility of propositions, and of logical relations between propositions, of all kinds, without regard to subject matter. On the contrary: the existence assumption embodied in the axiom is clearly required only for the special purposes of mathematics and the theory of classes. Counting the axiom of reducibility as part of logic thus seems quite inconsistent with the conception of logic that I have attributed to Russell.

A similar difficulty arises in rather a different way from the fact that *Principia* contains, and must contain, explicit statements of type restrictions. The difficulty here does not arise from the mere fact that there are type restrictions. I have suggested that it is a truth of logic (on the Russellian conception) that there are propositional functions; it is also a truth of logic that no contradiction is true. If propositional functions must, to avoid contradiction, be subject to type restrictions, then it must also be true (and presumably also a truth of logic) that there are type distinctions among propositional functions. The difficulty arises not from the mere fact that there are type distinctions; it arises from the fact that these distinctions have to be stated within *Principia*. The crucial fact here is that according to the conception of logic which I have attributed to Russell there can be no genuine meta-perspective on logic: logic applies to every statement, and thus also to statements which are intended to limit the scope of the variable used in other statements.

We saw this point stated explicitly in 'Mathematical Logic as Based on the Theory of Types' (see p. 147, above). The point recurs in the introduction to *Principia*, where Russell again argues that the unrestricted variable is fundamental, but goes on to qualify the claim:

We shall find that the unrestricted variable is still subject to limitations imposed by the manner of its occurrence, i.e. things which can be said significantly concerning a proposition cannot be said concerning a class or relation, and so on. But the limitations to which the unrestricted variable is subject do not need to be explicitly indicated, since they are the limits of significance of the statement in which the variable occurs, and are therefore intrinsically determined by this statement (*Principia*, p. 4).

The picture that this suggests is that the limitations imposed by type theory do not need to be stated but will, in a later terminology, make themselves manifest. Certainly this is what *Principia* requires, for statements of the limitations imposed by restrictions of type are, as we shall see, liable to be in violation of type theory.[46] But the expectations aroused by this statement are not fulfilled. *Principia* does contain statements of type restrictions. These statements, moreover, do not occur merely in the expository prose, which has perhaps a purely heuristic function. On the contrary: the numbered sentences which are the heart of *Principia* themselves contain notions which are required to set up type theory, and which threaten to violate it. Thus *9.131 is a definition of 'being the same type as'; and the primitive proposition (axiom) *9.14 makes essential use of the notion, asserting 'If "ϕx" is significant, and if a is of the same type as x, "ϕa" is significant, and vice versa.' (for reasons already noted, p. 152, above, the proposition stated in *9.14 occurs again, with the number 10.121).

It is important to see clearly exactly why a statement establishing type theory – indeed the very notion 'is of the same type as' – violates type restrictions. If the clause 'a is of the same type as x' is not to be wholly otiose (and in fact it is not), then it must sometimes be true and sometimes be false. That is, there must be an object, call it b, of which it makes sense to say that it is of the same type as some given object a, but where this is not true; and there must be another object, c, which is of the same type as a, and where this can also be said. But then there is one propositional function, that expressed by 'x is of the same type as a' which can be significantly applied both to b and to c (truly in one case, falsely in the other). But by a crucial tenet of type theory itself (expressed in the 'vice versa' clause of *9.14) it ought to follow from this that b and c are of the same type. Since 'is of the same type as' is transitive, this conclusion is directly contrary to the initial assumption that b is different in type from a but that c is of the same type as a.

The difficulty here clearly arises from the attempt to state type theory within type theory. The argument above constitutes a *reductio ad absurdum* of the idea that we can treat 'is of the same type as' as expressing a propositional function which must itself be subject to the restrictions of type theory. Yet the universality of logic, as I have articulated it, seems to demand that *every* proposition fall within the scope of logic, and that every propositional function be subject to type theory. Once again, the demands of type theory seem to be inconsistent with the conception of logic that I have attributed to Russell. On this issue there is a clear contrast between Russell's conception of logic and the model-theoretic conception. On the latter conception we have available a metalanguage in which we can state type distinctions for the object language; the question whether our statements in the metalanguage violate the type distinctions of the object language simply does not arise. It is also worth noting that the difficulty that I raised for Russell might be resolved by combining the universalist conception of logic with a syntactic approach to type theory, so that type restrictions would not state anything about (non-linguistic) entities, but would simply lay down conditions of well-formedness on combinations of symbols. I shall not, however, investigate this possibility here.[47]

I turn now to the issues raised by the so-called axiom of infinity. Again, it is worth noting that no such axiom is mentioned in *Principles*. The main body of that work advances a view which lacks any distinctions of logical category. It is, according to that view, thus provable that there are infinitely many entities: '. . . if n be any number, the number of numbers from 0 up to and including n is $n + 1$, whence it follows that n is not the number of numbers. Again, it may be proved directly, by the correlation of whole and part, that the number of propositions or concepts is infinite.' (section 339). The first of these arguments is directly analogous to that used by Frege to show that his definition of natural number ensures that there are infinitely many natural numbers.[48] The correctness of this argument in Frege's logic, however, is directly connected with those features of that logic which make it contradictory. So also in the case of Russell's *Principles*. One way to make this point is to say that it is only because of the lack, in the view conveyed in most of *Principles*, of any type distinctions that the argument works; once type distinctions are introduced to avoid paradox, the argument fails. Unlike Frege, Russell is aware of the need for type distinctions, or some analogous way of avoiding the paradox. He is, however, not satisfied by the systems of types that he considers, and most of *Principles* proceeds as if Russell had never discovered the paradox. Certainly this is true of the present point. The issue of the axiom of infinity does not arise in *Principles* because Russell believes – or is willing to write as if he believes – that the infinitude of entities is provable by the general methods of logic.

In *Principia*, by contrast, type theory makes it impossible to prove that there are any infinite classes unless there are infinitely many *individuals*. This matter, Russell insists, cannot be settled by logic: 'This assumption [the axiom of infinity] . . . will be adduced as a hypothesis whenever it is relevant. It seems plain that there is nothing in logic to necessitate its truth or falsehood, and that it can only be legitimately believed or disbelieved on empirical grounds.' (*Principia*, vol. II, p. 183). Russell does not, however, assume the infinitude of individuals as an axiom (although he does use the expression 'the axiom of infinity'). He says, rather, that both this so-called axiom and the axiom of choice are to be taken 'as hypotheses', i.e. as antecedents to conditionals, wherever they are needed (besides the passage from *Principia* vol. II, p. 183, quoted above, see also vol. I, p. 482).

Russell's attitude towards the axiom of infinity does not threaten the conception of logic that I have attributed to him. It does, however, threaten the fundamental project of logicism: it might be said that *Principia* represents not so much the culmination of Russell's logicism as Russell's abandonment of logicism. It is, however, a subtle question, whether a form of (pseudo) logicism that is forced to take the axiom of infinity as an extra-logical assumption can play the philosophical role that I claimed Russell's early logicism played. One of the arguments that I attributed to Russell was simply that mathematics is an example of a body of absolute truth, whose truth was in no way dependent upon (or conditioned by) the spatio-temporal; this example undermines a crucial idealist doctrine. Stated like this, the argument no longer holds. Mathematics will no longer stand as an undeniable example of knowledge which is absolute, valid beyond the realm of the spatio-temporal, and non-trivial (i.e. obviously genuine knowledge). Mathematics, i.e. logic plus the axiom of infinity, is presumably dependent upon whatever evidence we may have for there being an infinitude of individuals, and individuals presumably exist in space and time (hence the statement in the passage quoted above that the infinitude of individuals is an empirical matter). It is, however, possible that the basic point of Russell's claim would still hold. Logic (not including the axiom of infinity) is not shown by the need for the axiom of infinity to be other than wholly general and absolutely true. It is perhaps less obvious than before that logic is an example of genuine knowledge, rather than being analytic in Kant's sense, but the point is at least arguable. It is thus possible that logic, including the theory of propositional functions but excluding the axiom of infinity, could play the anti-idealist role for which Russell originally cast mathematics. The fate of the other argument that I attributed to Russell is equally unclear. This argument had to do with the crucial role of mathematics in showing that consistent theories of space and time are available. Now if it were thought that the consistency of the infinite, and indeed the transfinite, depended simply upon the fact that their existence is a truth of logic, then clearly the need for an extra-logical assumption of infinity would be fatal. Or again, it might be thought that the crucial question posed by the need for an extra-logical assumption of the infinite is the consistency of this assumption (given the truths of logic); to this question Russell clearly has no answer. An interpretation somewhat more sympathetic to Russell, however, might claim that the power of his position comes from the fact that he is able to show that particular arguments purporting to show the inconsistency of the infinite are one and all erroneous. This fact continues to hold. The logic of *Principia*, though it cannot prove that there are infinitely many entities, can define the notion of the infinite; the understanding embodied in this definition is sufficient to show that traditional philosophical arguments against the infinite are misconceived.

The details of the impact of type theory upon Russell's conception of logic and of logicism are very complex. But even from the outline given above it is clear that the picture which I sketched of the motivation of Russell's logic and of the Russellian conception of logic is seriously threatened by the introduction of type theory. Should we infer from this that Russell's views on these matters shift between *Principles* and *Principia*? Is it incorrect to attribute the earlier picture to Russell at the time of *Principia*? I suggest that it is wrong in principle to insist that there must be a definite answer to a question of this sort. In the case of this particular question I suspect that no clear-cut answer would emerge, even if all the facts were known. The most significant facts in this case are, first, as we have seen, that the development of type theory does undermine Russell's earlier conception of logic and his philosophical claims for logicism; second, he does at times show at least some awareness of this; third, within the relevant period Russell does not find any other conception of logic, or any other view of the significance of logicism, which is remotely plausible. This third fact is in some ways the most significant, for it means that Russell continues, at least when his attention is not fully focused on the issue, to talk as if he still held the old conception of logic, and the old view of logicism. Insofar as any general philosophical conception of logic influences him at this time it is this one. He does not really discard the old picture, for he has nothing with which to replace it; on the other hand, he cannot continue to hold this picture with a clear conscience.

One way of thinking about this situation is as an example of what is, I think, a more general truth. When philosophy takes on a technical guise there is always the danger that the technical endeavour will take on a life of its own. One may become caught up in the technical endeavour, and cease to think very hard about whether it will still serve the purposes that originally motivated it, or any others. When the resulting mathematical achievement is *Principia Mathematica*, the neglect of philosophy may be pardonable, even laudable; commentators, however, should be wary of assuming that so great an achievement, simply in virtue of its magnitude, *must* have a philosophical point. It is entirely possible that changes in the enterprise, perhaps dictated by technical needs, cause it to lose contact with the considerations that gave it its original point. Something like this, I think, happened to Russell's logicism.

One piece of evidence in favour of the general reading that I am advancing is that Russell never attempts, in *Principia*, to give an account of logic, even when such an account seems to be called for. Thus his statement of the conditions that a logical system must satisfy, the analogues of completeness and consistency, reads like this:

The proof of a logical system is its adequacy and its coherence. that is: (1) the system must embrace among its deductions *all those propositions which we believe to be true and capable of deduction from logical premises alone* . . . and (2) the system must lead to no contradictions (*Principia*, pp. 12–13, my italics; cf. also pp. v, 59–60).

The first of these two criteria is the analogue of completeness: our system of logic must be powerful enough. But Russell has no characterization of what *powerful enough* comes to, because he has no way of characterizing logic (which the system is presumably trying to capture). He cannot characterize it semantically, as suggested by the model-theoretic conception, for this conception is still wholly alien to this thought. Yet neither can he characterize it in terms of the universalist conception, for these terms do not fit the type-theoretic system of *Principia*. Instead he offers a statement of what a system of logic ought to be able to prove which is completely without content; as an account of logic it would be absurd. Taken quite literally it makes any (axiomatizable) theory at all reducible to logic, provided we can persuade ourselves to believe that that theory is reducible to logic or that its axioms are principles of logic; given our belief, logic just expands (so to speak) to embrace the relevant axioms. But what, then, is the content of the *belief* that such a theory is reducible to logic? What is it that we are trying to persuade ourselves to believe? Russell, so determinedly anti-psychologistic, would hardly advance a view according to which the scope of logic is dependent upon the beliefs which we have; what the passage indicates, I think, is that he simply has no account of logic which he can accept.[49] He realizes, more or less clearly, that his previous view of logic will not do, and so realizes that some alternative account is required, but he simply has no coherent alternative to offer.

A second piece of evidence for the reading that I am advancing is the eagerness with which Russell later adopts a new view of logic – a view which he admittedly does not fully understand at the time. In the final chapter of his *Introduction to Mathematical Philosophy*,[50] written in 1918, Russell discusses the nature of logic (and thus, given logicism, of mathematics) as follows:

> All the propositions of logic have a characteristic which used to be expressed by saying that they were analytic, or that their contradictories were self-contradictory. This mode of statement, however, is not satisfactory . . . Nevertheless, the characteristic of logical propositions that we are in search of is the one which was felt, and intended to be defined, by those who said that it consisted in deducibility from the law of contradiction. This characteristic, which, for the moment, we may call tautology . . . (*Introduction to Mathematical Philosophy*, p. 203).

Russell eagerly claims that logic consists of tautologies (he is influenced in this by his earlier conversations with Wittgenstein; at the time he wrote this, however, he had not read the *Tractatus Logico-Philosophicus*.) He insists upon this in spite of the fact that, as he says, he does not know how to define 'tautology' (p. 205). It ought to be a puzzle to us that so great a thinker as Russell can insist, in diametrical opposition to his earlier views, that logic has an essential characteristic which he cannot define, and cannot explain in a fashion which is at all illuminating.

Without a clear understanding of the notion of tautology, how could he possibly have reason to believe that logic consists of tautologies? Part of the answer to this puzzle no doubt lies in the impact that Wittgenstein's personality had on Russell before the First World War, an impact that was evidently not dependent upon Russell's understanding of Wittgenstein's views. But a crucial part of the answer also must be Russell's recognition that his thought about the nature of logic was bankrupt: his old view will no longer work, he has nothing to take its place, and yet his work crucially depends on logic having some kind of special philosophical status. Under these circumstances he clutches at the word 'tautology', hoping, perhaps, that Wittgenstein will emerge from the trenches with a definition of the word which will enable it to play the role that Russell needs it for.

My conclusion, then, is not straightforward. If one focuses on *The Principles of Mathematics* a rather clear picture emerges of Russell's conception of logic and of the general philosophical motivation of Russell's logicism; the two are connected in complex ways which I have tried to indicate. This clear picture is, however, only possible because the main doctrines of *Principles* ignore the difficulties posed by Russell's paradox and related paradoxes. No doubt Russell thought that he would find a solution to the paradoxes which did not threaten anything which he took to be philosophically fundamental. This hope, however, was misplaced; the theory of types, I have argued, *does* undermine philosophically crucial aspects of Russell's early conception of logic. The magnificent structure of *Principia* is thus left without a clear and coherent philosophical motivation.[51]

Notes

1 Given the length of Russell's active philosophical life, and the multiplicity of positions that he held, few claims about his views can be made without qualification as to time. I mean primarily his views in the first decade of this century, when he did all of his serious work on logicism – *The Principles of Mathematics*, 'Mathematical Logic as Based on the Theory of Types' and the *Principia* itself.

2 Cambridge University Press: 1903; 2nd edn, George Allen and Unwin, London: 1937. Abbreviated in the text simply as *Principles*.

3 George Allen and Unwin, London: 1959, pp. 74–5.

4 'My Mental Development', in *The Philosophy of Bertrand Russell*, ed. P. A. Schilpp (Evanston, Illinois: 1944), p. 13.

5 The contrast between Kant and Russell here is complex; their agreement on the synthetic status of mathematics masks two points of disagreement (as well as a more basic conflict over the significance of the distinction between the analytic and the synthetic, which I shall discuss later). Kant holds that being analytic and being independent of space and time are co-extensive properties of judgements (see especially *Critique of Pure Reason*, A 158 = B 197, where Kant makes it clear that all synthetic judgements are dependent on intuition and thus on space and time; analytic

judgements, by contrast, are repeatedly said to be dependent only on concepts, and thus not on intuition). Logic, for Kant, has these two properties: it is independent of space and time and it is analytic. For Kant, however, the status of logic is different from that of mathematics, which lacks both properties. Russell, by contrast, argues that logic and mathematics have the same status. Both, he insists, are independent of space and time. For Russell, however, being independent of space and time is not co-extensive with being analytic; he denies that either logic or mathematics has this latter property.

6   Russell's general view of Kant is largely endorsed by Michael Friedman in his 'Kant's Theory of Geometry', (*Philosophical Review*, vol. XCIV, no. 4, October 1985, pp. 455–506). Friedman's work is, however, far more sympathetic to Kant than is Russell's.

7   I say 'Russell's development' because, in spite of what Russell says in the passage quoted, this notion is not to be found in any explicit form in Peano's work. On the other hand, Russell's treatment is itself less explicit than that of Frege, but I assume that it is independent of the latter. The best source for Russell's development of (a theory equivalent to) quantification theory is 'The Logic of Relations', first published in French in Peano's journal, *Rivista di Mathematica*, vol. VII (Turin, 1900–1), pp. 115–48; reprinted in *Logic and Knowledge*, ed. R. C. Marsh (George Allen and Unwin, London: 1956), pp. 3–38.

8   Since our concern is with the post-Kantian idealists, as well as with Kant, it is important to note that the use of the infinitesimal in mathematics was explicitly discussed by Hegel, who found it to be contradictory. See especially *Hegel's Science of Logic* (George Allen and Unwin, London: 1969), which is a translation by A. V. Miller of Hegel's *Wissenschaft der Logik*, section 2, ch. 2, C.

9   The case of geometry deserves special mention. The argument that geometry is logic requires the distinction between pure geometry and applied geometry: the former is simply a branch of mathematics, whereas the latter, for Russell, is part of physics (roughly, it tells you which geometry in the first sense is applicable to the real world). No such distinction was accepted by Kant, for example: his view is that there is only one sense of geometry, and that it gives knowledge of the real (physical) world.

     The issue of geometry makes it clear that Russell's logicism is not exactly the same as Frege's. Frege was also willing to accept a version of Kant's claim that geometry depends upon the forms of our intuition. This difference in content stems in part from a difference in philosophical context and motive. Frege was not concerned with post-Kantian idealism; his target was naturalism and psychologism. See Hans D. Sluga, *Gottlob Frege* (Routledge and Kegan Paul, London: 1980), especially ch. I.

10   Hegel, ibid., p. 190; cf. also pp. 197–8.

11   The context of this quotation is as follows: 'Zeno's distinctive characteristic is the dialectic. He is the master of the Eleatic school, in which pure thought comes into its own in the movement of the concept in itself, and in the pure spirit of inquiry; he is the originator of the dialectic.' Hegel, *Vorlesungen uber die Geschichte der Philosophie*) (*Lectures on the History of Philosophy*), vol. I (p. 295 of the edn by Suhrkampf Verlag, Frankfurt am Maine: 1971; the translation is my own).

12   *An Essay on the Foundations of Geometry*, Cambridge University Press: 1897, p. 191. It is worth noting that Russell sees nothing new in the idea that there are contra-

dictions in space; it is, he says 'an ancient theme – as ancient, in fact, as Zeno's refutation of motion' (p. 188). One of Russell's arguments (on pp. 189–90) closely resembles F. H. Bradley's discussion on pp. 31–2 of *Appearance and Reality* (2nd edn, Oxford University Press: 1897; ninth impression, 1930), and has more distant affinities with Zeno's argument and with Kant's second antinomy.

13 Besides *Foundations of Geometry*, see also 'On The Idea of a Dialectic of the Sciences' notes of Russell's dated 1 January, 1898. These were not published at the time, but are in *My Philosophical Development* (see n. 3), pp. 43–53.

14 Russell puts forward this claim in opposition to Kant. The idea that it conflicts with Kant's view relies, as I have indicated, upon an interpretation of Kant which I do not wish to endorse. The alternative interpretation sees Kant as claiming that the mathematical theories of space and time are, on their own terms, consistent, and that inconsistency arises only from the metaphysical interpretation given to these theories. The important point here, however, is *Russell's* interpretation of Kant.

15 At this point we can see that it is in fact crucial to Russell's purposes that mathematics be genuine knowledge; this is one of the reasons that he insists that mathematics and logic are both synthetic in character. Kant holds logic to be analytic, and not genuine knowledge; he asserts, for example, 'no one can venture with the help of logic alone to judge regarding objects, or to make any assertion' (*Critique of Pure Reason*, A 60B 85). Since Kant holds logic to apply beyond the spatio-temporal, he might be thought to hold it to be (in his sense) 'unconditioned' (as Parsons points out, the applicability of logic to things-in-themselves is implicit in Kant's view that we can *think* of things-in-themselves; see 'Kant's philosophy of arithmetic', reprinted in *Mathematics in Philosophy*, Cornell University Press, Ithaca, New York: 1983, pp. 115–19). But since logic is analytic, it is not unconditioned *knowledge*, and so not a counter-example to his general position.

16 Russell sometimes offers a different sort of argument, which I do not emphasize, against Kant's view of mathematics. If mathematics depends upon the forms of our intuition, and this is a psychological feature of the human mind, then it looks as if mathematics is dependent upon psychology. Russell does not always clearly distinguish this anti-psychologistic argument from his anti-idealist arguments. See e.g. *Principles*, section 430.

17 At this point I am of course simplifying a very complex story. In particular, the view of Carnap in *Logical Syntax of Language* (Routledge and Kegan Paul, London: 1937) does not depend on logicism in anything like the sense which I am presupposing. See Michael Friedman, 'Logical truth and analyticity in Carnap's *Logical Syntax of Language*, in eds W. Aspray and P. Kitcher, *Essays in the History and Philosophy of Mathematics* (University of Minnesota Press: 1987).

18 Carnap's 'Autobiography', in *The Philosophy of Rudolf Carnap*, ed. P. A. Schilpp (La Salle, Illinois: 1963), pp. 46–7:

> Wittgenstein formulated ... [the view] that all logical truths are tautological, that is, that they hold necessarily in every possible case, therefore do not exclude any case, and do not say anything about the facts of the world ... [T]o the members of the Circle, there did not seem to be a fundamental difference between elementary logic and higher logic, including mathematics. Thus we

arrived at the conception that all valid statements of mathematics are analytic in
the specific sense that they hold in all possible cases and therefore do not have
any factual content.

What was important in this conception from our point of view was the fact that
it became possible for the first time to combine the basic tenet of empiricism
with a satisfactory explanation of logic and mathematics.

19 Section VI of the introduction to the *Critique of Pure Reason*. This section was added
    in the second or 'B' ed of the Critique, but contains nothing that is not consistent
    with the 1st edn text; the passage is at B 19.

20 See e.g. *Principles*, 434. This view was one which Russell held consistently through-
    out the period leading up to *Principia* (and, in fact, until he came under the influence
    of Wittgenstein's new views on the status of logic; see pp. 164–5, below). For a later
    reference, see *The Problems of Philosophy* (Williams and Norgate, London: 1912; new
    edn, Oxford University Press: 1946), pp. 79, 83–4. In the former of these passages,
    Russell makes clear his view that deduction can give *new* knowledge, i.e. knowledge
    not contained in the premises.

21 The notion of analyticity is not discussed at all in *Principles*, which is one sign of the
    lack of importance that it had in Russell's thought. He does discuss it, as one could
    hardly avoid doing, in his book on Leibniz (*The Philosophy of Leibniz*, Cambridge
    University Press: 1900; new edn, Allen and Unwin, London: 1937). His discussion
    there contains a number of arguments against the philosophical significance of the
    notion.

22 It must seem paradoxical to speak of the author of *Our Knowledge of the External
    World*, the advocate of reduction of physical object-statements to sense-data
    statements, as anti-epistemological in his orientation. Various considerations mitigate
    this paradox. One is that all of Russell's work in the epistemological vein are written
    after the completion of *Principia*; there was a shift in his concerns around this time,
    perhaps traceable in part to the lectures that Moore gave in 1910–11 (later published
    as *Some Main Problems of Philosophy*, George Allen and Unwin, London: 1953). A
    second is that the notion of a sense-datum can be seen, in a curious way, as the natu-
    ral outcome of the view that we have a direct and unproblematic relation to the
    objects of our knowledge. If one holds this view then it may seem obvious, upon re-
    flection, that the objects of our knowledge are not such things as tables and trees. The
    fact of sensory illusion seems to show this (it may be said, indeed, that one who holds
    the view of knowledge that I have mentioned is the appropriate target for the argu-
    ment from illusion). Thus one searches for suitable objects of knowledge–relata
    which can preserve the relation of knowing as a direct and unproblematic one. The
    result is the notion of a sense datum, as conceived by Russell and Moore – not as a
    subjective or mental entity, but as an objective non-mental thing with which our
    minds are in direct and unmediated contact. The non-mental nature of Russellian
    sense-data is of course crucial to this way of understanding matters, and is often
    overlooked. A third fact is probably most important of all from the present perspec-
    tive. Russell's epistemological worries do not rapidly extend themselves to serious
    questions about our knowledge of abstract objects. Here the answer is that we simply
    are in direct contact with them, that we 'perceive' them in some non-sensuous

fashion, continues to satisfy him at least until the 1920s. This is the point which is most relevant to the discussion of logicism and also, although less obviously, to his anti-Kantianism.

23   See 'The nature of the proposition and the revolt against idealism', in *Philosophy in History*, eds R. Rorty, J. Schneewind and Q. Skinner, Cambridge University Press: 1984.

24   For discussions of this conception of logic, see van Heijenoort, 'Logic as language and logic as calculus', *Synthese* vol. 17 (1967), pp. 324–30; and Goldfarb, 'Logic in the twenties: the nature of the quantifier', *Journal of Symbolic Logic*, vol. 44 no. 3, September 1979, pp. 351–68.

25   This point is closely connected with that made by Frege, when he insists that his logic *expresses a content*. See especially 'On the aim of the "conceptual notation"', trans. in ed. T. W. Bynum, *Conceptual Notaion and Related Articles*, Oxford University Press, Oxford: 1972: 'my aim [in the *Begriffsschrift*] was different from Boole's. I did not wish to present an abstract logic in formulas, but to express a content through written symbols.' To say that a statement of logic expresses a content is presumably also to say that it is true or false on its own account, without the need for an interpretation.

26   This version is from 'Mathematical logic as based on the theory of types', reprinted in ed. Marsh *Logic and Knowledge* (George Allen and Unwin, London: 1956), p. 71. For other versions see e.g. 'On "insolubilia" and their solution by symbolic logic', reprinted in ed. Lackey, *Essays in Analysis* (George Allen and Unwin, London: 1973), pp. 2056, and *Principles*, section 7.

27   For the development of the issue of (semantic) completeness in its modern sense, see the paper of Goldfarb's cited in n. 24, and also the introductory note by Burton Dreben and Jean van Heijenoort to Gödel's proof of completeness, in vol. I of *Gödel's Collected Works*, ed. Solomon Feferman et al., Oxford University Press: 1986.

28   I say 'would have' rather than 'did' because there is no reason at all to believe that Russell articulated the sorts of considerations that I am giving. In particular, there is, as I have said, no reason to think that he considered any other conception of logic as possible.

29   At this point the idealist interpretation of Kant is again arguably mistaken. In particular, the view that things-in-themselves are independent of all our cognitive faculties seems to neglect Kant's distinction between sensibility and the understanding, and between the schematized and the un-schematized categories. At least in some places, Kant's view seems to be that things-in-themselves are independent of sensibility (and therefore of the schematized categories), but not of the understanding (and the un-schematized categories. See especially *Critique of Pure Reason*, A 253–4 = B 309–10.

30   *Studies in Hegelian Dialectic*, Cambridge University Press: 1896, 2nd edn, 1922, p. 27. I cite McTaggart not only because he is clear and (on this point) representative, but also because we know that Russell took him seriously, read his work, and was influenced by his interpretation of Hegel. See e.g. *My Philosophical Development* (cited, n. 3), p. 38.

31   See Russell's letter to Jourdain, dated 28 April 1909: 'I do not prove the independence of primitive propositions by the recognised methods; this is impossible as

regards principles of inference, because you can't tell what follows from supposing them false: if they are true, they must be used in deducing consequences from the hypothesis that they are false, and altogether they are too fundamental to be treated by the recognised methods.' This portion of the letter is printed in *Dear Russell – Dear Jourdain*, by I. Grattan Guiness (Duckworth, London: 1977), p. 117.

32   See *Our Knowledge of the External World* for some discussion of this point.

33   A. N. Whitehead and B. Russell, *Principia Mathematica*, vol. I, Cambridge University Press: 1910; 2nd edn 1927. All my references are to material printed in the 1st edn and reprinted 'unchanged except as regards misprints and minor errors' in the 2nd (introduction to the 2nd edn, p. xiii); my pagination, however, is that of the 2nd edn. I make the simplifying assumption that it is Russell, rather than Whitehead, who is responsible for the parts of *Principia* that are my concern.

34   See Quine, *Philosophy of Logic* (Prentice Hall., Englewood Cliffs N J: 1970), pp. 64–8. Elsewhere Quine argues at some length that Russell's strategy of taking propositional functions as fundamental, and classes as defined, has no advantages (and some disadvantages) compared with that of taking classes as fundamental outright. See especially *Set Theory and its Logic* (Harvard University Press, Cambridge Mass.: 2nd edn, 1969), ch. XI.

35   Here I presuppose that propositional functions are not linguistic entities, a claim that has been doubted by a number of commentators. See *Principia* vol. II, p. xii, where a distinction is made between a propositional function and the *symbolic form* of a propositional function. The context of this passage may make it less than conclusive. The general tenor of Russell's discussions of propositional functions, both in *Principles* and in *Principia*, however, is that they have the same status as propositions, and are indeed exactly like propositions except that propositional functions have variables in one or more places where the corresponding proposition has an entity.

36   It is important to note that propositional functions are not *constituents* of propositions (see *Principia*, pp. 54–5); this fact is crucial to the basis of type theory. But we must acknowledge propositional functions if we are to have any account of generality.

37   *Set Theory and Its Logic*, pp. 257–8; my italics.

38   See for example Quine's *Philosophy of Logic*, Prentice Hall, Englewood Cliffs N J: 1970.

39   Here again there is a clear contrast between Russell and Kant (and equally between Frege and Kant). For Kant, logic has no objects of its own, and does not even deal with objects; its concern is with the understanding and its form (see especially *Critique of Pure Reason*, preface to the 2nd edn, at B ix). Russell's propositions and propositional functions, by contrast, are logical objects (as are Frege's *Wertverläufe*). One way to understand the significance of Russell's paradox, and related paradoxes, is as showing that Kant was right on this issue, and Russell and Frege wrong. The assumption that there are logical objects, when combined with the generality which both Russell and Frege took as characteristic of logic, leads to paradox; see section III, below.

40   See especially T. G. Ricketts, 'Objectivity and objecthood', in *Synthesizing Frege*, eds L. Haaparanta and J. Hintikka (Reidel, Dordrecht: 1986).

41   'Russell's Mathematical Logic', in ed. P. A. Schilpp *The Philosophy of Bertrand Russell*, The Library of Living Philosophers, Evanston, Illinois: 1946, p. 126.

42 In the preface to the 1st edn of *Principia*, Whitehead and Russell say that '[t]he proofs of the earliest propositions are given *without the omission of any step*' (p. vi; my italics). The reasons they give for this care are also important. They do not appeal to any abstract standards of syntactic rigour, but to more practical considerations: 'otherwise it is scarcely possible to see what hypotheses are really required, or whether our results follow from our explicit premisses', and 'full proofs are necessary for the avoidance of errors, and for convincing those who may feel doubtful as to our correctness' (ibid.). How far they are from wishing to put forward a formal system in the modern sense may also be gathered from the Preface and from the discussion, in the introduction to the 1st edition, of their use of symbolism. They say in the introduction, for example, 'In proportion as the imagination works easily in any region of thought, symbolism (except for the express purpose of analysis) becomes only necessary as a convenient shorthand writing to register results obtained without its help.' (p. 3).

43 Like the so-called axiom of infinity, the so-called axiom of choice is not mentioned in *Principles* but is recognized in *Principia* as required for mathematics; like the axiom of infinity, again, it is not in fact taken as an axiom of *Principia* but is used as an hypothesis as required (see below, pp. 161–2. I shall not discuss the axiom of choice for two reasons. First, the philosophical issues which the need for this 'axiom' raises are raised also by the need for the axiom of infinity, which is perhaps more interesting for our purposes. Second, the fact that the axiom of choice is not discussed in *Principles* is not due to some difference between that work and *Principia* which implies that the issue does not arise in the former. It is, rather, simply that Russell was not aware, when he wrote *Principles*, that the axiom had to be assumed as an independent principle. As he himself says in the introduction to the 1937 edn, he 'did not become aware of the necessity for this axiom until a year after the *Principles* was published' (p. viii). I see no reason to doubt his later statement on this point. By contrast, the need for the axiom of infinity in *Principia* but not in *Principles* indicates a crucial difference between these works, as we shall see.

44 The word 'order' is consistently used in this sense in the introduction to the 2nd edn of *Principia*. Ramsey adopts this usage, and confines the word 'type' to distinctions among propositional functions which are based on distinctions among the entities to which they can be significantly applied; see 'The Foundations of Mathematics', (first published in the *Proceedings of the London Mathematical Society*, series 2, vol. 25, and reprinted in *The Foundations of Mathematics and other Logical Essays*, ed. R. B. Braithwaite, Littlefield, Adams and Co., Totowa, NJ: 1965), especially pp. 23–8. In his usage, there is thus a clear distinction between type and order, and many later authors have followed him in making this distinction. In the first edition of *Principia*, however, Russell's use of the words 'type' and 'order' does not consistently follow this rule. In particular, he often uses 'type' for both kinds of distinctions among propositional function (e.g. in 9.14, which will be discussed below, pp. 160–1). Although I follow Ramsey's use of the word 'order' here, my later discussion, like that of the 1st edn of *Principia*, uses the word 'type' in a non-Ramseyan way to include distinctions of order.

45 Two propositional functions are said to be co-extensive if they are true of exactly the same things; the extension of a propositional function consists of those things of

which it is true. If the notion of the extension of a propositional function were taken as fundamental, it would provide us with an analogue of set theory with no more ado. Russell's method of dispensing with the assumption that there are classes (or sets or extensions) is to define class symbols in such a way that a sentence involving such a symbol expresses a (more complex) proposition about propositional functions.

46 This point was perhaps first made by Wittgenstein; see 'Notes on logic' (printed as appendix I to *Notebooks 1914–16*, University of Chicago Press: 1961, 2nd edn: 1979) pp. 98, 101.

47 A syntactically specified version of *Principia* would also be clearly inadequate for mathematics because of Gödel's incompleteness theorem, which states that any (consistent) formalism fails to prove some arithmetical truth. *Principia* is not syntactically specified, and it is by no means evident that one should think of it as a (rather careless) formalism at all. It is thus by no means clear that *Principia*, as its authors intended it, is vulnerable to an argument based on Gödel's theorem.

48 Compare Frege, *Foundations of Arithmetic* (trans. J. L. Austin, Blackwell Oxford: 1950, 2nd edn: 1953), section 82.

49 The question of the nature and status of logic occupied Russell after the completion of *Principia*. It appears that this was to have been one of the issues discussed in the unwritten third portion of Russell's projected 1913 book, *The Theory of Knowledge*. See *The Collected Papers of Bertrand Russell*, vol. 7, ed. E. R. Eames (George Allen and Unwin, London: 1984) which contains as much as Russell wrote of the book, and also discusses his plans for the remaining portions.

50 George Allen and Unwin: 1919.

51 I should like to express my gratitude to the organizers of the conference in Munich where this paper was read, and to the Volkswagen Stiftung for making the conference possible. I cannot mention all those at the conference who gave me criticism, advice and encouragement, but I should like to thank them all, and espcecially Peter Clark and Bill Hart. For criticism of earlier drafts of this paper I am indebted to Francis Dauer, Michael Friedman, Warren Goldfarb, Leonard Linsky, Thomas Ricketts and, especially, Burton Dreben.

8
Through a Glass Darkly: Vagueness in the Metaphysics of the Analytic Tradition

Mark Sacks

1 The Backdrop

The concern of this paper is not with the extent to which philosophers of the analytic tradition have been vague about their metaphysical assumptions; thereby leaving an unarticulated, sometimes unnoticed backdrop to their work. My concern is rather with a certain vagueness within that backdrop, and with the significance of such vagueness for the aims of analytic philosophy.

It seems at times that it is more a common style of doing philosophy, than a common philosophical commitment, which unites Analytic Philosophy into a single tradition. Perhaps there is no single set of presuppositions common to all analytic philosophy. Nevertheless, it is possible to delineate certain general commitments which establish the concern with which something recognizable as mainstream analytic philosophy wrestles.

Twentieth century thinkers inherited both the Cartesian split between the knowing subject and the external world, and the emphasis on the sciences aimed at understanding the latter, the material world. In the analytic tradition concern with the dichotomy between language and the world came to replace the more traditional concern with the dichotomy between knower and the world, between subject and object. But in turning to investigate language the analytic philosopher was certainly not turning away from the scientific enterprise. On the contrary, the analytic philosopher, in turning to language, was sharpening the tools with which the scientific enterprise could investigate the world.

The world seemed to be responding well to scientific treatment; it seemed to offer answers to ever more precise and rigorous questions with which scientists were probing it. There seemed to be no ineliminable vagueness in the empirical world. All this boded well for the view that the world was fully determinate; that any question would have a precise answer.[1]

Accepting this view of the world, and the obvious capacity of empirical science to cope with the investigation of it, the philosopher, as someone whose task it was to pursue that investigation, was clearly made redundant. This left various options open to the committed philosopher.

Rather than opposing or evaluating the scientific enterprise, or extending it into new fields, analytic philosophy accepted natural science as paradigmatic, and retreated to the linguistic, to ask what language must be like if it is to be adequate to the scientific task. There was in this something of the traditional conception of philosophy as the *foundation* of other sciences; other sciences requiring the grounding provided by the philosophical enterprise. But in the context of the analytic tradition this took on a new guise.

If the world is fully determinate, the perfect target for scientific inquiry, it is necessary to ensure that we approach it with implements that are as finely tuned as possible, to make sure that it is not the insensitivity of the mapping mechanism that produces an inaccurate picture. The tools – language – must be suitably sensitive for the task. Primarily, language must be such as not to contain within it any blind spots. It must not contain any ineliminable vagueness. For any point, at which language is ineliminably vague, is thereby a point at which the full determinateness of the world goes unfathomed, unmapped. The requirement is that language come as close as possible to being as free of vagueness as the world towards which our inquiry – couched in terms of it – is directed. If language is the instrument by means of which we tackle the world, it must be shown to be as fine an implement as the delicate job at hand requires. In doing this analytic philosophers were turning reflexively to language as our *lens* on to the world; intent on securing its transparency. Disinclined to spend too much time on the dark side of the lens – they were intent on seeing the world through it.[2]

It should be noted that in fact what we have here is a parallel to the old sceptical problem about the reliability of our access to the world. The question is unchanged: whether that access is adequate to the job of capturing the way the world is. The difference is that the source of possible trouble is now thought to be not the mind, located behind the lens, but rather language itself, a point beyond which the analytic philosopher was loath to retreat.[3]

What assurance is there that language displays contents of the sort required to represent the world accurately? Even on an empiricist conception of language, where language is learned through our encounter with the world rather than being innate, there is still no guarantee that the subsequent linguistic cooking of elements gleaned from experience will render results adequate to picturing the empirical world. There is still no security that the linguistic mechanism, even if its elements are derived wholly from the empirical world, will yield the sort of output that can adequately map the empirical world. This is not merely because the linguistic 'cooking' apparatus is itself said to be innate rather than learned from experience.[4] That much was granted by some forms of classical empiricism (e.g. Locke). The point is rather that even if the synthesizing mechanism of language could, in its entirety, be the result of the encounter with the empirical world rather than innate, this in itself does not guarantee that it will be such as to have a structure that will enable us to see the empirical world, that gave rise to it, as it is. It is that perspicuity that the traditional empiricists accepted without question. And so for them the problem seemed to be only that it was not possible to glean enough from the world. The reflexive turn to language puts just that assumed perspicuity into question. Once it is recognized that language, as it stands, may not be totally transparent, that some traditional metaphysical problems may have been the result of linguistic knots, of an opacity of the natural lens, then it can no longer be thought that the mere fact that language is learned rather than innate, guarantees that it is up to the task of accurately representing that from which it is learnt.[5] And if there is no such security in the case of natural language which was learned from experience, this is likely to be a problem in any other, artificially designed language. It is because of this that, despite the fundamentally empiricist outlook, the analytic philosopher must face the possibility that the output of our linguistic synthesis ('cooking') might eventuate in a picture which, even if ultimately gleaned from experience, is nevertheless not applicable to it as an accurate representation.

There is, however, this important difference. Whereas it is difficult for us today to see why innate ideas might have been thought to give us access to the way of the world, we can more easily participate in the initial sense of optimism that there was about the likelihood of ideas that come to use from the world providing us with an accurate epistemic route back to the way of that world. This perhaps has something to do with the fact that in a secular age the trust, which we place in the reliability of causal chains, is greater than any we have in God (who was required to explain why our innate ideas match the world).

It was this optimism regarding the potential for a perspicuous language, that led philosophers of the analytic tradition to concentrate on putting language in order, eliminating what vagueness had been allowed to lurk in language. As long as language is vague, it will not be able to serve the scientist who wished to use it to investigate the fully determinate nature of the empirical world.

Now vagueness in language comes in two sorts. To the extent that the vagueness of the given language is *eliminable*, ordinary language philosophy will do, aimed at eliminating that vagueness from the existing language, in the belief that the cleansed language will be adequate for the job. To the extent, however, that the language is thought to be *ineliminably* vague, there will be no option other than to discard that language and to come up with some other language better suited to the scientific purposes. While ordinary language philosophers like

Austin pursued the former with regard to our natural language, positivists like Carnap pursued the latter option. For the coherence of either project, it is necessary that the existence of a language without ineliminable vagueness be possible.

This in itself is of course not a sufficient condition for these projects. (It is at least necessary also that such a language be rich enough to allow complex communication of sufficiently complex ideas, and that there be nothing that precludes us from mastering such a language.) Were it to be shown that such a language is not possible, a problem would ensue for the entire programme of providing science with the perfect linguistic apparatus. And to the extent that this is so, there will be no further room to push on with the kind of reflexive turn that the analytic tradition adopted in the service of science. Of the possible forms that the linguistic turn can take, that adopted by the analytic tradition will have proved to be a dead end.

Dead ends aside, the broad conception of the programme rests upon two presuppositions which constitute a metaphysical backdrop: (i) that there is a tenable dichotomy between language and the empirical world, such that it makes sense to think of the one as a description of the other, and (ii) that some such language can in principle be rendered as determinate as the world that is to be described. Let us take these as two basic tenets of the analytic tradition.

Perhaps the two prime examples of this concern to tie language reliably to empirical reality by eliminating vagueness from the former in preparation for handling the full determinateness of the latter, are provided by Frege and the early Wittgenstein. The general need for a fine-grained and precise framework must explain the way in which Frege came to occupy a central place in the history of the analytic tradition. Similarly, Wittgenstein's *Tractatus* exemplifies – perhaps *par excellence* – the concern to guarantee that language be able to track empirical world. The picture theory, indeed, provides insight into the underlying metaphysical concern to be assured that there is no ineliminable vagueness in language.

That language is not so determinate, that our lens on to the world cannot be made so transparent as the picture theory would have us believe, is something that philosophers only gradually came to see. Among those philosophers whose work forced us to question the assumption of the transparency of language, which early analytic philosophers accepted, were Goodman, Quine and, of course, the later Wittgenstein.

2   The Presuppositions

The Fregean view captures well the reflexive turn to language as a tool which in principle can serve to give a picture of the world which matches the world itself for determinacy. For Frege the bits of language whose job it is to depict bits of the world, are *sentences*. It is sentences, on their own, that depict facts. Sentences are the units of significance. The meaning of the individual word consists in the contribution it makes to the sentences in which it can occur. Sentences are either true or false. And it seems clear that if those units of significance are to be either true or false, they must have determinate meaning. Were a sentence to prove incomplete as the bearer of content, completeness requiring some additional element, then accordingly the sentence on its own – without that additional complementary element – would not have a determinate truth-value. The sentence would then be true, or false, only *relative to that additional element*, whatever that may be.[6]

It is, however, easy today to see reasons why we should doubt whether the sentence *is* the unit of significance, the bearer of determinate content. Goodman's 'new riddle of induction' was initially introduced as showing that the same facts equally well confirm two different and incompatible hypotheses. The question posed was: What leads us to select the one hypothesis rather than the other? Whether this poses a new riddle of induction is not at all clear. But there certainly is a sense that Goodman is getting at something new that we do not find in Hume. It might be that what Goodman says about *induction* is not very new (except in dress), and that what *is* new in Goodman's riddle is not particularly about induction. (And this extra element cannot be merely the point that experience underdetermines theory: that much is obvious from Hume.)

Goodman's riddle unpacks in different ways. The simplest interpretation is the one which asks how we know which hypothesis – green or grue – is the one that the world will conform to in the long run. All emeralds up to now were just as grue as they were green, so – assuming that today is 31 December 1999 – 'why not expect the first one tomorrow to be grue, and therefore blue?'[7] This indeed comes down to a problem rather similar to the original Humean problem. But on a different interpretation the problem soon diverges quite distinctly from Hume's, and indeed can be seen to apply to more than the issue of induction. This interpretation is more obviously concerned with *language* and its ability to provide a determinate reading of the way the world is.

On the first interpretation of Goodman's riddle, language remains in principle sensitive to the extra-linguistic facts. We might not know, on inductive grounds provided to date, whether to go for the green or the grue option. But there is reason to think that sooner or later the world will let us know at least which was wrong. This does not, of course, mean that the problem is merely pragmatic. Precisely because of the 'sooner or later' clause, there remains a severe problem. But this is just the problem of induction. Suppose, on this reading, that all emeralds do *not* appear blue on the designated morrow: Well, then the hypothesis that they would is refuted. But no sooner have we done so, than we realize that we cannot now live monogamously with the old green hypothesis – a new grue hypothesis has emerged about whether the sun will rise on green or on blue emeralds on the morrow.[8] And of course the situation is no better if on the morrow, as January 2000 dawns, all emeralds change to blue. OK – we were wrong about emeralds being green: but whether we were right about them being grue is totally unclear, given that we do not know how long they will go on being grue, i.e. currently blue, with a history of green. For all we know, they might be gruered: history of being green, currently blue, but with a rosy future ahead of them... Still, in principle these hypotheses are sensitive to the facts – the problem is only that we never have in hand at once all the facts we can hope to have in hand over the passage of time.

The second direction for interpretation is slightly different: as a first step it is noted that even if we do have all the facts in hand that we could ever have, there still remain green and grue descriptions of what it is that we have in hand – there are different mappings of one and the same factual bulk.

It might help to bring out the direction of this second interpretation by showing that Goodman's original examples involve elements that make it easy to equivocate between the two interpretations, almost as if he was not altogether sure which problem he was introducing. After the year 2000, the choice will be made as to whether the green or the grue hypothesis is to be rejected. That element of the case introduces the sensitivity of language to the facts. One hypothesis will be selected over the other in the long run, it is just that on the current information we cannot tell which. This is the (more or less new) problem of induction. Now to introduce this problem, as various writers have pointed out, the expiry date need not have been placed far into the future; it would suffice to talk of emeralds as of now. Yet placing the 'best before' date far into the future does enable Goodman to capture something of the second interpretation. Until the year 2000, all emeralds will carry on fitting both green and grue hypotheses. For the duration of this period there are two descriptions of emeralds which are incompatible with each other, but which map on to the world equally well. Of course this persists only until the year 2000. But just as the first interpretation did not require the extended time lag until 2000, so the second interpretation does not require an upper time limit beyond which the facts come to bear on the competing descriptions. There could be two descriptions of the world, in competition with one another, without either being shown at any point to be the wrong one: Both fit *all* the facts. To see this we might reconstruct the example, tailoring it to the second interpretation. Let 'grue' mean blue if unexamined, and green upon examination and thereafter. The examination of any emerald, whenever carried out, will then confirm equally the hypothesis that all emeralds are green, and the hypothesis that all emeralds are grue. *Both* hypotheses can be mapped on to the world: yet they cannot both be true of one and the same world. Of course, this is only the first step, and so far we have only the underdetermination of theory by experience.

But given that such green and grue mappings are possible, it is a small step to see that rather than being associated with different linguistic strings, each mapping might have had the same linguistic string, such that speaker *a* in using the string meant one thing by it, and speaker *b* meant another by his use of the same string. Here we are thinking not of a single set of facts and two corresponding sentences expressing two different hypotheses, but rather of a single set of facts and a single sentence used to describe it. The question then arises which of two or more hypotheses that sentence (say, 'All emeralds are green') expresses: that those bits of the world are one way, or another way. The very fact that *one and the same* sentence could fit the evidence for it in one of several ways, each attributing to the sentence a different meaning, suggests that it is not the case that the sentence taken on its own is the bearer of determinate content. As soon as this possibility emerges, it is quite clear that while the case of green and grue does serve to indicate a problem about induction, it also provides the material for a problem about the determinacy of linguistic content. How do we tell that two speakers, using the same words, mean the same things by them?

Thus we see an interpretation of Goodman's riddle, or at least of the underlying insight, which poses a severe problem for the outlook of early analytic philosophy, insofar as on that view it was assumed that the sentence is the unit which taken on its own has determinate semantic content, and which renders language fully determinate in content and perspicuous to the world. The question arises what, if anthing, could eliminate gruesome content, and render determinate content to each sentence.

One familiar answer is that offered by Quine, urging that in taking the statement as unit we have drawn our grid too finely. There is no one sentence that on its own is judged to fit or capture the way of some extra-linguistic terrain. Language meets the tribunal of sense experience as a whole. A conflict with experience would then force us to make some changes in the linguistic framework, but there is no one statement that would be singled out as the refuted bit of language. Any statement can be held true, as long as we make the required adjustments elsewhere.[9]

This view can accommodate the fact that the individual statement does not have determinate content or truth-value. The conception of language is such that the individual statement no longer needs to play that role. All that matters is that that statement fits in with the other sentences of the language, such that that language – as a whole – accommodates all sensory experience, taken as a whole. To put it differently: faced with a sentence that could be given an alternative gruesome reading, either reading could be accepted as true with the other as false, providing we were prepared to make the required changes elsewhere in the language. And to the extent that we keep the language fixed, the chances are that one of the possible readings will have to be rejected. In this way taking the language as a whole as the unit of significance can bestow on the statements in it a determinacy which they cannot be shown to have when taken in isolation.

This in itself does not, however, eliminate all possible vagueness from the sentence. It might be that both a green and a grue interpretation of a sentence fit, while requiring absolutely no accommodating changes elsewhere in the language. It is perhaps not clear how we can make good this alleged difference between the interpretations, since we could now not identify or perhaps even state that difference in the language. But the fact that we could not identify or state that difference would not mean that it was not there – just to the extent that two people had in mind different meanings associated with one and the same sentence. Quine might then seem to be rid of this vagueness which persists despite holistic nesting in language, by his rejection of meanings. This, however, will not really help in the long run.

Even if linguistic holism can determine the content of the *sentences* which are fitted into it, this still does not offer a satisfactory result overall. The question was whether *language* can be rendered determinate – free of ineliminable vagueness – as required for the purposes of capturing the way of the assumed determinate world. As long as the units of significance were individual sentences, it mattered that they were ineliminably vague. That vagueness is eliminated on the holistic thesis by way of *intersentential constraints*.[10] Sentences are rendered determinate in the context of the whole language, so sentences taken on their own are not the vehicles of significance – the language as a whole is.[11] It is of the units of significance – the intended bearers of content – that we must establish that they are not ineliminably vague. And so the holistic thesis, just insofar as it takes the language as a whole rather than the individual sentence as the unit of significance, carries with it the corollary that what now matters is whether the language as a whole, taken on its own, is not ineliminably vague in just the way that the individual sentence was. That is, can a language as a whole not be indeterminate between a green and a grue interpretation of *it*?

It seems clear that it can be, and indeed that without further work it *will* be, since nothing has changed except the *size* of the bit of the linguistic item which we are considering as the unit of significance. It is to be expected that once we have embarked on the project of eliminating systematic vagueness of one bit of language by contextualization of it in some larger unit, then the same will occur in the case of the larger unit, and so a regress is born.

Quine seems reasonably happy to endorse something like this. He rejects the museum myth according to which words are labels which we append to meanings which reside in our heads like fixed exhibits in a museum.[12] On that view a person's words and sentences have determinate meanings, in his mental museum, even in cases where we are unable through our behavioural observations to establish what those meanings are. In preference to the museum myth, Quine adopts Dewey's naturalist approach:

> For naturalism the question whether two expressions are alike or unlike in meaning has no determinate answer, known or unknown, except insofar as the answer is settled in principle by people's speech dispositions, known or unknown. If by these standards there are indeterminate cases, so much the worse for the terminology of meaning and likeness of meaning.[13]

Quine presents cases like that of *gavagai*, the translation of which from one language into another can be performed in a variety of different ways, just so long as we make the appropriate adjustments in the translations of other terms from the first language into the second. It might be that we could in this way come up with two translations of a language, different from each other, but both of which accorded perfectly with all observed behaviour, as indeed with all dispositions to behaviour on the part of the speakers concerned.

On these assumptions it would be forever impossible to know of one of these translations that it was the right one, and the other wrong. Still, if the museum myth were true, there would be a right and a wrong of the matter; it is just that we would never know, not having access to the museum. See the language naturalistically, on the other hand, and you have to see the notion of likeness of meaning in such a case simply as nonsense (pp. 29–30).

Let us assume that we adopt the naturalistic view of language. There is then no sceptical problem as to how we can ever know which of the two possible translations captures the right meaning. For there is then no right meaning. But even so, the fact that there are alternative equivalent translations is still enough to show that the translated language cannot have the kind of perspicuity, the kind of determinate grip on the world that we are after.

We were after a language which would be as sensitive to the facts as the purposes of depicting them required. We now see that, given a candidate language, the problem is that it can itself be translated in a variety of ways, each of which depicts the world differently, while at the same time accommodating all the behavioural dispositions. It would seem, then, that the given language is ineliminably vague, insofar as it can be translated in these different ways, neither of which is wrong. Or, in terms of the earlier perspective: the sentence, indeterminate when taken on its own, can be made determinate by taking it up into a larger context of language. But there are two or more incompatible translations of that language that will do the job equally well, neither of which are wrong. The reason that neither is wrong is that, once it is accepted that both translations accord with all possible evidence, there is nothing left for them to be wrong about.

The problem is even more acute. Although the problem of the inscrutability of reference is introduced in a way that depends on the indeterminacy of translation, and for those purposes it is convenient to appeal to radical translation, Quine recognizes that the problem emerges just as clearly in the case of our home language. The mere fact that several of us use the same sounds does not show that we mean the same thing by them. Any of my sentences could be translated by you in such a way that none of my words referred to what you would be referring to if you employed the same words; overall behavioural accord being secured by compensatory adjustments elsewhere. 'In short, we can reproduce the inscrutability of reference at home.' (Ibid., p. 47).

Quine sees, or rather half-sees, that if this is the case with my neighour's understanding of my homophonic utterances, then it should be equally the case with my understanding at t_2 of my own utterances at t_1.[14]

Quine is not sufficiently explicit about this. Just as when I encounter a native in foreign lands I must translate their language into my own, so – closer to home – when I encounter someone else, I must translate their language into my own. In just the same way, as a matter of fact, when at t_2 I encounter (in memory or print or some other such storage device) my own words from t_1, I can understand what they mean only by translating them into my own language at t_2. The fact that the same words are used might be of little significance.

As a rule, of course, I translate 'rabbits' at t_1 as 'rabbits' at t_2, assuming that they carry the same significance. But the problem is that at t_2 I might translate the 'rabbits' of t_1 – which then referred to rabbit-stages – as 'rabbits' at t_2 – which now refer to rabbits – and providing that there are sufficiently rigorous appropriate shifts in the translation of other words, there is no way that the resulting translation manual from my-English-at-t_1 to my-English-at-t_2 will fail to work. That is, there is no way that I will discover any such pervasive shift in the significance of my words and sentences. Precisely because of this, it might be felt that we have no need to worry about such shifts. But nevertheless, the result will be that my language has no determinate content, since reference and meaning need not be the same on any two occasions. Indeed, the very idea that language has any abiding content seems to collapse. Whether or not this need worry us as a practical matter is not the point; it is clearly of serious import for our view of language as a determinate tool for mapping the world.

Now the only way out of this problem that Quine offers is an assumption of a backdrop language – our native language in which we are at home – which we hold fixed and in terms of which we translate any other language, or theory. This background serves as our frame of reference.[15] We cannot ask whether the term 'rabbit' refers to rabbits, or rabbit-stages, absolutely. We can ask this only relative to some background language.[16]

Any answer to questions of reference or significance of the terms of a language, will depend on taking up a translation of that language into some background language. The ontology of a given theory, or language, is thus relative to some other background language. As Quine readily points out, we now have an infinite regress. We determine the interpretation of the language relative to some background language – but then clearly the same must apply when we turn to this background language. Questions of reference for it will make sense only relative to a further background language:

And in practice we end the regress of background languages, in discussions of reference, by acquiescing in our mother tongue and taking its words at face value.[17]

A given language is made determinate relative to some background language, ultimately coming to rest in a blindly adopted background language which cannot be made fully determinate itself for lack of any further language into which to regress. However, on Quine's view, this does not reveal that language to be indeterminate. He holds that it makes no sense to say what the objects of a theory are, *except* by saying how to interpret that theory in another. Talk of the ontology to which a language is committed is meaningful only relative to the background theory with its own primitively adopted and ultimately inscrutable ontology. And so he considers that there is no room to raise questions about the significance of our own terms, close to home, in our own language, simply because we then have no background into which to regress, into which to provide a uniform translation of all terms:

> Paraphrase in some antecedently familiar vocabulary, then, is our only recourse; and such is ontological relativity. To question the reference of all the terms of our all-inclusive theory becomes meaningless, simply for want of further terms relative to which to ask or answer the question.[18]

This seems to show how we can have relative determinacy, that is, determinacy relative to our inherited framework. A given language could then be used to depict the ontology of the world as cut up by that framework. And there is indeed a sense in which Quine can be seen to offer something like a Kantian empirical realism, whereby we have a language to depict the world which that language has carved out. It remains to be seen whether or not this is adequate.

The problem of how we can know that our language is adequate to the task of presenting to us the full determinateness of the empirical world disappears once we realize that at any given time that empirical world is no more detailed or fully determinate than the language with which we approach it – precisely because it is the determining, containing, language that also determines the way the world is carved to begin with. It is no surprise to find that language is adequate to the job of presenting the world in all its detail: this is underwritten by the very way in which it is language that cuts the world up to begin with. What we have here is the old commitment ot transcendental idealism – the world in itself is not the world of which we have empirical knowledge – along with an empirical realist claim, that the world of which we do have knowledge is constituted in part by the framework we apply to it, so that the success of its application is not surprising.[19] The difference being that whereas Kant is concerned with the constitutive role of the mind, Quine is concerned with that of language.

It is important, however, to recognize that this adequacy of a language to capture the way of the empirical world, is confined to the inherited framework which renders both determinate. Consequently that empirical realism is only as extensive as that inherited or blindly adopted framework. If it turns out that different speakers of English might be rendering language determinate relative to different inherited background languages into which they were translating English sentences, it will hardly be of significance to point out that each within the confines of their nesting could be an empirical realist. The weight is thus put on the assumption of some one background language as something that is common to us all, or at least to a sufficiently large community, in the way that for Kant the same structure of mind is supposedly shared by us all, thus giving his empirical realism general intersubjective validity.

Now in response to the question of how we avoid radical translation applying at home, indeed to one individual on various occasions, Quine says that such questions – being relative – only make sense when we have some language to regress into, which in the case of our home language is lacking. But the latter assertion surely begs the question.

Why is it that my sentences – and perhaps yours – are all part of a common background mother tongue? The whole point is that this is what we want to establish. After all, it could well be that we should arrive on a planet to find people speaking a language which uses English sentences; the use of which would not necessarily mean that homophonic translation would be right. Now why am I not in just this situation in encountering utterances of my new neighbour, or for that matter utterances of my old neighbour, or indeed of my own past self? It will not do here to appeal to the notion of a common background language – that is just what is being questioned.

The point is that there is no reason to think that there is only one background language. There might well be two, or more. This is *in itself* enough to render any language hopelessly indeterminate and ambiguous, since it could equally well be nested, and so be made determinate, in either of two background languages – which renders each language indeterminate between the two.[20] Now add to this the consideration that given two or more mother tongues in this sense, they might be homophonic. If they are, then every encounter with a neighbour or my own past self is a possible encounter with a *gavagai* native.

And of course, once *this* is recognized, the idea that all languages are made determinate by translation into some background language, and so on back till we reach the mother tongue, will no longer render convergence into some common background language. There might be a regress ending in more mother tongues than there have ever been mothers; indeed as many mother tongues as there are moments of linguistic utterance. Every sentence is given determinate content within a language, which in turn has determinate content in virtue of its being taken up within other containing languages, themselves perhaps nested within yet others and finally within some blindly accepted language. But there is no reason to think that that background containing language is invariant from one generation/person/person-stage to the next. This rather undermines the value of the determinacy that each background language can bestow on the languages nested within it.

The result is an indeterminacy which is no better – indeed is no different from – the original indeterminacy of a sentence taken on its own. As anticipated, the indeterminacy at the level of sentences is now replicated at the level of whole languages; it makes no difference how big the bit of language in need of holistic nesting is.

Now it might be thought that the problem here is precisely in that the desired determinacy of language is being sought by contextualizing bits of language within other (larger) bits of language; that what is missing is some further, extra-linguistic constraint. The extra-linguistic constraint, on the received model, could come from two sources. The obvious source, which is responsible for Cartesian individualism, is in the goings-on behind the linguistic lens, para-digmatically, meanings in the head of the speaker. The idea would be that what goes on there will secure a determinate content for each sentence. Alterna-tively, we can look to the broader context in which the sentence occurs. This itself covers various possibilities, depending on how we construe the notion of a broader context.

Clearly, the former option, the appeal to mental goings-on, is precisely the sort of thing that Quine, preferring a clean-shaven ontology, sets out to avoid. Indeed, the analytic tradition generally would have preferred to render language fully determinate without appeal to goings-on elsewhere, particularly in the mind, on the assumption that the latter are not necessary, and only cloud the lens. The idea is that a scientific language would do better dropping 'meanings' – dark en-tities in the mind – *in order* to obtain the kind of fully determinate language required. The idea is nice. But since it does not work, perhaps meanings – those dark goings-on behind the linguistic lens – have been the missing ingredient?

It should be borne in mind here that what we are looking for is not simply an account of meaning; but rather one which will also satisfy the various constraints set by the aims of the analytic tradition. 'Meanings', as things in the mind, are admittedly not the sort of entities with which the scientific outlook would be comfortable. There is for this reason an understandable tendency among advocates of analytic philosophy towards behaviourism and nominalism. How-ever, on the other hand, any indeterminacy of content that resulted from the exclusion of mental events, occurrences behind the linguistic grid, would be open to the charge of crippling inadequacy it terms of the aims of the analytic tradition. So it has to be seen whether appeal – however unfortunate – to meanings as things in the mind might not serve to eliminate vagueness from language.

Thus in attempting to identify whether a certain token – word or sentence – means one thing rather than another, we are forced out of the narrow confines of language. Language must be anchored, and this leads us to see whether behind the linguistic grid, in the mind, we might not be able to find some fact about the individual that would secure some determinate meaning to his utterances.

The hopelessness of this endeavour is well known by now.[21] Unlike Quine, Wittgenstein, in the rule-following sections of the *Investigations*, endorses no bias against mental occurrences in trying to work out what constraints there are in interpreting rules, in grasping concepts. It soon becomes clear that the presence in my mind of some inner experience could not possibly determine meaning. Even if whenever a certain word or sentence is entertained, some inner experience occurs, there is no reason to think that it will be the same experience on every occasion; and even if it is, even if every concept is correlated with a unique sign wired into my brain, there is no way of assuring that that sign is being interpreted in the same way on two different occasions. What is in the mind, just as much as linguistic strings, can be mapped on to the world in all sorts of gruesome ways. And of course, if this can happen from one occasion to the next in the case of one speaker, there is no reason why it should not happen across different speakers, even if they have the *same* inner experiences accompanying all the same linguistic strings.

There is thus little hope that anchoring sentences to inner mental events, or indeed to inner brain states, can fix determinate content. The fact that sentence and inner feature are anchored to one another does not anchor the pair to one meaning rather than another. And as Wittgenstein points out,[22] anchoring sentence and inner event to an inner representation of a mode of projection aimed at fixing one determinate meaning will add complexity, but not the desired determinacy. We would still have various ways of projecting the projection-schema. What goes on in the head, then, will not serve to eliminate vagueness from language.

In the face of this we can either give up the idea that we ever mean anything determinate by what we say, the words we entertain, or must find some other way of doing the job, presumably by finding some better candidate as the determining context in which to place the linguistic item.

It might be tempting to think that it is in search of such a candidate that Wittgenstein appeals to the context of the communal grid. We cannot say that it is because of some content in the mind, common to different person-stages, that they mean the same; let us therefore try a different context, which reaches out beyond any one individual, into the society that different individuals constitute. We then say that it is not the mental states or brain states that secures determinate meaning, but intersubjective checkability. A communal grid determining the sense of a certain concept is placed over the individual, thereby leading to univocality that could not be secured by anything located within the individual. Two individuals or two person-stages using the same word are deemed to be meaning the same by it until some behavioural deviation forces us to admit otherwise. As Kripke points out, this involves an inversion; from the desired situation in which it is sameness of meaning that leads to agreement between people-stages, we have resorted to saying that it is agreement between people-stages that leads us to attribute sameness of meaning (an attribution that will persist until behavioural discord forces re-evaluation).

Unfortunately, the sameness of meaning, which we end up attributing in this manner, is not the sameness of meaning we had in mind to secure at first. We started out assuming the notion of sameness of meaning required for the analytic goal, and end up with one that renders that goal unattainable. Behavioural agreement is as close as we can draw the net around meaning-agreement, which is what we were after. But in the space left over after all constraints of behavioural accord have been exerted, there is still room for meaning variation. It is not as if once we have secured behavioural accord between all users of a word, they cannot but agree on the meaning of the word. Nor is this simply a problem of finite observation; that what looks like accord today might break down tomorrow, revealing the discrepancy in meaning between the parties. Even at the end of the day, when all the observational data were in, behavioural accord in the use of the word 'plus' would not suffice to show that we mean the same thing by that word. Even where we cannot help agreeing; we cannot be certain that we are agreeing on the same thing. It might still be that I-at-t_1 mean one thing by 'plus', and that I-at-t_2 mean something quite different by it. As long as there is no behavioural discord, the difference in meaning will go undetected.

For the most part, of course, Wittgenstein limits himself to cases in which there is *manifest* discord at the behavioural level – a mismatch emerges which gives good reason to conclude that it is not the same rule that is being followed by, say, the student (in *PI*, § 185). But the point is that we could in principle (unverifiability aside) reach a stage beyond which no evidence of discord would emerge. Yet there is no reason to think that in such cases meaning breakdown does not still occur. Only a behaviourist premise, legislating against unverifiable facts, could eliminate that possibility. But Wittgenstein adopts no such premise. It is in the end only on the basis of behavioural accord that we can attribute sameness of meaning; but this, as Kripke emphasizes, is a behavioural conclusion, not a behaviourist premise.

Now if behavioural accord was supposed to go some way towards securing meaning agreement in just the determinate sense that was once naively assumed – which is what would be supposed if behavioural accord was being offered, as Kripke suggests it is, as a sceptical solution to a sceptical paradox – then the point just made, that it does not secure meaning in that sense, would be problematic. For as it stands the sceptical solution does so little to ensure sameness of meaning (as opposed to sameness of behaviour) that it is in danger of collapsing back into the sceptical problem. It seems more reasonable, however, to think that Wittgenstein does not feel the need to answer the sceptical paradox at all. To assume that he is trying to do that, is to assume that he was still wedded to a picture of meaning determinacy that was once his – precisely the view of the analytic tradition that is under investigation here.

Perhaps, unlike Kripke, Wittgenstein is no longer concerned to capture as much as possible of these ideals. Rather than meeting the challenge of a sceptical paradox, he is perhaps content to dismantle the picture whereby language affords us determinate meaning. The idea is perhaps not to pose a problem that needs to be solved, as Kripke assumes, but rather to point out that if we think of meaning along traditional lines, we are involved in that paradox; so that perhaps we should recognize the dead-end and adopt a view of linguistic meaning which no longer aims for such absence of indeterminacy. Rather than seeing him as having a concern to answer a sceptical paradox, we might see Wittgenstein as rejecting that notion of meaning, and instead *endorsing* that ineliminable vagueness of language. On this new view, we move around, closing the societal net as tightly as possible around sameness of meaning, fully aware of the fact that this is not going to be tight enough to exclude meaning variance:

> But here we must be on our guard against thinking that there is some *totality* of conditions corresponding to the nature of each case (e.g. for a person's walking) so that, as it were, *he could not but* walk if they were all fulfilled. [*PI*, § 183].

The view of meaning fundamental to the analytic tradition gives significance to the sceptical paradox. Suggesting that Wittgenstein is out to provide the best answer possible to that paradox, suggests that his concerns are still those of the analytic tradition and that his allegiance is to it. Hence the paradox is still of significance to him on this interpretation. However, it might be that Wittgenstein is simply out to debunk the ideals of that tradition, by pointing out a paradox which is significant for anyone still committed to its ideals. In offering societal constraints on meaning Wittgenstein is then not so much proposing a sceptical solution to that paradox – the need for which would be felt only by someone still committed to the old framework in which meaning was to meet the ideals of analytic philosophy – but rather is opting out of that tradition altogether, and for a different account of meaning attribution.

However, regardless of whether or not this is what Wittgenstein was after, the point is that the kind of meaning convergence offered by societal constraints is quite different from the kind of univocality of meaning that was initially assumed to guarantee agreement. The latter would render language fully determinate, but it is not to be had, as is shown by the sceptical paradox in which it culminates. What *is* to be had is the former, the attribution of sameness of meaning on the basis of behavioural accord. Such accord does not indicate that two person-stages do in fact mean the same by the same phrase – only that it no longer matters for purposes of pragmatic communication if they do not, since whatever differences there are cannot be captured in language.

> The essential thing about private experience is really not that each person possesses his own exemplar, but that nobody knows whether other people also have *this* or something else. The assumption would thus be possible – though unverifiable – that one section of mankind had one sensation of red and another section another (*PI*, § 272).

But, of course, what does not matter for practical purposes, might still matter for theoretical purposes. Any difference in content between different speakers, and indeed different speaker-stages, can no longer be captured. And that is enough to undermine the view that language constitutes a perspicuous fully-determinate lens with which to map the way the world is. Its contents can alter from one occasion of use to the next. The fact that any such difference in content will remain undetected just insofar as it does not result in any behavioural discord, only seems to render such vagueness more damaging to the ideal of language as fully determinate. The less detectable such differences of content are in practice, the more pernicious they become in principle to the ideals of analytic philosophy.[23]

Now of course the difficulty here seems to be that mental entities, first introduced to help in eliminating indeterminacy of meaning, are now, having failed to do what common sense told us they might do, still around, and it is by appeal to them that language is now being revealed to be essentially indeterminate even in the face of added constraints on the far side of the linguistic lens (total behavioural accord). This might be thought to reinforce our reasons for eliminating mental events. It might be thought that we would be better off dropping from our ontology those dark entities in the mind, in order to reopen the way for the fully determinate language desired.

Even if it were the case that the introduction of meanings was not necessary for other reasons, merely eliminating mental entities would not be enough on its own to eliminate essential indeterminacy. Eliminate meanings – mental events – and total behavioural accord still permits of totally different mappings from one speaker's sentences to those of another. We are, in essence, back with Quine: just as different manuals of translation can be devised for a native language, each of which allows for total behavioural accord, so the same radical translation can be reproduced in our home language which equally well passes the test of behavioural accord. The indeterminacy of language – its essential vagueness – has already been seen not to be due to the *presence* of mental entities. All we have now seen is that equally this indeterminacy was not merely due to the *absence* of such entities either; i.e. that it cannot be eliminated simply by appeal to such entities.

In the face of these sorts of insights, one of the basic tenets of analytic philosophy seems to be undermined. Before turning to see whether determinacy of meaning cannot after all be secured by appeal to the wider context, beyond the linguistic lens, it is helpful to turn briefly to the other tenet of analytic philosophy. The idea of the linguistic grid, as fully determinate, is conjoined with a general picture of language as set apart from the world it is to depict. Once language is suspected of not having that kind of determinacy, the idea of language as the detached picturing framework, loses much of its point. But in any event, the view of language as set apart from the world so as to constitute a scientific lens on to it, poses problems quite apart from the question as to whether it can have the kind of determinate content which would be essential to the enterprise.

At first the dualism of world and linguistic lens on to it offered the philosophers of the analytic tradition an escape from the more traditional mind–world dichotomy. It is, however, a difficult dichotomy to maintain. It is not at all clear how language can be disentangled from the world. In a very obvious sense, language is just another phenomenon in the world. And if we insist on seeing language as at the same time somehow set apart from the world, how do we then explain the special way in which it ties up with the world? These problems are of course not unique to the analytic tradition. But they become particularly acute in the analytic tradition, given the prominence in it of language as a perspicuous picturing device. This is particularly obvious in the case of the *Tractatus* and Russell's logical atomism, and in the desperate eagerness with which Carnap and other logical positivists embraced Tarski's definition of truth.

Now as the recognition dawns that language cannot be fully determinate in the manner required by the ideals of the analytic tradition, so the dichotomy of language–world loses its prime appeal, and the tenuous nature of that distinction is more easily recognized. In the *Investigations* we find Wittgenstein breaking down a dichotomy he himself had previously been more inclined to accept. Language is no longer the self-sufficient vehicle of meaning, which needs only to be tested against the world for its truth. He describes language games showing that utterances can be ascribed meaning only in their context in communal space – logical space is no longer enough – a context which leaves no room for a clear division between the linguistic and the non-linguistic elements of the world. This suggests a view of language as so inextricably enmeshed with the world that its content cannot be determined in isolation from the contribution of the supposed 'extralinguistic' environment.

Wittgenstein's appeal is mainly to 'extralinguistic' social constraints. A more extreme approach, which has been given much sympathetic attention in recent years, attempts to argue that determinate meaning can be secured only by appealing to the wider context, beyond the linguistic lens, in both the social and the physical world. The root idea is, simply, that meanings aren't in the head.[24] What is contained in the head – mental state – underdetermines *meaning*,[25] since it leaves out the contribution of the extralinguistic domain.[26] More recently appeal to wide contexts as playing an essential role in determining meaning has been used to argue against the Cartesian individualist view of meaning (whereby meaning is assumed to be rendered determinate solely on the basis of constraints present on the near side of the individual's linguistic lens).[27] It is important to recognize the bearing that these attempts have on the aims of the analytic tradition.

There are two points to be made here: (a) if no determinate meaning can be attributed to an utterance or gesture in abstraction from the world around it, this fit – or contextualization – will not serve to give it determinate meaning of the sort that the analytic philosopher was after. In the first place, regardless of the contribution of the broader context, there remains the narrow content, the contribution of psychological states. These will always mean that no matter how impressive the extent of behavioural accord, there will remain room for meaning variation, as was seen in Wittgenstein's own treatment. In the second place, apart from the effect of events in the mind, it seems that there would always be different ways of interpreting the meaning of a certain nexus of interaction between symbols, symbol-manipulators, and the environment in which they are acting. The integration of language (meaning) into the world, or of world into language, adds only complexity, not determinacy.[28] We might no longer be dealing with placing sentences in the larger context only of other sentences, but rather in the context of the language which is itself placed in the larger context of the supposedly extra-linguistic world, just insofar as it is inseparably bound up with it. This, however, is *just* the situation the radical translator is in, whether at home or abroad. There still remain various ways of mapping the web of interactions between symbols, symbol-manipulator and the containing background. The fact that that background is assumed to be the real physical world makes no difference; if various speakers point to a cube in the middle of the room, saying that *that* is what they mean by a word – 'cube' – the constraints on sameness of meaning will be no better – indeed will be no different – than if they had each proceeded on the basis of some identical brain state or mental event. Either way, all we can do is apply behavioural tests, and if there is behavioural accord, that is as far as we can go. Various ways of mapping our behaviour with the cube are compatible with that. It simply does not seem to matter *where* the item is located; it still has to be interpreted. With interpretation comes the problem of ineliminable vagueness; yet prior to interpretation there is no room to talk of the item making a contribution towards one meaning rather than another.

(b) But even if broader ('extra-linguistic') content *could* determine meaning, this would not help the analytic project. That project was based, as we said at the beginning, upon the idea of language as (i) set apart from the world, while (ii) offering a determinate meaning such that it could capture the way of the fully determinate empirical world which was the object of scientific inquiry. The problem then emerged about the assumed determinacy of that language. Ineliminable vagueness of the language would short-circuit the entire analytic project. In an attempt to capture that determinacy we tried locating the bits of language in some wider, duly restrictive, contexts: among other sentences (within the linguistic lens), among events in the mind (on the near side of the lens) and finally among the totality of elements in the world (on either side of the linguistic lens). But now *this* extreme holism – well founded perhaps on general grounds – is mere desperation *qua* attempt to save the programme of analytic philosophy.[29]

For if determinate meaning requires such broad contextualization of language to the 'extra-linguistic', then the price of securing the determinateness required for the second basic tenet of the analytic tradition, is such as to undermine the first tenet. Once language is made determinate – assuming for the moment that this could be done by wide contextualization (total holism) – it is no longer in a position to depict the world. (Whereas as long as it is in a position to do that, it is not determinate enough to do so according to the scientific ideals.) It is no longer set apart from the world – with determinate meaning – such as to provide a tool with which to explore that object domain.

The escape from traditional metaphysics led to the replacement of the mind–world dichotomy with a different dichotomy, that between language and world. The project based on that dichotomy has, perhaps, in the span from early Wittgenstein to the late, run its course. But from the fact that that dichotomy does not hold up – or that holding it up leaves language indeterminate – it does not follow that the dichotomy between mind and world, between subjectivity and objectivity, does not hold up either.

Indeed, the failure to render language determinate seems to underline the peculiar nature of our subjective stance in the world. It would seem then that at the end of an analytic tradition which was given a free hand to eliminate subjective elements, events in the mind, and nevertheless failed to render language determinate, it will be difficult to avoid metaphysical returns. The old dichotomy of subject–object remained in the wings throughout the analytic tradition. If it be the case that language, set apart from the world as a blue-print, cannot have the determinacy to capture the assumed determinacy of the world, then we have to admit that the ideals of that tradition are unobtainable. And if, somehow, once language is integrated into the world, that determinacy *could* be afforded then, while this would not help to secure the analytic philosophers' ideal, we might be led on to a somewhat different project.

The search for determinacy ultimately seems to put pressure on the distinction between the linguistic and the extra-linguistic. Certainly language does not seem to be capable of bearing determinate content as long as we insist on that distinction. And it is not clear what an indeterminate language is; anything needed to render its content determinate would seem to have a claim to be part of language. This threatens to break down the distinction between language and world. There seems to be no non-programmatic reason to resist this. As soon as we stop to reflect, it seems that only an unquestioned dogma or an unpacked metaphor – language as a picture, or a web, or net – can keep the two apart.[30] Rejecting this language-world dichotomy – so central to the orientation of analytic philosophy – leaves us to deal with the issue of meaning in a significantly different stage-setting. In this way, concentrating on the issue of the ineliminable vagueness of language as the detached picturing framework serves to reveal the sense in which we might feel that the analytic tradition has run its course.

Finally, it is of interest to note that Quine simply accepts the dichotomy between world and language, saying that language meets the tribunal of – presumably non-linguistic – experience as a whole. It is perhaps ironic that the very dichotomy which seems to emerge as a dogma is the cornerstone of his 'Two dogmas of empiricism'. This drives home the sense in which the progress of philosophy is perhaps no more than the plight of its presuppositions.

Notes

1 The idea that the world is fully determinate, such that for any fact in the world there is a reason why it is so rather than some other way, or that the world abides bivalence, was not new. However by the early part of the twentieth century the conviction that the principle of sufficient reason held true of the world seemed to be fully borne out by empirical successes of science, and no longer required rationalist principles to be adduced in its favour.

2 The metaphor of a lens is not intended to carry weight in what follows or to be taken too seriously. Indeed the point is ultimately to argue that it cannot bear much weight. It is introduced as a suggestive caricature of a philosophical model.

3 Whether the analytic philosopher can refrain from retreating further, to the concern with what goes on in the mind behind the lens, a retreat also to the more traditional questions in the philosophy of mind, is something to which we will return.

4 The temptation to think that it must be innate has to do with the fact that it seems that without that mechanism we would not have the capacity for learning a language, for synthesis of primitive concepts. We could only have learned the mechanism, if we already had some more basic mechanism of that kind. (Of course Fodorians will go further, providing an argument along these lines for the innateness not merely of the language-learning mechanism, but of the primitive concepts as well.)

5 Nor would it do to say – as some are tempted to – that survival is the test of language accuracy. For one thing, survival requires only that the picture of the world which we

entertain and act upon is compatible with the world; and compatibility with the world is not the same as having a language which enables us to track the world scientifically. It might be that it is precisely the vagueness of the language, which ill-equips it to providing a scientific map of the empirical world, that enables us to survive in it. And, perhaps more poignant; what evidence is there to think that we have passed any significant test of survival at all? Would our satisfaction over our own survival not look shortsighted from the temporal perspective to which reptiles, for example, are entitled? (That they do not have the linguistic framework to express this perspective is not an objection – rather it serves to underline the very point just made).

6   This will be so whether we make truth or meaning prior; whether we give a truth-conditional account of meaning, or an account of truth in terms of meaning.

7   Quine, 'Natural Kinds', in *Ontological Relativity and Other Essays*, p. 15.

8   This is not the same situation as arises on the second interpretation: the world is genuinely changing, hypotheses are being refuted and replaced by new ones, rather than a lot of gruesome candidates striving in vain for the refutation that never comes their way to put them out of the misery of their competition.

9   'Two dogmas of empiricism', p. 43.

10 It is interesting to draw a parallel between these intersentential constraints and the holism of intersubjective constraints relevant to an understanding of Wittgenstein's *Investigations*.

11 'Two dogmas', p. 42.

12 'Ontological Relativity', in *Ontological Relativity and Other Essays*, New York: Columbia University Press, 1969, p. 27.

13 Ibid., pp. 28–9.

14 I say 'half-sees' because Quine seems to think that this problem emerges *only if* one has given up the traditional museum view of meaning:

> I have urged in defense of the behavioral philosophy of language, Dewey's, that the inscrutability of reference is not the inscrutability of a fact; there is no fact of the matter. But if there is really no fact of the matter, then the inscrutability of reference can be brought even closer to home than the neighbor's case; we can apply it to ourselves ('Ontological Relativity', p. 47.)

> This is too weak. Even if there is some fact of the matter, it could still be the case that what I have in mind when I say 'rabbit' on one occasion might not be the same as what I have in mind when I next utter the word. Even if I did have the same thing ('picture'-'exhibit') in mind on the two different occasions, there is no guarantee that I would interpret them the same way on the two occasions. This is the now common point to which I shall return below in the discussion of Wittgenstein.

15 'Ontological Relativity', p. 48.

16 Ibid., p. 49.

17 Ibid., p. 49.

18 Ibid., p. 54. Earlier, on p. 51, Quine accepts that we should not speak of a theory as a set of fully interpreted sentences.

19 On this interpretation of Quine, see my *The World We Found*, London, Duckworth, 1989, ch. 2.

20 It might of course be urged that any two background languages could be mapped on to some common map, just insofar as both are distinguished as languages. This is the kind of line Davidson advocates in 'On the very idea of a conceptual scheme'. But this would not eliminate the indeterminacy between them – we might be left with an irreducible disjunction which left all translated languages indeterminate between the possible disjuncts. Besides, it might be the case that the different basic languages are *not* distinguished. This could perhaps be *precisely* because they are homophonic.

21 Wittgenstein, *Philosophical Investigations*, §§ 139; 140; 151–78, and Kripke, *Wittgenstein On Rules and Private Language*, pp. 40–54.

22 *Philosophical Investigations*, e.g. § 141.

23 These are the very ideals from which Wittgenstein, on the present suggested reading, seems to be turning away. Kripke seems more committed to those ideals, and so it is unfortunate that he does not mention this weakness of the proposed sceptical solution to the paradox.

24 Putnam, 'The meaning of "meaning"', p. 227.

25 Ibid., p. 271.

26 Rather than questioning what sense there is in calling this an extra-linguistic domain, Putnam rather heavy-handedly thinks of it as 'the real world', thus slipping into a realism that is not warranted (ibid., p. 245).

The fact that the same basic idea about meaning is present in Wittgenstein's *Philosophical Investigations* seems to be proof that the importation of realism is a consequence of a separate commitment, rather than a conclusion from the same premises.

27 Evans, *The Varieties of Reference*; Burge, 'Individualism and the mental', and various other papers. (See, e.g. Pettit and McDowell, 1986.)

28 For something of an acknowledgement of this, see Putnam, "The meaning of "meaning", pp. 257–8, on 'Radical Translation'.

29 It should be clear, from what was said above, that I am not attributing to Wittgenstein in the *Investigations* any such attempt. On the contrary, he seems to have ushered in a declaration of the bankruptcy of that project, precisely by attacking both the assumption that language can be rendered determinate, and that language can be set apart from some 'extra-linguistic' world.

There is something both curious and fitting about this: it is perhaps *fitting* that the philosopher who did more than any other to crystallize the conception of language in the analytic tradition was also the man who some time later established the futility of its aims. It is possibly because this is not noticed that we find the curiosity that Wittgenstein was taken to be the father of ordinary language philosophy, an enthusiastic if programmatically misguided attempt to pursue the goals of analytic philosophy as identified here. Doubtless this resulted from not realizing just how radical Wittgenstein was being, assuming that the aims had remained the same, and only the kind of analysis that was supposed to render language transparent had changed.

30 Davidson, in 'On the very idea of a conceptual scheme' declares the scheme-content distinction to be the third dogma of empiricism.

References

Burge, T., 'Individualism and the mental', in *Midwest Studies in Philosophy Volume IV Studies in Metaphysics*, eds. French et al., Minneapolis: University of Minnesota Press, 1979, pp. 73–121

Burge, T., 'Cartesian Error and the Objectivity of Perception', in Pettit and McDowell, 1986

Butterfield, J., ed. *Language, Mind and Logic*, Cambridge: Cambridge University Press, 1986

Davidson, D., 'On the Very Idea of a Conceptual Scheme'. in *Inquiries into Truth and Interpretation*, Oxford: Clarendon Press, 1984

Evans, G., *The Varieties of Reference*, ed. J. McDowell, Oxford: Clarendon Press, 1982

Goodman, Nelson, *Fact, Fiction and Forecast*, 3rd edn. Indianapolis: Bobbs-Merrill, 1973

Kripke, Saul, *Wittgenstein on Rules and Private Language*, Oxford: Basil Blackwell, 1982

McGinn, C., 'The structure of content', in Woodfield, 1982.

Pettit, P., and McDowell, J., eds. *Subject, Thought, and Context*, Oxford: Clarendon Press, 1986

Putnam, Hilary, 'The meaning of "meaning"', in *Mind, Language and Reality: Philosophical Papers*, vol. II, Cambridge: Cambridge University Press, 1975

Quine, W. V. *Ontological Relativity and Other Essays*, New York: Columbia University Press, 1969

Quine W. V. *From a Logical Point of View*, Cambridge, Mass.: Harvard University Press, 1953

Sacks, M., *The World We Found*, London: Duckworth, 1989.

Wittgenstein, Ludwig, *Tractatus Logico-Philosophicus*, London: Routledge and Kegan Paul, 1961

Wittgenstein, Ludwig, *Philosophical Investigations*, Oxford: Basil Blackwell, 1976

Woodfield, A. ed. *Thought and Object*, Oxford: Clarendon Press, 1982

9

Clarity

W. D. Hart

In the remarkable foreword to *Must We Mean What We Say?*, Stanley Cavell notes '. . . that each philosophy will produce "terms of criticism" directed against other philosophies, or against common sense, which are specific to that philosophy, and hence defining for it'.[1] Praise for clarity and, perhaps even more, condemnation for its opposed vices have been perceived as characteristic of philosophy done in an analytic style; indeed, some opponents of that style once marshalled under a banner proclaiming that clarity is not enough.[2] Analytic philosophers also seem to think of themselves as somehow more self-conscious about their standards than those they exclude from their ranks. For that reason, it is striking that the corpus of analytic philosophy includes no settled articulate analysis of clarity, nor even much in the way of rivals for that office. It is all very well to smile at the amateur who insists that we *begin* by defining our terms, for inquiry into what is obscure, but familiar, aims to *end* with analysis; but how many analytic knights have even set off in quest of the holy grail of clarity?

Critical history is sometimes a suggestive way to order data against which to test an analysis. But since it is hard to believe that anyone could be sufficiently and equally intimate with all of even the major texts in the analytic corpus, it is as well to remember that any such order is likely to be highly selective, schematic, and biased by philosophical pre-occupations. Still, if we are to begin, we must plunge in somewhere. We might divide the history of analytic philosophy into four major moments. Most contemporary philosophers in the analytic style trace their intellectual lineage back to Frege, and despite strenuous scholarly efforts, Frege's philosophical style still feels as if it sprang fully grown from the brow of Zeus. Although most of even the great minds of his day ignored Frege, Russell did not, and obscure though the high classical Russell is, it is perhaps a datum that he was an analytic philosopher. Wittgenstein's *Tractatus* is more obscure even than most Russell (except his ramified theory of types), but its author acknowledges his debt, as he puts it, to 'Frege's great works' and to the writings of his 'friend Bertrand Russell';[3] and the *Tractatus* is distinguished among early analytic works by a relatively developed doctrine of clarity. G. E. Moore seems never much to have shared the preoccupations of Frege, Russell and the younger Wittgenstein with the new logic; but he was preoccupied with a kind of analysis, and he wanted a kind of clarity. The era 1879–84 to about the end of the First World War, sparsely populated by Frege, Russell, Moore and Wittgenstein, is sometimes called 'logical atomism', though that phrase may prompt people to think more of Russell's 1918 lectures and of the *Tractatus* than of Frege or of Moore.

Logical positivism, centred around Schlick and especially Carnap, is perhaps the most interesting public movement in analytic philosophy between the two world wars. Russell had been kicked out of academic life, and made his living writing the books which earned him his reputation for clarity. Wittgenstein withdrew during most of the 1920s and , despite his return, his work was not openly available until after the Second World War. Interest in Ramsey persists; one wishes he had lived to stand up to Wittgenstein. But beginning between the wars, Carnap was to develop one of the most articulate and influential conceptions of clarity yet to emerge in analytic philosophy.

The period from the end the Second World War until 1987 splits more or less in two. In 1987 one thinks of its first half as the time of ordinary language philosophy, or Oxford philosophy, or even linguistic philosophy. But this was also the time when Quine began to receive more general attention, and it was also the time when Wittgenstein's later works, which contain a highly distinctive conception of clarification, began to be made public. The second half is probably too close for its structure to be salient: in geographical terms, one might call it the American hegemony.

Doubtless there are many reasons of various sorts why this history can be parsed into these segments, but at least one theme persists. If one leafs through this century of philosophic prose, the notations of the new logic stand out in all four phases except perhaps the third. It was in these terms that Russell challenged Frege, and in these terms that Russell, with Whitehead, took up the cause. Indeed, an English-speaking philosopher at the time of the publication of *Principia Mathematica* could be excused for expecting the new logic to become an English enterprise. But with Russell banished and Ramsey fated, only Turing remained. Not even the First World War could destroy the power of German logic, mathematics and science, and these set philosophical ideals for the Vienna Circle, and in Berlin, Prague and Warsaw. It took Hitler to drive analytic philosophy out of continental Europe. During the generation in which Carnap, Reichenbach, Hempel, Tarski and other refugees taught the symbol-slingers of the American hegemony, Oxford Dons, largely innocent of mathematics and natural science, defined the ordinariness of their language partly by strident contrast with that of the new logic. Even if we cannot answer with certainty, it is enlightening to ask how the development of the new logic integrates with analytic ideals of clarity.

I

Frege was a philosophical original, but he may have drawn on his mathematical education for some of his philosophical ideals. The theorem is an ideal of mathematical statement. It is typically a single sentence meant to be strong enough to stand by itself: what it says should be impersonal, unambiguous and impervious to context; above all, it should be true utterly without qualification. To be sure, its statement may require technical terms for which a novice will need explanations, and if the statement is not utterly fundamental, he may also need to be shown that it is true; but thereafter it should become for him a fixed point of invariable content and unqualified truth. In these respects, theorems do not differ importantly from axioms, nor from the laws of natural science. It can come to seem as if their constituent concepts lock seamlessly and indissolubly into perfect truths. This unqualified and impervious perfection might remind those acquainted with mathematics of what Descartes and Leibniz, who, like Frege, were mathematicians as well as philosophers, were trying to express when they associated clarity and distinctness with truth. So, prescinding from all scholarly claims, we might try to give credit here by speaking of the theorem as a semantic ideal of rationalism. There have always been philosophers who have suspected that philosophy could only be worth doing, were it to become capable of measuring up to that mathematical ideal of exposition. That suspicion seems an important theme in the history of the analytic style.

A sceptic might ask whether this ideal of exposition deserves its seductive power any more than charm or elegance. Understanding may sometimes suffice by itself to command assent; but is it then enough to justify a claim to truth? Is what is obvious true? It sometimes happens that in the attempt to articulate a theorem, an axiom, a law or a principle, success in articulation (or comprehension) is so tangled up with conviction as to feel as if saying is believing. This surely is part of what Gödel was describing when he said that the axioms of set theory force themselves upon us as being true.[4] Whatever the details of Descartes's exposition of his doctrine of clear and distinct ideas, surely he too meant something like this phenomenon by clarity. Doubtless too it is part of what was meant at various times by self-evidence, *a priori* knowledge, and perhaps even necessary truth and analyticity. But more was always meant by these. They included a trust that some thoughts which are convincing merely in being thought are, perhaps for that reason, known to be true. One might call this an epistemic thesis of rationalism. The espistemic thesis makes explicit an enduring motive for attachment to the semantic ideal. The semantic ideal is about the isolatability of unqualified truth. It makes no reference to knowledge or justification, a commitment left to the epistemic thesis.

Frege seems to have shared both the semantic ideal and the epistemic thesis with rationalists like Descartes and Leibniz.[5] Whether he wrote much about clarity or not, something like a doctrine of clear and distinct ideas was at the root of Frege's epistemology. In this, he may have thought of his new logic as a sort of prophylactic. The vernacular might almost be pictured as leading a wayward life of its own. Despite the blinding and primitive clarity of the unbridgeable distinction between objects, denoted by what we now call singular terms, and functions, among which the concepts are references of grammatical predicates, the vernacular is promiscuous enough to engender singular terms like 'the concept referred to by the predicate "is a horse"'. We must say that the concept *horse* is not a concept. Frege saw Benno Kerry's 'predicament' as 'an awkwardness of language' rather than of his own views.[6] The rigour of Frege's new logic would be proof against such monstrous hybrids. He seems to have trusted in the clarity of basic logical reason enough to take a high hand with Kerry's paradox and the vernacular itself.

Something of the same confidence may have sustained Frege at analysis. Toward the end of his introduction to the *Grundlagen*, after a swipe at empiricist philosophers, Frege writes, 'to those who feel inclined to criticize my definitions as unnatural, I would suggest that the point here is not whether they are natural, but whether they go to the root of the matter and are logically beyond criticism.'[7] It is as if a sort of critique of, or by, pure logic forces even nature (in the guise of ordinary artless thought) to pull back to reveal the root of number.

What is questions go back at least to Plato's dialogues, and they were at least often taken as requests for definitions of some sort. In that way, it was not especially novel for Frege to have introduced his *Grundlagen* by asking what the number one is. But one of the maxims with which he closes that introduction, never to ask for the meaning of a word in isolation but only in the context of a proposition, may have inaugurated something which became special in analytic philosophy. When Plato portrays Socrates as asking what virtue or knowledge is, it seems understood that an identity is expected by way of an answer. Frege's maxim can open out the range of *what is* questions: first settle a basic sentence-form in which the term in question occurs; then state conditions necessary and sufficient for the truth of sentences of that form. Thus a theory of descriptions can be envisaged, while the question 'What is the?' is not even grammatical; what Russell will call definitions-in-use may be the first articulate alternatives to definitions by genus and differentiam. (But recall also that Frege took biconditionals as identity sentences whose flanking singular terms are sentences.) However, it must be admitted that by sections 62–8 of the *Grundlagen*, Frege winds up rejecting a definition-in-use of the definite description 'the number of F's'; an innovator need not work out all the potentialities of his insights.

Frege devised his new logic in no small part in order to have means from which to devise an answer to the question with which he introduced the *Grundlagen*. Of course his means are not an arbitrary or free *jeu d'esprit*; what in particular become on his account *Wertverläufe* were intended to be cleaned up, or cleared up, versions of the extensions of concepts about which traditional logic talked so much.[8] It is also clear that he intended to 'prove the worth' of his analyses of the concept of number and related concepts by deriving from them and his new logic the essentials of Dedekind's axioms for number theory.[9] In other words, Frege had in practice what Tarski later thought of as conditions of material adequacy, which Carnap took as making explication possible. Section 3 of the *Grundlagen* makes it plain that Frege thought his deductive organization of the truth of logic and arithmetic answered to the unique, independent, objectively correct order of those truths from the somehow recognizable primitive truths to more familiar ones. This order by epistemic priority is also an idea of analysis. One aspect of the subsequent development of the constructional tradition (especially through Carnap's *Aufbau*[10] to Goodman's *The Structure of Appearance*[11] and Quine) is a loss of confidence in epistemic priority. But the rigour of Frege's derivation was also to make a mathematical sort of clarity possible in philosophy. Rigour makes it routine to check the correctness of an argument, and there is a sense in which Frege set the terms for modern standards of rigour; although no merciful teacher formalizes his text, a correct proof should admit of recasting in a precise codification of some recognized part of mathematics. In this aspect, Frege's clarity is an ideal of public science, where publicity is a dimension of clarity.

Frege's construction founders on the paradoxes of set theory. It may be that Russell's paradox so disheartened Frege because he saw in it a refutation of the epistemic thesis of rationalism: the clarity he crystallized in his logic did not after all guarantee truth and knowledge; perhaps there is no *a priori* knowledge after all (though in a half-hearted way, Frege then tried to found arithmetic in geometry which, he agreed with Kant, was synthetic *a priori*). *Principia Mathematica* grew up in the rubble of Frege's construction. In his preface, Russell writes that the chief reason for a doctrine of the principles of mathematics is inductive; problematic principles, if consistent, are justified insofar as they are needed to derive received mathematics. Even if Russell felt a more than inductive confidence in the vicious circle principle, confidence in *a priori* knowledge was similarly shaken by the disestablishment of Euclid's parallels postulate in the triumph of general relativity. Where John Stuart Mill's denial of *a priori* knowledge may have seemed an heroic, even Quixotic, denial of patent data, Quine's is not.

How should an understanding of the nature and importance of clarity be transformed by empirical maggots eating away at the epistemic thesis of rationalism? Russell was perhaps at least as much the heir of British empiricism as a founder of analytic philosophy; he was at least as much after certainty as after clarity. Perhaps it is not, or not merely, an accident of slovenliness that *Principia Mathematica* struck Gödel as 'so greatly lacking in formal precision in its foundations' and as 'in this respect a considerable step backwards from Frege'.[12] Besides, was Russell patient or steady enough for the meticulousness of Frege or the scrupulosity of Moore? It was Wittgenstein who in the *Tractatus* extracted from Russell's logic a transformation of Frege's conception of clarity.

In his preface, Wittgenstein writes that the whole sense of his book is that what can be said at all can be said clearly, and that whereof one cannot speak one must be silent. This sense is embedded in a scholastic structure of numbered theses.[13] One attempt to outline part of that structure briefly might begin with the thoughts that truth is correspondence to fact, that to understand a proposition is to know what would be the case if it were true (4.024), and that we can typically understand sentences which we have never encountered before without having them explained to us one by one (4.027). From the first two, one might infer that the sense of a proposition is the possible fact which would be actual if the proposition were true (4.03, paragraph 2). The third might then seem to require that there be something in the sentence which somehow 'gives' us an acquaintance with the possible fact, and then it might be hard to think how the gift could be made unless something were common to both the sentence and the possible fact (2.161). This is the core of the picture theory of meaning (and, better, thought) and the root of the conception of logical form in the *Tractatus*.

Logical form must be shared by any sense and any sentence which can express that sense (2.18). What makes falsity possible, and it is always possible in any genuine picture (2.221–5), is that not everything is common to picture and depicted (2.173, 3.13); an elementary propositional sign consists of names distinct from the objects they denote. But for any propositional sign to express a sense, it must have the logical form of that sense. So any description of a logical form would have to describe its own logical form. But such a description would thus say something about itself, and no proposition can make a statement about itself; this last, Wittgenstein tells us, is the whole of the theory of types (3.332). But if logical form is ineffable because it is shared, for the same reason it is exhibited in, because it is present in, sentences as they stand (4.12); this contrast between what is shared between picture and depicted (and thus cannot be said) and what is not shared but said by the picture of the depicted, is the root of Wittgenstein's distinction between saying and showing.

Frege's logic foundered on the paradoxes. Russell had to weaken Frege's logic enough to block the derivations of the paradoxes while at the same time keeping it strong enough to derive received mathematics. The upshot was Russell's (ramified) theory of types. Wittgenstein seems to have thought that its core, its 'whole', was no less *a priori* than Frege had thought his own logic before Russell refuted it; perhaps Russell (and Frege) learnt a lesson which passed Wittgenstein by. At any rate, Wittgenstein thought that the core of the theory of types, which is logic, has the consequence that how language and thought are possible, that is, can represent reality, is ineffable. When informally Frege allows singular terms like 'the concept *horse*', he permits what he would call proper names for concepts. Frege's concepts evolve into Wittgenstein's logical forms; where Frege's concepts have holes, Wittgenstein's logical forms are patterns of holes. Frege used 'incomplete' as a metaphor for concepts in his sense. This metaphor answers to the blank left in a sentence when a proper name, in Frege's sense, is omitted from the sentence. 'Hole' is another metaphor for the incompleteness answering to this blank. But Wittgenstein seems to have thought of these holes, or argument-places for objects, on the model of an array of points in space that would become a fact when objects occupied those points.[14] Then the form, which corresponds to one of Frege's concepts but whose value is a fact or possible fact rather than a truth-value, is the array of points in empty space; that last is what is meant by a pattern of holes. All this is more motivating metaphor than explicit doctrine. By the theory of types, logical forms cannot be, in Wittgenstein's sense, named. So of course Kerry can generate paradox from Frege's informal usage. Wittgenstein may have detected the same fallacy in both Kerry's and Russell's paradoxes, namely, a garbled attempt to say what is clear when shown. Wittgenstein may have thought of himself as working Frege's metaphysics grounded in logic through to its correct end. On the other hand, the *Tractatus* is a book about logical form, so, like the theory of types, stating it violates it (6.54); we may doubt that Wittgenstein much improved Frege's metaphysics.

An ordinary sentence does not look much like a nexus of names for simple objects, that is, like an elementary propositional sign (4.011). There is in the *Tractatus* an argument, apparently in no small part from Russell's theory of descriptions (which was for Russell an important stage on the way towards this theory of types), for the necessity of simple objects, their names, and elementary propositional signs in which the only signs are such names. The basic idea seems to be that language must make contact with the world; that is the purpose of its referential apparatus. Quantification is parasitic on a prototype (*Urbild*; 3.24, 3.333) of singular terms, and definite description cannot be basic here either. This is not merely because, by Russell's theory, quantification underlies definite description. Rather, there are three ways a sentence of the form 'The *F* is *G*' can be false; according to Russell's theory, it may fail because there is no *F*, or because there is more than one, or because, although there is exactly one, it is not *G*. So a sentence in which reference is accomplished by definite description does not say a single unique and determinate thing; no such sentence could in Wittgenstein's view be basic. Truth-functional molecules are not atoms; they lack what Wittgenstein calls determinateness of sense. So, since sense must ultimately be determinate, there must be elementary propositions in which reference is accomplished by names which cannot be anatomized (3.261) by definite descriptions; that is how what can be said at all can be said clearly. Wittgenstein says at 3.23 that the requirement that simple signs be possible is the requirement that sense be determinate. It is not the purpose of idiomatic speech to reveal the vast range of elementary propositions on which its expression of thought depends. We can thus see the possibility of an enterprise aimed at laying out these elementary propositions. This enterprise Wittgenstein calls complete analysis; it will clarify thought by laying bare its determinate sense and showing its logical form. He may have thought of complete analysis as the work of a philosophical dogsbody; at any rate, he himself does not undertake it, but leaves it as a task for whatever remains of philosophy.

The requirement that sense be determinate is, in part, a requirement that each elementary proposition have determinate sense independently of whether any other is true or false; the statement that the F is not G would deny exactly one thing only if it were somehow already given that, say, there is an F and it is unique. There also descends from the theory of types an equation between a sentence having sense and its having a truth-value. It follows that each elementary proposition is true or false independently of whether any other is true or false; the elementary propositions are logically independent of each other.[15] It should thus be clear that Wittgenstein's (apparently undefended) requirement of definiteness of sense is a version of the semantic ideal of rationalism; both emphasize unqualified isolation. It is the root of the logical atomism of the *Tractatus*. Wittgenstein took what he saw as the indisputable core of Russell's revision of Frege's logic, and from this core extracted an ideal of clarity and its necessary metaphysics. His tool for extraction is the requirement of determinateness of sense; this is his understanding of the semantic ideal of rationalism, and that is an ideal of clarity. But note too in this connection that it is no accident that the *Tractatus* is a sequence of separated and numbered theses; the *Tractatus* also embodies an extreme mathematical ideal of philosophy, perhaps even to the point of parody.

II

Having completed *Principia*, Russell soon set out to do for our knowledge of the external world what he had done for mathematics; this is the motivation behind his lectures under that title at Harvard in 1914, and it was also part of Whitehead's motivation in writing *The Concept of Nature*. Carnap says explicitly that both led the way toward his first major (and perhaps best) book, the *Aufbau*; certainly part of the aim of the *Aufbau* is to do for empirical knowledge what *principia* does (or seemed to do) for mathematics. The second chapter of *Our Knowledge of the External World* is called 'Logic as the essence of philosophy'. What he means there by 'logic' comes down mostly to what he calls 'the principle of abstraction ... which might equally well be called "the principle which dispenses with abstraction"'. By the end of the fourth chapter, it is clear that this is essentially what we now call the technique of equivalence classes.[16] By 1924 Russell saw in it a contrast which gave content to the maxim always to substitute a logical construction for an inferred entity;[17] we would now call his logical constructions equivalence classes. Essentially this technique underlay Frege's analysis of number. The method of equivalence classes, and its generalization to similarity classes, is the main technique of the *Aufbau*, and remains the prime resource of the constructional tradition in analytic philosophy.

But the Vienna Circle also had a critical axe to grind; they wanted to do away with metaphysics. (This may have begun as revenge on distribution requirements for science students at the University of Vienna. They took a licence for this revenge from the *Tractatus*, but it is not clear that they even understood how much metaphysics Wittgenstein works out in order to silence metaphysics.) An exposition of the conventional wisdom about the logical positivists' elimination of metaphysics begins with 'the' distinction between analytic and synthetic truths.

Notwithstanding the authorities of Frege and Russell, the positivists thought that in the *Tractatus* there is an 'interpretation' of *Principia* which justifies the claim that mathematics is not true because it corresponds to mathematical fact or describes mathematical reality. Instead, it is true by virtue of what it means. In *The Logical Syntax of Language*, Carnap appeals to this view in rejecting Ramsey's 'theological mathematics'; in A. J. Ayer's words in *Language, Truth and Logic*, mathematics 'is not about the world'.

The verifiability theory of meaning was restricted to synthetic propositions; here, meaning is evidence, a doctrine the positivists traced back to British empiricism. Where hypotheses do not differ in possible evidence, they do not differ in meaning, and thus do not differ at all. The slogan that a difference which makes no difference is no difference was the banner under which the positivists stigmatized the sceptical problems of philosophy, like the problem of the external world and the problem of other minds, as pseudo-problems. (But those for whom this Carnap is a bit of a smart alec might look again at the wisdom of his observation in the closing paragraphs of the *Aufbau* of the phoniness of most 'philosophizing' about death.) It was partly to eliminate the pseudo-problems of philosophy that in the *Aufbau* Carnap set out to reconstruct matter, 'other' people and society from 'one's' own experience. Empiricism required that while in *Principia* mathematics had been constructed from logic alone, the external world would be constructed from more. In Russell's case, sense data were that more. In Carnap's case, *Gestalt*-like experiences were that more. But it is worth noting that in sections 153–5 of the *Aufbau*, Carnap contemplates defining his single extra-logical primitive notion in terms of the system of concepts he has defined from it and a new logical primitive. Had he done so, what had seemed primitive would have become derived. This suggested reversal may have been part of what ultimately led Goodman in *The Structure of Appearance* to reject any commitment to epistemic priority.[18]

It may also be a bit surprising, and perhaps more so to those more familiar with some of Carnap's later work like *Meaning and Necessity*, just how extensionalist the *Aufbau* is. This was not a new issue. In response to C. I. Lewis's critique of the material conditional and to his logic of modality, Russell had replied that extensional methods sufficed to represent logic and mathematics adequately.[19] To be sure, Carnap's desire was to construct things as much as possible from what was epistemically prior to them; meaning, recall, is evidence. Nonetheless, the value of construction outweighed, as in Frege, fidelity to the natural order of our notions. Thus, for example, in sections 86 and 115 he constructs sight from what he himself describes as an 'inessential' feature of it without the slightest connection with its special phenomenal peculiarity. This construction, he says, will attract objection only if one confuses the logical value of a definition with its epistemic value; 'a translation which is carried out with the aid of constructional definition as translation has to guarantee nothing but the invariance of truth values of the statements, and not also the invariance of the sense.' Otherwise, perhaps, one could not expect to construct 'enough' from so slender a base as Carnap wanted.

Wittgenstein was Carnap's main authority for the principle of extensionality, namely, that one proposition may occur in another only, as we might now say, truth-functionally. This thesis seems much stronger than merely requiring no more than extensionality of constructional definitions. There is also an exegetical puzzle here. For despite the justice of Carnap's appeal to Wittgenstein on behalf of extensionality, it is natural to understand Wittgenstein's complete analysis as requiring a very strict sort of synonymy. The solution may be that for Wittgenstein, to analyse a proposition is to replace its propositional sign by another, and indeed strictly synonymous, propositional sign; but it is not to *state* that the second is the complete analysis of the first. For such a statement would mean at least in part that the second makes obvious the logical form of the first, and to try to say this would be to try to say what can only be shown. For Wittgenstein, what can be said clearly conforms to extensionality, but there are things which cannot be said. Surely the 'mysticism' of this last would have made Carnap uncomfortable.

Carnap's argument for the principle of extensionality in sections 43–5 of the *Aufbau* feels slipperly, but with hindsight it is tempting to speculate how much he was there struggling toward the distinction he highlighted in *The Logical Syntax of Language* between the material and the formal modes. It was, odd as it may now sound, part of Carnap's purpose in making this distinction to demonstrate that language could be discussed in language; Wittgenstein had seemed to argue from the distinction between saying and showing that thought and language cannot grasp themselves. It is perhaps even more surprising that, for Carnap in 1933 Gödel's 1931 technique of arithmetizing syntax was a breakthrough in no small part for the answer it seemed to provide to the strictures imposed by Wittgenstein's distinction between saying and showing on the possibility of stating philosophy.[20] Logic again seemed to have led, or even rescued, philosophy.

The Logical Syntax of Language was also a move in the dynamic internal to logical positivism. As Russell spoke of logic as the essence of philosophy, so the Circle agreed that philosophy is the logic of science. Carnap set out to convince them that the logic of science is the logical syntax of the language of science. To legitimize a discussion of the logical syntax of the language of science in what could only be the language of science, he had to answer Wittgenstein. Against this background, it is no accident that it was in the 1930s that Quine began to teach us how the distinction between use and mention is fundamental in achieving that precision and clarity in which Gödel found Russell more wanting than Frege.[21] It was by confusing use and mention, Quine argued, that Russell could think of what is in fact inferring to an equivalence class as dispensing with an abstraction.[22] To this day, a sensitivity to matters of use and mention in abstract discussions remains a trusty test of having mastered analytic clarity. Even if it seems preposterous that anyone confuse himself with his name, it is remarkable how slow and painful the birth of the distinction between use and mention, and the recognition of its pervasive importance in abstract issues, seems to have been.

Schlick said he agreed with Wittgenstein that in a quite definite sense we cannot 'go beyond language' and he argued that truth is consistency (coherence) with protocol statements which are immune from revision.[23] When Carnap argued that the logic of science is the logical syntax of the language of science, he was in part setting himself against what some logicians, and some recent metaphysicians who call themselves realists, have come to call semantics; the view persists that metaphysics can be got from relations between words and the world. It seems to have been the logical precision of Tarski's work on defining truth for formalized languages which persuaded Carnap of the possibility of semantics; if mathematical logic can include a theory of truth, then truth is not to be rejected with metaphysics. It seems also from Tarski that Carnap got words for the apparatus of material adequacy conditions which he would build up into his ideal of explication.

Quine has noted that Tarski's Convention T for the material adequacy of definitions of truth will not select among co-extensive but non-synonymous definitions of truth. Quine remained committed to extensionalism; recall how for him the Wiener-Kuratowski definition of the ordered pair (which Russell called a trick) is a paradigm of philosophy. We think of Carnap as becoming increasingly intensionalist over the years; indeed, 'Empiricism, semantics and ontology' exhibits Carnap's intensional ideology in defence of 'non-theological', non-metaphysical, non-Platonic mathematical truth against Quine's extensional ontological critique. But we should not forget how explication, a term Carnap taught many of us, was meant to clarify. Carnap's paradigm became the refinement of 'vague' qualitative adjectives like 'cold', 'cool', 'warm' and 'hot' to a numerical quantity, temperature. Here the purpose is hardly synonymy, especially to the point of preserving vagueness; it is rather an improvement in exactness, rigour and precision. The point is to increase such clarity to where science, which is always mathematical, will be possible. Thus Carnap's aim in *The Logical Foundations of Probability* (1950) was a logic of induction that would become as much a logic as Frege's treatment of deduction had by then become.

III

Carnap's *Logical Foundations of Probability* was published three years before Wittgenstein's *Philosophical Investigations* appeared posthumously. It seems plain that the older Wittgenstein had lost his youthful enthusiasm for the new mathematical logic. Indeed he seems at pains to insist on the separation of whatever it is he is about from not merely logic, but from all science. It was true to say, he writes in section 109, that our considerations could not be scientific ones. We must, he tells us, do away with all explanation, and description alone must take its place; natural history, contrasted with science, often seems his half-metaphorical ideal. We want, he says, in 122, the kind of clarity which consists in seeing connections. The concept of a perspicuous representation is, he writes, of fundamental significance for us. It earmarks the form of account we give, the way we look at things. Carnap's *Foundations* and Wittgenstein's *Investigations* are monuments by mature major philosophers in the analytic tradition. Moreover, each is special at least in that it includes a comparatively articulate conception of clarity from within the analytic tradition. What is striking is how different these conceptions are. Exactness, rigour and precision were Carnap's scientific ideals of clarity (and he had got these ideals partly from the younger Wittgenstein). But Wittgenstein says at *Zettel* 464 (of the pedigree of psychological concepts), 'I strive not after exactness, but after perspicuity.' Carnap's scientific ideal of clarity can seem the easier to grasp (or burlesque). Wittgenstein's struggle toward something else is harder to make out; how perspicuously can we represent his idea of perspicuity to ourselves?

The word 'picture' is often a term of criticism in the *Investigations* and the later corpus.[24] Article 115 is a central text here: 'A *picture* held us captive. And we could not get outside it, for it lay in our language and language seemed to repeat it to us inexorably.' Observe the connection which Wittgenstein makes, or sees, between a picture and captivity. We know from experience that we need only say to students, for example, that all mathematical truths are necessary, and they will nod; not only do they not object, but they ask for neither justification nor explanation. If one asks why they agree, they seem nonplussed. Wittgenstein seems to have been struck, remarkably enough, by facts like these. We might conjecture that he wanted to put into words, to describe the natural history of, the silent background behind what we called the epistemic thesis of rationalism. He engaged, in a way, in a critique of *a priori* knowledge.

What goes without saying escapes, for that very reason, critical examination. Burton Dreben has in discussion called this sort of critical examination 'breaking hold of a picture'. But this should not be identified too easily with rejecting a picture, with judging that it misrepresents its supposed subject matter. Wittgenstein noted a remarkable fact: there are views which, as it were, seize conviction without argument. Article 129 reads, 'The aspects of a thing that are the most important for us are hidden because of their simplicity and familiarity. (One is unable to notice something–because it is always before one's eyes.) The real foundations of his inquiry do not strike a man at all. Unless *that* has at some time struck him. –And this means: we fail to be struck by what, once seen, is most striking and most powerful.' It would be a distortion at least of emphasis to say that Wittgenstein set out to refute natural or compelling views, as if he were out like some adolescents to *épater les bourgeois*. It was a maxim of Freud's that where id was, ego shall be; part of his point was that enlightenment liberates from unacknowledged captivity, and enlightenment is a kind of clarity.

We have already seen examples of the power of pictures to captivate conviction. It stems from the roots of Frege's picture of functions, objects and their notations that the concept *horse* is not a concept. This result is Kerry's paradox, but though it is a paradox, Frege's picture so grips his conviction that he blames the paradox not on his picture but on language. When Wittgenstein wrote at 3.23 in the *Tractatus* of 'the requirement that sense be determinate' he seems hardly to have noticed especially that he had written of a *requirement*. Perhaps he was expressing something like an insight of an intellectual analogue of psychoanalysis when he wrote at 107 in the *Investigations*, 'For the crystalline purity of logic was, of course, not a *result of investigation*; it was a requirement.' Wittgenstein knew full well, and said, that it was a consequence of what he had said in the *Tractatus* that he cannot say it. Its grip on his conviction was strong enough that nonetheless, he did not throw away the ladder, but instead published it. Kerry's paradox and Wittgenstein whistling in the dark what cannot be said are paradoxes; antinomies; philosophical problems. Typically we solve a paradox by converting it into a *reductio ad absurdum* of an enthymeme behind it which went without saying. That, for example, is how we now motivate limiting the size of a set (that is, Zermelo-Fränkel set theory) from Russell's paradox. But only description (of the natural history of belief) is likely to bring the enthymemes (like the comprehension schema) to light for critical revision. When Russell wrote *Principia*, he took it for granted that for every (meaningful) predicate, there is a set that is its extension; indeed he took it so for granted that he never bothered to say so. Yet nowadays we take Russell's paradox as a *reductio ad absurdum* of that enthymeme; the denial of an enthymeme in a paradox is a theorem of contemporary set theory.[25] To be sure, the example of Wittgenstein's juvenile requirement of determinateness of sense illustrates that paradox and antinomy are probably too narrow, too sharp to represent all philosophicl problems perspicuously. Still, he tells us at 109, the description which must take the place of explanation gets its light, its purpose, from the philosophical problems. 'For the clarity that we are aiming at is indeed *complete* clarity. But this simply means that the philosophical problems should *completely* disappear.' (133). This complete disappearance is perhaps more the complete end of captivity than the complete erasure of all pictures; for we want to understand, to *command a clear view*, a perspicuous representation (122).

As an example, let us touch all too briefly on Wittgenstein's discussion of reading between 156 and, approximately, 178. This discussion is embedded in a discussion of understanding and following a rule which stretches, approximately, from 134 to 242. It has become a commonplace that the issue between 134 and 242. It has become a commonplace that the issue between 134 and 242 includes mental processes. But we must not take it for granted that we know what the problem is or how Wittgenstein conceived it. He writes:

> How does the philosophical problem about mental processes and states and about behaviourism arise? – The first step is the one that altogether escapes notice. We talk of processes and states and leave their nature undecided. Sometime perhaps we shall know more about them – we think. But that is just what commits us to a particular way of looking at the matter. For we have a definite concept of what it means to learn to know a process better. (The decisive movement in the conjuring trick has been made, and it was the very one that we thought quite innocent.) – And now the analogy which was to make us understand our thoughts falls to pieces. So we have to deny the yet uncomprehended process in the yet unexplored medium. And now it looks as if we had denied mental processes. And naturally we don't want to deny them. (*PI*, § 308)

So at least, we do not want to deny mental processes. But what analogy falls to pieces? In introducing the topic of reading, Wittgenstein writes:

> First I need to remark that I am not counting the understanding of what is read as part of 'reading' for purpose of this investigation: reading is here the activity of rendering out loud what is written or printed; and also of writing from dictation, writing out something printed, playing from a score, and so on (*PI*, § 156).

His discussion of reading is embedded in his discussion of understanding *not* as an example of understanding. Something else, perhaps more general, seems to be at issue. His examples are of people who are given notations (in writing, print, speech or a musical score) and who give back notations (in speech or writing) or music. He might have been willing to count some instances of transliterating, transcribing and copying as reading; a native speaker of English who cannot translate Greek into English but who can pronounce Greek could in the relevant sense read Greek. The discussion in 156–78 is very closely prefigured in the discussion of reading on pages 119–25 of the *Brown Book*. Here, immediately before, where conventional composition would place a statement of the issue, Wittgenstein describes a player piano thus:

> In the working of the pianola we have a clear case of certain actions, those of the hammers of the piano, being guided by the pattern of the holes in the pianola roll. We could use the expression 'The pianola is *reading off* the record made by the perforations in the roll', and we might call patterns of such perforations *complex signs* or sentences ... we should say that the pianola *can* read *any* pattern of perforations of a particular kind, it is not built for one particular tune or set of tunes (like a musical box) (*Brown Book*, p. 118).

The terms 'guided' will return in sections 170, 172–3, 175 and 178 of the *Investigations*. Perhaps it is an analogy between mental processes supposed in reading of Wittgenstein's sort and the action of the pianola which he will at 308 say falls to pieces, though of course 308 does not illuminate only 156–78. The pianola has an ancestor in the gramophone at 3.013–4.0141 in the *Tractatus*. The two sorts of machine, taken merely as machines, are thoroughly analogous. It is on the model of the gramophone that in the *Tractatus* Wittgenstein explains how understanding is possible. Liken an ordinary sentence to a musical score. For us to be able to understand or mean that sentence, it must already have a complete analysis into (a truth-functional combination of) elementary propositional signs. This complete analysis is the thought by having which we understand or mean the sentence; liken the thought to the long wound-up groove of nitches and notches on the gramophone record, where the arrays of nitches are like arrays of names in an elementary proposition. The gramophone is a process for producing from the groove a performance of the music noted on the score. Understanding is the process whereby the mind projects the thought into logical space to the possible fact which is the sense of the ordinary sentence. In understanding an ordinary sentence, the mind projects the thought that is the complete analysis of the sentence to the possible fact that is the sense of the sentence; in thus getting the sense from the sentence, the mind understands the sentence. Wittgenstein seems to intend 'project' here literally. There must on this view be mental processes, like the action of the gramophone, by which language is understood, though we are not conscious of such processes taking place in us. Wittgenstein's use of the gramophone here pretty clearly has its roots in Hertz's discussion of thought and dynamical models in sections 418–28 of his *Principles of Mechanics*. We know from 4.04 that this part of Hertz's book inspired Wittgenstein's picture theory of meaning (and thought and understanding) in the *Tractatus*. Wittgenstein could have been led to Hertz by chapter LIX of Russell's *Principles of Mathematics*.[26]

Suppose we set out to investigate an analogy between the action of the pianola and Wittgenstein's sort of reading; how shall we proceed? At 374 Wittgenstein writes, 'And the best that I can propose is that we should yield to the temptation to use this picture, but then investigate how the *application* of the picture goes.' To investigate how this application goes here, we might begin by describing salient features of the action of the pianola. For example:

1 There was a *first* perforation on a first roll to activate the mechanism of the pianola, and there was a first note it played; there is a definite time before which the mechanism in the pianola had never been activated but at which it was first activated.

2 There is a fact of the matter about whether the pianola is actually *producing* or *deriving* the notes coming out from the perforations on the roll, or whether there is instead a gramophone in there playing a recording of piano music which would go on even if the roll were not engaged.

3 We could open up the pianola and trace out the continuous chain of contacts from the holes in the roll through the teeth on the cylinder via various gears and cogs to the hammers which strike the strings. There is *a quite special process* going on *inside* the pianola by which the notes coming out are *connected*, *guided*, *influenced* and *caused* by the perforations in the roll.

One might call the terms italicized in these three remarks a system of description. Most of us are not intimate with the nuts and bolts, the hook-ups of cogs and gears, inside a pianola. But we know there is a fairly complicated mechanism in there, and we have a definite idea of what it would be like to learn the details of that mechanism. From 156 to about 178, Wittgenstein (and his interlocutor) extract the underlined terms from the system of description, which even those of us largely innocent of the insides of a pianola are confident apply to its commonly unknown complex detail, and ask what, if anything, in Wittgenstein's sort of reading seriously answer to those terms. If only for reasons of space, you are trusted to see whether your reading (with understanding) of 156–78 is organized by taking them in this way. The upshots of these investigations one by one seem always to be pretty much the same. If one ignores whatever preconceptions one might have and attends carefully to one's experience in reading aloud words one does not understand, then the most accurate and detailed description generally true of what one experiences is that one sees the print and says the words. Seeing and speaking are it; the most unbiased and scrupulous introspective observation reveals nothing in consciousness remotely like the cogs and gears inside the pianola. The *insistence* that there *must* be between seeing and speaking something like the continuous linkage of cogs and gears but hidden in the unconscious or the brain is bald assertion without evidence. Wittgenstein is in a way super-empirical. He will cite no psychological phenomenon unless it is patently open to anyone's introspection of his own experience. These super-empirical reminders of the obvious (128) are assembled for a particular purpose; nothing one so finds in oneself answers at all to even the grossest linkages in the pianola. It is also super-empirical that Wittgenstein refuses to speculate; circumspect speculation will not yield the certainty with which the picture of the pianola grips (*a priori?*) conviction about reading. This refusal to speculate includes a refusal to deny the existence of a continuous linkage like cogs and gears between seeing and speaking in reading; we do not want to deny mental processes. Wittgenstein emphasizes observation and, in particular, encourages meticulous introspection, but it is to be super-empirical in perhaps something like the way natural history is thought to have a priority over scientific theory; and he refuses to speculate beyond his super-empirical data. It seems to be this observation which is to enlighten the dumb background of the epistemic thesis of rationalism and the free falling *a priori*; he rubs our noses in the failure of bad pictures to apply to their supposed subject matter. Wittgenstein can remind one of Hume: as Hume emphasizes that we do not experience the continuance of a single object which we experience only at different times, so Wittgenstein emphasizes that we experience nothing deserving to be called a connection between seeing and saying in reading. Like Hume too, Wittgenstein does not try to fill the gap; his question might rather have been what gives us the idea that there is a *gap* here?

One might in this connection worry about the second point above in the picture of the pianola. Surely, the interlocutor might say, there is a difference between reading even in Wittgenstein's sense and reciting from memory while pointing one's face at print; in the second, but not the first, case one could go on even if the print were covered up. Remember that in the *Brown Book* Wittgenstein distinguishes the pianola, in which any suitable roll will work, from a music box whose cylinder limits its repertoire; how seriously are we to take the suggestion that a man might recite from memory any of indefinitely many passages, even ones we compose on the spot? More deeply perhaps, what does one experience when one recites from memory? One may perhaps visualize the text one memorized, and that could be just like Wittgenstein's sort of reading all over again. But mostly, one just says the words. The words just come. Wittgenstein might ask what convinces us that they must have come from somewhere. Conservation of energy is a law of thermodynamics; but, he might say, to insist on conservation of being in psychology is to be held captive by a picture.[27]

Is Wittgenstein really super-empirical? When he writes in 109 that the philosophical problems are not empirical problems, he may mean not that they are to be solved by *a priori* reasoning, or meaning analysis, but rather that they are problems in part because pictures captivate conviction without empirical evidence that they apply to their subject matters. When he writes that we must do away with all explanation, that description alone must take its place, and that the problems are solved, not by giving new information, but by arranging what we have always known, he may mean, for example, that accurate description of what we experience when we read aloud words we do not understand does not bear out applying the picture of the pianola to reading.

Perhaps; but it is as well to recognize that this exegesis ignores utterly the fact that throughout sections 89–113, Wittgenstein emphasizes the description of, in particular, our use of *words*. At 115, he said that the picture which held us captive lay in our *language*. He could mean only that language is the primary conduit through which all our cultural heritage descends; does the fact that we learn about mass mostly by reading make mass a linguistic phenomenon? It could be that he was himself most captivated by philosophical problems about meaning and understanding, that is, problems whose subject matter includes language; at 120 he writes, 'Your questions refer to words; so I have to talk about words.' Then, like most good poets at criticism, he could have seen the problems of philosophy as his problems writ large; his problem about reading in his sense is a problem about reading *words* and other notations. But there comes a time when the sympathy necessary for believing a text worth attention is wise to distinguish between correct exegesis of a text and exegesis of a correct text. If Wittgenstein thought that commanding a clear view just of our use of our words would all by itself solve all philosophical problems, and that philosophy is a battle against the bewitchment of our intelligence by means only of language, where language is distinguished from the rest of the world engaged with by arts and sciences which deans distinguish from philosophy, then Wittgenstein was himself held captive by a picture which falls to pieces when we look at his practice in 156–78. It is crucial there that we really do take his advice and introspect; to investigate whether a picture applies to a matter is to investigate that matter as well as that picture.

Having sketched briefly an illustration of Wittgenstein working to break the grip of a picture, let us return to the question how perspicuously we can represent his ideal of perspicuity. At *Zettel* 464 he said (of the pedigree of psychological concepts) that he strives not after exactness, but after perspicuity. There is a genuine contrast here. Presented with a derivation from first principles in *Principia Mathematica* or some fully rigorous formal system, it is all too easy to get lost and miss the forest for the trees. A well-done informal sketch of the same proof highlights its important ideas and its point in part by omitting trivial details. The sketch achieves perspicuity by sacrificing some rigour; to some extent, rigour and perspicuity vary inversely.

Wittgenstein's perspicuity gets its point from the philosophical problems. On Carnap's model of clarity by explication, increasing exactness decreases vagueness. But increasing perspicuity is to decrease misunderstanding, confusion and paradox. We are to clear up problems at least in part by breaking the grip of inapplicable pictures so as to clear the way for getting clear about their subject matter. Such clarification should not be pictured on the model of simplifying exposition so as to ease the way of students, a pedagogical model likely to attract epithets like 'merely subjective'. The crux here is rather understanding, as in the fact that no one understands the turbulent flow of fluids or exactly why the iambic pentameter line is so natural to English literary verse. Such understanding is, of course, a mental state, but it is no less objective than the genus, knowledge, of which it is a species. Wittgenstein's contrast in 109 notwithstanding, some descriptions are explanations because they articulate deep understandings. Understanding is the measure of perspicuity.

Peter Hylton says that there is no useful distinction between philosophy and meta-philosophy.[28] For example, the remarks in the last paragraph are no more remarks in some meta-philosophy about an ideal of perspicuity for philosophical practice than they are remarks in philosophy of science about explanation or than they are remarks in aesthetics about literary criticism. But it is more important for understanding the organization of the *Investigations* to see that the sort of understanding in which, according to 89–113, we are to be left when a philosophical problem has been cleared up is the same sort of understanding about which 134–242 are to leave us clear; it is good composition (dare one say grammar?) to have followed the first sequence with the second. If only to save space, let us here speak somewhat dogmatically. The idea is that understanding comes down to a sort of *engagement*. What we do not get, we bracket. We do not go on from it, even by way of vitriolic denial. We ignore it and go past it. We leave it out. If one insists that there must be a state of our minds, understanding, which explains how we can go on 'correctly', then one is not doing away with all explanations; Wittgenstein does not speculate. The evidence (dare one say, in the *ordinary* way, the criterion) of understanding something is that we take it up and go on from it, if only by way of denial.[29] Philosophical problems are ways of conceiving things from which we do not go on. When a problem is cleared up, a way is clear. The evidence that a way is clear is that we go on. At 123 Wittgenstein writes, 'A philosophical problem has the form: "I don't know my way about."' Of course clarity is not enough: one wants depth too. The measure (the criterion) of depth is the extent to which we go on, which will be vanishing if we do not go on at all.

Wittgenstein took his representation of problems, solutions and perspicuity (but not understanding) from Heinrich Hertz. In the introduction to *The Principles of Mechanics Presented in a New Form*, Hertz describes the 'wearisome frequency' with which one hears that

the nature of force is still a mystery, that one of the chief problems of physics is the investigation of the nature of force, and so on. In the same way
electricians are continually attacked as to the nature of electricity. Now,
why is it that people never in this way ask what is the nature of gold, or
what is the nature of velocity? Is the nature of gold better known to us than
that of electricity, or the nature of velocity better than that of force? . . . I
fancy the difference must lie in this. With the terms 'velocity' and 'gold' we
connect a large number of relations to other terms; and between all these
relations we find no contradictions which offend us. We are therefore
satisfied and ask no further questions. But we have accumulated around
the terms 'force' and 'electricity' more relations than can be completely
reconciled amongst themselves. We have an obscure feeling of this and
want to have things cleared up. Our confused wish finds expression in the
confused question as to the nature of force and electricity. But the answer
which we want is not really an answer to this question. It is not by finding
out more and fresh relations and connections that it can be answered; but
by removing the contradictions existing between those already known, and
thus perhaps by reducing their number. When these painful contradictions
are removed, the question as to the nature of force will not have been
answered; but our minds, no longer vexed, will cease to ask illegitimate
questions.[30]

Hertz's discussion of thoughts and dynamical models in sections 418–28 of his
Principles inspired what is non-Fregean in Wittgenstein's theory of understanding in the *Tractatus*. But the connection did not end there. Wittgenstein writes:

Consider as an example the question 'what is time?' as Saint Augustine and
others have asked it. At first sight what this question asks for is a definition,
but then immediately the question arises: 'What should we gain by a definition, as it can only lead us to other undefined terms?' And why should
one be puzzled just by the lack of a definition of time, and not by the lack
of a definition of 'chair'? Why shouldn't we be puzzled in all cases where
we haven't got a definition? Now a definition clears up the *grammar* of a
word. And in fact it is the grammar of the word 'time' which puzzles us.
We are only expressing this puzzlement by asking a slightly misleading
question, the question 'What is . . .?' This question is an utterance of
unclarity, of mental discomfort, and it is comparable to the question
'Why?' as children so often ask it. This too is an expression of mental discomfort, and doesn't necessarily ask for a cause or a reason. (Hertz,
Principles of Mechanics.) Now the puzzlement about the grammar of the
word 'time' arises from what one might call apparent contradictions in that
grammar.

It was such a 'contradiction' which puzzled Saint Augustine when he argued: How is it possible that one should measure time? For the past can't be measured, as it is gone by; and the future can't be measured because it has not yet come. And the present can't be measured for it has no extension.

The contradiction which here seems to arise could be called a conflict between two different usages of a word, in this case the word 'measure'. Augustine, we might say, thinks of the process of measuring a *length*; say, the distance between two marks on a travelling band which passes us, and of which we can see only a tiny bit (the present) in front of us. Solving this puzzle will consist in comparing what we mean by 'measurement' (the grammar of the word 'measurement') when applied to a distance on a travelling band with the grammar of the word applied to time. The problem may seem simple, but its extreme difficulty is due to the fascination which the analogy between two similar structures in our language can exert on us. (*Blue Book*, p. 26).

It does not seem too much to say that when we juxtapose these two passages we can see Hertz's idea of a contradiction evolving into Wittgenstein's idea of a problem, Hertz's idea of accumulations of relations between terms evolving into Wittgenstein's ideas of the grammar of a word and, via fascination with an analogy between two structures in our language, of captivity by a picture lying in our language. For both, their problems are solved not when we acquire new information, but when the source of the question in our treatment of what we already 'knew' is defanged; for both, that is how clarification happens. Let us resist the temptation to take a cheap shot by saying that, 109 notwithstanding, Hertz knew that problems of Wittgenstein's sort are not peculiar to philosophy as opposed to science. For it is probably more liberating (from a bad picture) to say that philosophical problems crop up everywhere, no matter how deans section off the departments. The point is hardly to urge scientism; the point is to understand, whether we label it science, art or philosophy. There is in this picture of going on together a grain of salt to be taken with the semantic ideal of rationalism. For Wittgenstein's index of understanding, and so of clarity, is that we can go on from what is clear. This going on from a remark is an embedding of it in an endlessly unfolding context. That embedding might in turn be contrasted with the isolation and fixity that the semantic ideal predicates of, say theorems. But, of course, theorems do not thereby become unclear; indeed they may become starting points of new proofs, or tests of generalizations of their original habitats, or parts of the cannon of mathematics taught at school, or otherwise embedded in their own unfolding contexts. The isolation of a theorem is only relative, like that of an italicized or displayed bit of text.

The question of clarity answers to history; that is, on Wittgenstein's view, whether a remark or thought or view is clear turns on whether there is a subsequent history of its being taken up and developed (perhaps by denial). Have we gone on from the *Investigations?* Some of us return to it from time to time and offer up at it sacrifices called interpretations, but that return does not feel like the right sort of going on. Both Marx and Freud made claims to the objectivity of science for their work, as did Darwin for his. The issue here is not the silly question whether Wittgenstein made science out of philosophy. Poetry is not, and should not be, a science; but poetry has gone on from Wilfrid Owen at least in that near-rhyme is now a received poetic technique. Evolutionary biology (with genetics) does seem to have acquired a life of its own after Darwin. Perhaps it is not quite as oblivious of its descent from Darwin as physics is largely oblivious of its impulse from Newton, but evolutionary biology has gone on from Darwin. In contrast, the schools founded by Marx and Freud never seem to lose concentration on their founders. As it were, Marx is a fetish of marxism, and psychoanalysis is obsessed with Freud. (How much is either like being held captive by a picture?) It feels wrong to say that Wittgenstein founded a discipline, as Newton and Darwin did. It feels wrong to say that there begins with the *Investigations* a school in anything like the way Marx and Freud founded schools. The curse of discipleship apart, philosophers seem always too much like intellectual atoms, or even monads, for philosophical disciplines or even schools to work for long; the antithesis to this thesis is that philosophy is, and ought to be, the slave of its history, liberation from whom comes only by incorporation, that is, rigor mortis. Philosophy is not a co-operative activity in the way that molecular biology has become, and the intellectual isolation of philosophers might remind one of Leibniz's monads. Yet the problems we treat are historically given, and the judgement of our treatments lies in whether they become part of the subsequent history of philosophy. Isolation and historical embedding contrast like thesis and antithesis. It may be fair to say that a trend in ordinary language philosophy was away from explanation and toward describing something remotely like what Wittgenstein called grammar, namely, how we put words together. But equally a thrust in the American Hegemony has been toward theory and, increasingly, speculation. Both felt in part like going on from the *Investigations,* but as if one were pushing off with a ten-foot pole. 34 years is a brief span in the history of philosophy. But the proliferation of commentaries suggests that Wittgenstein's private language argument threatens to become as much a stumper, as much an abiding object of baffled interpretation, as book zeta of Aristotle's *Metaphysics* or Kant's transcendental deduction. Over these 34 years, most of us have made up our minds one way or another about what we take to be the central ideals and methods of Frege and Carnap. Perhaps we have practised differently from them, but in part we have done so out of how we made up our minds about them. By that standard, most of us seem largely to have passed Wittgenstein by, and this includes those who get stuck at interpreting the

Investigations. Is there a way of grasping the *Investigations* which is *not* an *interpretation*, but which is exhibited in actual cases? Are 34 years long enough in our history for us to judge that by its own lights the *Investigations* is not clear? Or do we shun its clarity out of fear of desolation? Is its depth the depth of the void?

IV

If clarity is a virtue, then there should be an explanation of what it is good for. Rationalists may once upon a time have believed that clarity is a condition such that a thinker can tell from his thought alone whether or not it is clear, and such that any clear thought is true. But the idea of an internal property of thoughts that suffices to settle how things stand out there in the world seems as magical, and thus as difficult to take seriously, as action at a distance. But if rationalism of that sort is too naive, while clarity is nonetheless a virtue, then what is clarity good for? On Carnap's conception of clarity as exactness, rigour and precision, clarity paves the way for the mathematical methods of natural science. On Wittgenstein's later conception of clarity as perspicuity, clarity paves the way of understanding. His index of this is that the conversation down the ages that is culture can take up, incorporate and go on from what is clear; clarity is a virtue of unfolding understanding. Since the natural sciences with the arts constitute central, if not the main, parts of culture, perhaps we could say that Carnap's conception of clarity stands to the elder Wittgenstein's as species to genus. Then we might explain that clarity is good for continuing our talk together. If that sounds too obvious, Wittgenstein might remark that our continuing conversation down the ages is all the depth there is to us.

Notes

This essay was conceived some months after that wonderful week in Munich, so while it was not refined in the warm critical fire there, it is grateful to its god-parents, the Volkswagen Foundation, the Institute for Philosophy, and Kardinal Wendel Haus, and it was inspired by the open, honest spirit which refused to chop logic and who hovered over those memorable sessions. It is especially indebted to Tyler Burge and (then and later) to Peter Hylton, and (later) to David Wiggins and Malcolm Budd. But for me, that spirit always speaks with Burton Dreben's accent.

1   Stanley Cavell, *Must We Mean What We Say?*, Cambridge University Press, 1976, p. xviii.
2   H. H. Price, 'Clarity is Not Enough', *Proceedings of the Aristotelian Society*, supplementary vol. XIX, 1945, pp. 1–31; reprinted in H. D. Lewis, ed., *Clarity is Not Enough*, George Allen and Unwin, London, 1963.

3   Ludwig Wittgenstein, *Tractatus Logico-Philosophicus*, Pears and McGuinness, trans., Routledge and Kegan Paul, London, 1961, p. 3.

4   Kurt Gödel, 'What is Cantor's Continuum Problem?', in Paul Benacerraf and Hilary Putnam, eds, *Philosophy of Mathematics*, 2nd edn, Cambridge University Press, 1983, pp. 483–4.

5   Note the juxtaposition of mathematical and philosophical ideals in articles 2 and 3 of Gottlob Frege, *The Foundations of Arithmetic*, J. L. Austin, trans., Basil Blackwell, 1950.

6   Gottlob Frege, *Translations from the Philosophical Writings of Gottlob Frege*, Geach and Black, eds, Basil Blackwell, 1970, p. 46.

7   Frege, *Foundations of Arithmetic*, p. XI.

8   cf. Frege, *Translations*, p. 31. Black and Geach render *Wertverlauf* as 'value-range'.

9   Richard Dedekind, *Essays on the Theory of Numbers*, Chicago, 1901.

10 Rudolf Carnap, *The Logical Structure of the World* and *Pseudoproblems in Philosophy*, Rolf A. George, trans., California, 1969.

11 Nelson Goodman, *The Structure of Appearance*, 2nd edn, Bobbs-Merrill, 1966.

12 Kurt Gödel, 'Russell's Mathematical Logic', in Benacerraf and Putnam, p. 448.

13 Wittgenstein, *Notebooks 1914–1916*, von Wright and Anscombe, eds, Harper, 1961, 9.11.14, p. 28.

14 cf. W. D. Hart, 'The whole sense of the *Tractatus*,' *The Journal of Philosophy* (6 May, 1971), p. 283.

15 For a slightly less breathless account than the few preceding paragraphs, see W. D. Hart, 'The whole sense of the *Tractatus*', *The Journal of Philosophy* (6 May, 1971), pp. 273–88.

16 See, for example, Donald Monk, *Introduction to Set Theory*, McGraw-Hill, 1969, pp. 57–61.

17 Bertrand Russell, 'Logical atomism', in Robert C. Marsh, ed., *Logic and Knowledge*, George Allen and Unwin, 1956, p. 326.

18 See, for example, Goodman, *Structure*, pp. 136–42.

19 Bertrand Russell, *Introduction to Mathematical Philosophy*, George Allen and Unwin, London, 1919, p. 154. See also W. V. Quine, 'Three Grades of Modal Involvement', reprinted in *The Ways of Paradox and Other Essays*, revised and enlarged edn, Harvard, 1976; and *Mathematical Logic*, revised edn, Harper, 1951, para. 5.

20 Rudolf Carnap, *The Logical Syntax of Language*, Countess von Zeppelin, trans., Littlefield, Adams and Co, Patterson, New Jersey, 1959, paras 18–19.

21 In addition to the work by Quine cited in note 19 above, see his 'Whitehead and the Rise of Modern Logic', reprinted in *Selected Logic Papers*, Random House, 1966.

22 Quine, *Set Theory and its Logic*, revised edn, Harvard, 1969, ch. XI.

23 Moritz Schlick, 'The Foundation of Knowledge', in A. J. Ayer, ed., *Logical Positivism*, The Free Press of Glencoe, 1959, pp. 214–16.

24 Some of the places in the later corpus where Wittgenstein uses 'picture' to describe accounts which compel conviction are:
    Philosophical Investigations: sections 1, 59, 136, 173, 295, 305, 335, 337, 349, 374, 397, 422–7, 490, 515, 604, 607.
    Zettel: sections 27, 251, 276, 331, 554.

Blue and Brown Books: pp. 56, 81, 139.
Remarks on the Foundations of Mathematics:
Part I: section 22.
Part IV: sections 9, 18, 27, 37.
Part V: section 45.
Lectures and Conversations on Aesthetics, Psychology and Religious Belief: pp. 7, 16, 55, 56, 71, 72.
In some of these cases, Wittgenstein modifies 'picture' with an overt adjective of criticism.

Work	*Passage*		*Adjective*
Investigations	section	136	bad
		337	misleading
		604	false
Zettel	section	27	fishy
		276	queer
Remarks	Part IV, sect. 9		false
	Part IV, sect. 37		frightfully confusing; frightfully misleading

Other relevant uses of 'picture' include:
Investigations: sections 115, 144, 191, 275, 295, 349, 352, 374, 397, 402, 422–7, 524, 663.
Zettel: sections 275, 323, 461.
Blue and Brown Books: pp. 23, 56, 135, 139.
Remarks: Part IV, section 10.
There are other occurrences of 'picture' which are probably not relevant.

25 In addition to the text by Monk cited in note 16 above, see George Boolos, 'The Iterative Conception of Set', *The Journal of Philosophy* (22 April, 1971), pp. 215–30; and Dana Scott, 'Axiomatizing Set Theory', in *Axiomatic Set Theory*, American Mathematical Society, Proceedings of Symposia in Pure Mathematics, vol. 13, part II, 1974, pp. 207–14.

26 But cf. Brian McGuinness, *Wittgenstein: A Life, Young Ludwig (1889–1921)*, Duckworth, London, 1988, pp. 37, 39.

27 See Malcolm Budd, 'Wittgenstein on Meaning, Interpretation and Rules', *Synthese* 58 (1984), 303–23, especially 309ff.

28 Peter Hylton, 'The Nature of the Proposition and the Revolt against Idealism', in Richard Rorty, J. B. Schneewind and Quentin Skinner, eds, *Philosophy in History*, Cambridge University Press, 1984, p. 394.

29 '... language is a practical consideration. It may be observed that in all communication between men, certainty comes only from practical acts and from the verification which practical acts give us. *I ask you for a light. You give me a light*: you have understood me.' This was published in 1939 by Paul Valéry in 'Poetry and Abstract Thought'. It is reprinted in *The Art of Poetry*, Pantheon Books, 1958, p. 64.

30 Heinrich Hertz, *The Principles of Mechanics Presented in a New Form*, trans., D. E.

Jones and J. T. Walley, Dover, 1956, pp. 7 – 8. Of course things moved on after 1894. When in 1905 Einstein argued in the special theory of relativity that velocities do not add as supposed in classical mechanics, it could be said that he changed our understanding of the nature of velocity. Has Kripke, by saying that gold *must* have atomic number 79, made the nature of gold an issue?

Index